Women Making Shakespeare

RELATED TITLES

Shakespeare Up Close: Reading Early Modern Texts, edited
by Russ McDonald, Nicholas D. Nace and Travis D. Williams
Shakespeare's Theatres and the Effects of Performance, edited
by Farah Karim-Cooper and Tiffany Stern
In Arden: Editing Shakespeare, edited by Ann Thompson and
Gordon McMullan

Women Making Shakespeare

Text, Reception, Performance

Edited by Gordon McMullan,
Lena Cowen Orlin and
Virginia Mason Vaughan

B L O O M S B U R Y
LONDON • NEW DELHI • NEW YORK • SYDNEY

Bloomsbury Arden Shakespeare

An imprint of Bloomsbury Publishing Plc

50 Bedford Square	1385 Broadway
London	New York
WC1B 3DP	NY 10018
UK	USA

www.bloomsbury.com

Bloomsbury is a registered trade mark of Bloomsbury Publishing Plc

Editorial matter and selection © Gordon McMullan, Lena Cowen Orlin and
Virginia Mason Vaughan 2014
All other matter © Bloomsbury Publishing Plc

British Library Cataloguing-in-Publication Data

A catalogue record for this book is available from the British Library.

ISBN: HB: 978-1-4081-8533-9
PB: 978-1-4081-8523-0
ePDF: 978-1-4725-3938-0
ePub: 978-1-4725-3937-3

Library of Congress Cataloging-in-Publication Data

Women Making Shakespeare : Text, Reception, Performance / edited by
Gordon McMullan, Lena Cowen Orlin and Virginia Mason Vaughan.
pages cm
ISBN 978-1-4081-8533-9-- ISBN 978-1-4081-8523-0 (pbk.)– ISBN 978-
1-4725-3937-3 (epub) 1. Shakespeare, William, 1564-1616–Characters--
Women. 2. Women in literature. 3. Feminist literary criticism. I. McMullan,
Gordon, 1962- editor of compilation. II. Orlin, Lena Cowen, editor of
compilation. III. Vaughan, Virginia Mason, editor of compilation.
PR2991.W64 2014
822.3'3–dc23

2013029971

Typeset by Fakenham Prepress Solutions, Fakenham, Norfolk NR21 8NN
Printed and bound in Great Britain

CONTENTS

PREFACE

This volume was compiled in tribute to Ann Thompson. It
continues the process she began, with Sasha Roberts, in the
1997 anthology *Women Reading Shakespeare*. Thanks to
Ann and Sasha and others who sought to rehabilitate writers
such as Henrietta Bowdler and actors such as Helena Faucit,
we have become very aware both of the extent to which
women have 'made' Shakespeare and also of the considerable
amount of material yet to be uncovered and understood about
the ways in which that 'making' came about. With *Women
Making Shakespeare*, we aim to take the project forward.

Women Making Shakespeare offers a series of short
readings, histories and interviews that demonstrate the power
of women's engagement with Shakespeare from the sixteenth
century to the present. Contributors were invited to write
about any aspect of the agency of women in the field known as
'Shakespeare' – anything, that is, from Shakespeare's characterization of women to the history of women's involvement
in Shakespeare criticism, textual studies, performance or
reception history.

Thus these case studies address the difference women
have made to our understanding of Shakespeare across a
range of achievement: Shakespeare writing about, and for,
women; women printers and booksellers in Shakespeare's
day; women as pioneering Shakespearean critics; women
as editors of Shakespeare; women painting Shakespeare;
women teaching Shakespeare; women's use of Shakespeare
for memorialization; women as Shakespearean anthologists; women's literary groups and 'Shakespeare Clubs'; the
role of Shakespeare in the women's suffrage movement;
Shakespearean performance as women's war work; women's

theatrical management; women writing Shakespeare-inspired fiction; women in the contemporary publishing industry; women directing and acting Shakespeare in anglophone and non-anglophone contexts; women playing Shakespeare as a form of dissent; women as understudies; women as voice coaches; women in the Royal Shakespeare Company and at the reconstructed Globe; women on the operatic stage; women as film directors and film editors; women's engagement with postcolonial Shakespeares; and women in cross-gendered roles. Throughout, the contributors celebrate an astonishing range of women Shakespeareans, well known and less so, from Mary Cowden Clarke to Sarah Siddons, from Anne Radcliffe to Mary Dunbar, from Charlotte Stopes to Virginia Woolf, from Peggy Ashcroft to Ann Thompson herself.

Ann is the connecting factor between the contributors, as friend, colleague, mentor, exemplar, and as someone whose breadth of interests is intimated here. She studied at King's College London, taught at the University of Liverpool, and moved to a chair at the then Roehampton Institute (now University of Roehampton). In 1999 she returned to King's as Professor of English, becoming Head of Department and then Head of the School of Arts and Humanities (that is, in general parlance, Dean). She is the founding director of the London Shakespeare Centre, based at King's, and co-organizer of the London Shakespeare Seminar. Ann is, as we hardly need to tell the readers of this collection, a general editor of the Arden Shakespeare; she is also on the advisory boards of *Shakespeare Survey* and *Shakespeare,* and is a general editor of the Arden *State of Play* series. Lecture engagements have taken her to the United States, Canada, Switzerland, Germany, Japan, Taiwan, and elsewhere. She has written on Shakespeare and Chaucer, on Shakespeare and language, on editing Shakespeare, and on the difference women have made to the phenomenon known as 'Shakespeare'. As an Arden general editor, Ann has not only been instrumental in bringing an unprecedented number of women into the editorial field but has also, with Neil Taylor, produced a landmark three-text edition of *Hamlet.*

It was only as the idea of this collection developed that the full reach of Ann's professional acquaintance and influence became clear to us. Our authors represent some of the many who are grateful to Ann for friendship, intellectual stimulation, advice, mentorship and, occasionally, productive disagreement. To a person, they responded enthusiastically to our invitation – 'just try and stop me', said one – and we are grateful for the good will, energy and learning each brought to the undertaking. Ann has provided the impetus for a wide-ranging set of essays by a formidable group of scholars, and for that we again have reason to remark our admiration for her and our appreciation, in personal as well as professional terms.

Gordon McMullan, Lena Cowen Orlin and
Virginia Mason Vaughan

ACKNOWLEDGEMENTS

The editors wish to thank the contributors for their instant enthusiasm for the project and their extraordinary willingness to produce chapters to an unyielding ceiling of 3,000 words (including title and endnotes) – a limitation we imposed for three reasons: for speed of production, for maximum focus, and because everyone we contacted initially said an immediate yes, thereby giving us (highly welcome) space issues. This eager participation can be attributed, it goes without saying, to the contributors' considerable regard, and genuine fondness, for Ann Thompson.

We would like to give special mention to John O. Thompson, Ann's husband, who knew about the project from early on, and who guarded the secret impeccably until we finally spilt the beans.

And we would like particularly to thank Margaret Bartley, Arden's indefatigable editor, for her instant and wholehearted support for the project, and for the efficiency with which she has put the book through the press. She and her team at Bloomsbury and at Fakenham Prepress – Claire Cooper, Emily Hockley, Kim Storry, Rosemary Morlin, and no doubt others we have yet to encounter at the stage at which these acknowledgements have been written – have worked rapidly and with great efficiency, and we are very grateful to them.

PART ONE

Text

1

Edward III: Women and the Making of Shakespeare as Historical Dramatist

Jean E. Howard

Columbia University

If Robert Greene's sentiments are typical, the character of Queen Margaret helped to make Shakespeare famous, or at least notorious, in the early modern theatre scene. In his *Greenes Groatsworth of Witte* he refers to Shakespeare as 'an upstart Crow, beautified with our feathers, that with his *Tygers heart wrapt in a Players hide,* supposes he is as well able to bombast out a blanke verse as the best of you: and being an absolute *Johannes fac totum,* is in his owne conceit the onely Shake-scene in a countrie'.[1] Greene here parodies Richard Plantagenet's biting indictment of Margaret before she murders him: 'O tiger's heart wrapped in a woman's hide!' (*3 Henry VI,* 1.4.138).[2] Along with the many resentments buried in this passage is Greene's acknowledgement that this 'Shakes-scene' could write powerful verse and create an unforgettable character in the figure of Margaret.

In fact, the 'bad girls' of the first tetralogy – Joan of Arc, Margaret of Anjou, Elinor Cobham – hold their own, for sheer memorability, with villains like Richard III and military heroes like Talbot. All of these women are powerful, and all of them are vilified – for cruelty, for witchcraft, for adultery, for pride, for usurping men's roles and clothes or simply, in Elinor's case, for being a fashionista who dresses too well. But they are 'players', figures who lead armies, defy custom and make things happen. Their prominence, as Phyllis Rackin and I have argued, provides a marked contrast to the diminished roles of women in the second tetralogy.[3]

Recently, textual scholars have argued that Shakespeare also probably had a hand in another early English history play, the multiply-authored *King Edward III,* and that within that play he came to write, by desire or assignment, the scenes involving the Countess of Salisbury. Accepting this attribution, I will show how in making the Countess character the young Shakespeare was shaped by the theatre culture around him even as he was beginning to be a writer others would notice and even imitate through parody. I will argue that in writing the Salisbury scenes, Shakespeare (or whoever made the plot from which Shakespeare was working)[4] drew on a template established in a number of comic history plays written in the late 1580s and early 1590s. These plays depict the education of a prince by focusing primarily on his overcoming a foolish or ill-considered sexual liaison. By drawing on and modifying that template, Shakespeare was expanding his repertory of ways to represent femininity in the history play genre, an expansion whose effects we can see in the second tetralogy.

Most scholars date *Edward III,* printed in 1596, as a play written sometime between 1590 and 1595. As theatre historians have shown, this was a period of unusual instability and fecundity in the emerging theatre industry with at least six companies performing in city theatres, a number of playhouses and inns available as performance sites, and a host of playwrights making plays, many working collaboratively. *Edward III* was created in this tumultuous time of experimentation and risk. Its last three acts – the acts *not* written primarily by Shakespeare – look a lot like *1–3 Henry VI* in their focus on martial exploits and pitched battles for control of France. Heywood's *An Apology for Actors* describes the thrilling military actions of this part of *Edward III* (or of a lost play on the same subject):

> What English Prince should hee behold the true portrature of that famous King Edward the third, foraging France, taking so great a King captive in his owne country, quartering the English Lyons with the French Flower-delyce, … would not bee suddenly Inflam'd with so royall a spectacle, being made apt and fit for the like atchievement.[5]

But Heywood's description overlooks the play's first two acts in which a less heroic Edward loses his laser focus on foreign wars because, himself married, he becomes infatuated with a married woman, the Countess of Salisbury, and goes into a lovesick funk. These scenes, I suggest, have their theatrical origins in a string of comic histories that show a king's entanglement in and renunciation of an inappropriate sexual liaison and then his embrace of a proper dynastic partner. While the basic story of Edward's encounter with the Countess of Salisbury is drawn from Froissart, its essentially comic theatrical scaffolding – and its emphasis on the education of the monarch – are drawn from elsewhere.

I argue that the matter of Edward III offered Shakespeare the opportunity to write about a successful monarch and about the sexual script that structures such a monarch's formation as well as about the good women who are essential to that script in ways the 'bad girls' of the *Henry VI* plays are not. For example, in both its opening and closing moments *Edward III* foregrounds the importance of women as the bearers of genealogical rights and the vessels who carry legitimate children. When Edward announces his intentions to conquer France, he stakes his claim through his mother, Isabel, the daughter of the French King, Philip le Beau. Those claims are treated with the utmost seriousness. To allay the suspicion that the English might simply be refuting the Salic law to serve their own interests, the defence of the English position is put in the mouth of the French nobleman, Artois:

It is not hate nor any private wrong,
But love unto my country and the right
Provokes my tongue thus lavish in report.
You are the lineal watchman of our peace,
And John of Valois indirectly climbs.
What then should subjects but embrace their king?
Ah, wherein may our duty more be seen
Than striving to rebate a tyrant's pride,
And place the true shepherd of our commonwealth?

(1.1.33–41)[6]

Here, the French King is the tyrannous usurper and Edward the 'true shepherd of our commonwealth'. Moreover, the language describing Isabel's womb is both strikingly beautiful and strikingly horticultural. Artois says: 'Isabel / Was all the daughters that this Philip had, / Whom afterward your father took to wife; / And from the fragrant garden of her womb / Your gracious self, the flower of Europe's hope, / Derivèd is inheritor to France' (1.1.11–16). The womb here is like a garden, and from the soil of that French garden sprang the flower, Edward.

While the pregnant womb of Edward's *mother* is only narrated and not directly embodied on stage, the same is not true for his *wife*. In Act IV an English nobleman reports to Edward that while Edward has been in France, David of Scotland has been beaten:

by the fruitful service of your peers
And painful travail of the queen herself,
That, big with child, was every day in arms,
Vanquished, subdued, and taken prisoner.

(4.2.43–6)

Here the maternal body is figured not only as a generative body but as a warrior's body. Pregnant but in arms, the Queen has helped to vanquish England's long-standing northern foes. In Act V she appears in France, still pregnant, when the Black Prince arrives victorious over his French enemies to be reunited both with his father and his mother.

Edward III, then, is bookended by the beautiful image of Isabel's fragrant womb and by the striking presence of the pregnant Philippa onstage with her husband and eldest son – a carefully staged embodiment of the successful dynastic family. Moreover, this positive representation of women's generative power is both reinforced and complicated by other parts of the play. In Acts I and II, after the initial account of England's claim to France, King Edward has his dangerous and prolonged encounter with the Countess of Salisbury in which he tries to get her to commit adultery with him. This part of the play, I suggest, employs a dramatic template familiar from Greene's *Friar Bacon and Friar Bungay*, his *The Scottish History of James IV*, and the anonymous *Fair Em*, probably all late 1580s and early 1590s plays. In each, a King or a Prince is overcome with foolish or ill-considered sexual desire that must be vanquished before he and his realm can prosper. In each case the monarch's sexual desire is ultimately directed towards an appropriate dynastic mate, an action that also reincorporates him into a homosocial network of male peers, advisors, and allies.

Consider *James IV*. In the opening scene James has just married Dorothea, his English queen, but announces in an aside in the chapel where he was married that his 'wandering eyes bewitch'd [his] heart' and 'The Scottish Ida's beauty stale [his] heart' (1.1.81 and 84).[7] Fair Ida resists the King's blandishments, and James eventually returns his heart to Dorothea, but not before Scotland totters from what his counsellors call James' 'heedless youth' (2.2.210) and the power he gives to Ateukin, a fake wizard whom he commands to win Ida to him. Only in Act V, upon learning of Ida's marriage to the virtuous Lord Eustace, does

James have a miraculous change of heart, recall his love for Dorothea, and curse his own lust and the evils of sycophants and flatterers who supported him in his misdeeds. Similarly, in the anonymous *Fair Em* William the Conqueror sees the image of a woman in a shield, goes to the Danish court to marry her, but on seeing her face to face decides she is 'sluttish' and fixes his heart on Marianna, a virtuous woman betrothed to another. Eventually, William, through a disguise plot, is brought to recover his original love for Blanche, the King's daughter whose face he had seen in the shield, thus making an appropriate dynastic union, just as James had made in wedding Dorothea.

The play most similar in structure, as well as theme, to *Edward III*, however, is *Friar Bacon and Friar Bungay*. Besides the magician plot, there is another involving Henry III's son, Prince Edward. Edward is destined for marriage with Eleanor, daughter to the King of Castile. But while hunting in the English countryside, Edward falls suddenly and hopelessly in love with Margaret, the Fair Maid of Fressingfield. She, in turn, falls in love with Lacy, the Earl of Lincoln and Edward's friend. Only in the middle of the play does Edward undergo a sudden transformation as he listens to Margaret and Lacy both plead for death so that the other can be spared. In an aside the Prince says:

Edward, art thou that famous Prince of Wales
Who at Damasco beat the Saracens,
And brought'st home triumph on thy lance's point,
And shall thy plumes be pull'd by Venus down?
Is it princely to dissever lovers' leagues,
To part such friends as glory in their loves?
Leave, Ned, and make a virtue of this fault,
And further Peg and Lacy in their loves.
So in subduing fancy's passion,
Conquering thyself, thou get'st the richest spoil.

(8.112–21)[8]

Edward eventually makes a proper dynastic marriage to Eleanor of Castile.

In each of these plays, the education of a monarch or a monarch-to-be requires that he learn to curb his sexual passion for an inappropriate sexual partner, no matter how attractive and virtuous she may be. In every instance, the women the monarch illicitly desires are chaste; none is a sexual temptress or adulteress. But none of them, even those of high social standing, is an appropriate partner for the monarch whose marriage choices in each case must cement a foreign connection and extend his country's international alliance structure.

These comic histories are, I argue, part of what went into the making of the first part of *Edward III* and determine its comic arc. The play did not *have* to dramatize Edward's northern adventures at all, though they are mentioned in Holinshed and elaborated in Froissart and Painter's *Palace of Pleasure*. But one way in the early 1590s to dramatize a successful king was to stage his triumph over inappropriate sexual passion. This is exactly the narrative that organizes the first part of *Edward III* that scholars now attribute to Shakespeare. Riding north to relieve the Scottish siege of Roxburgh Castle where the Countess of Salisbury is courageously holding out, Edward falls passionately in love with her, only later coming to his senses. Several things, however, are unique about *Edward III*'s handling of this familiar dramatic template. First, the last three acts of the play show a king actually ruling well, an outcome more implied than demonstrated in many of the comic histories I discussed above. Having passed the sexual test that seems the pre-condition for successful rule, King Edward goes on to lead his armies to victory in France and resecures his dynastic family. Second, Edward's marriage is of long standing and neither newly achieved nor in prospect. That means that the fruits of a dynastic marriage are on stage for all to see in the person of his son.

Like the other plays in this grouping, Edward's pursuit of the Countess reveals both a lack of personal self-control and a danger to all the relationships that support his rule. Like Margaret, Ida and Marianne, the Countess of Salisbury is chaste, comparing herself at one point to Abraham's wife Sarah in her faithfulness to her husband. But Edward presses his suit recklessly, even pressuring her father, Warwick, on his allegiance to the King, to command the Countess to comply with the King's wishes. His behaviour alarms his counsellors, alienates his supporters and threatens to abort the French campaign.

Edward's reversal of perspective begins when, unexpectedly, the son, Prince Edward, arrives at Roxburgh Castle with men he has gathered for the French invasion. The sight of his son's face fills Edward with piercing remorse because the son's face recalls that of Edward's wife, the Prince's mother:

> I see the boy. Oh, how his mother's face,
> Modelled in his, corrects my strayed desire,
> And rates my heart, and chides my thievish eye,
> Who, being rich enough in seeing her,
> Yet seeks elsewhere

(2.2.75–9)

A moment later, after Edward greets his father, the King resumes his aside:

> Still do I see in him delineate
> His mother's visage: those his eyes are hers,
> ...
> Away, loose silks of wavering vanity!
> Shall the large limit of fair Bretagne
> By me be overthrown, and shall I not
> Master this little mansion of myself?
> Give me an armour of eternal steel,
> I go to conquer kings.

(2.2.86–97)

Usually early moderns assumed that the mother provided the matter upon which the form of the father was imprinted, but this scene reverses expectations. Edward's son bears the impress of the mother's features, and that son will bear Edward's lineage into the future.

I argue, then, that *Edward III* shows the effects of having been written in the vibrant theatre culture of the early 1590s, and it riffs on several received ways of dramatizing English kingship. It shows, I have suggested, familiarity in the Salisbury scenes with the protocols of comic history in the Robert Greene mode. The first two acts recall and modify the story of a King led astray by desire, the sturdy resistance of a virtuous woman, and the eventual reformation of the monarch. This story is then sutured onto a more martial story, familiar from the battle scenes of *1 Henry VI*, about struggles for territory in France and the consolidation of manhood in battle. Unlike the bad marriages of Henry VI and Edward IV and the threatening women of the Henry VI plays, *Edward III* features two virtuous wives, Salisbury and Philippa, and presents the fruits of dynastic union in the person of the valorous Black Prince.

If I am right that *Edward III* reveals its origins in the theatre culture of the early 1590s, it also has its effects on later drama. When Shakespeare created Prince Hal, he took his storyline of the reformed Prince from Holinshed and also from the first half of *The Famous Victories,* but the comic histories and *Edward III* also played a role, particularly in marking the culmination of reform in the acquisition of a French princess in a dynastic union. As in the comic histories, Hal must end a dangerous infatuation before he can be a successful ruler. But Shakespeare's innovation was to make that infatuation centre – not on a virtuous woman – but on a vice-ridden, but charismatic older man. Whether we see the tavern world as homoerotic or simply homosocial, Falstaff's hold on Hal has to be broken before the young king can establish ties with the 'right' kind of homosocial community: his counsellors, the Lord Chief Justice, the peers of England, and his brothers.

With that rapprochement, Hal is set to be a legitimate King whose comic education narrative ends with marriage to the French Princess. Henry's marriage to her fulfils the cultural logic of the stage's representation of comic kingship, though it does not erase the fact that Katherine of France is given by her father as a prize of war to her country's conqueror. One need not demonize women to treat them as the second sex, but that is another story.

Notes

1   Robert Greene, *Greene's Groatsworth of Wit* in E. K. Chambers, *The Elizabethan Stage* (Oxford, 1923), 4: 241–2.

2   *The Norton Shakespeare*, 2nd edn, eds Greenblatt, Howard, Cohen and Maus (eds) (New York), p. 340.

3   Jean E. Howard and Phyllis Rackin, *Engendering a Nation: A Feminist Account of Shakespeare's English Histories* (New York, 1997).

4   For the idea of the plot as a document preceding what was often the collaborative writing of a play, see Tiffany Stern, *Documents of Performance in Early Modern England* (Cambridge, 2009), pp. 8–33.

5   Thomas Heywood, *Apology for Actors* (London, 1609), B4r.

6   All quotations from the play are taken from *King Edward III*, ed. Giorgio Melchiori (Cambridge, 1998).

7   Robert Greene, *James the Fourth,* in Ashley Thorndike ed., *Minor Elizabethan Drama* (London: Dent and Sons, 1958), p. 235.

8   Robert Greene, *Friar Bacon and Friar Bungay,* ed. Daniel Seltzer (Lincoln, NE, 1963), pp. 50–1.

2

Beguiling Fictions

Dympna Callaghan
Syracuse University

> '*I'faith, is't true?*'
> OTHELLO 3.4.77[1]

> '*Is it true think you?*'
> THE WINTER'S TALE, 4.4.266[2]

Most modern readers regard the early modern opposition to literature as the manifestation of a benighted fanaticism, now mercifully extinct among all right-thinking people. Even twentieth-century literary Marxists, who viewed the Puritans as the vanguard of the political changes that eventually led to parliamentary democracy, stumbled with some embarrassment over the historical contradiction that this brand of Protestantism was accompanied by an often violent antipathy towards literature – at least until later in the seventeenth century when Milton handily saved the day. Importantly the Puritans opposed not just specific books but the entire category of literary expression. My own view is that we do not take the Puritan suspicion of '*poesie*' (a term which covered all forms of imaginative writing) with nearly the seriousness it deserves. There is after all *something* if not actively suspect, then at least worthy of investigation and intellectual attention, about the whole business of being absorbed in fictionality, which is further complicated by the long-standing denigration of fiction as feminine. Although storytelling was always disparaged by virtue of its association with women (for example, old-wives tales and nursery stories), with the advent of the novel, the argument that fiction was itself feminine gathered momentum.[3] Whether understood to be 'natural' or culturally 'produced', assertions about the affinity between femininity and fiction seem to be at least in part based on empirical evidence: Amazon reports most readers of fiction are women, and according to Franco Moretti, this has been true for at least 300 years.[4]

If the consumers of Autolycus's ballads in *The Winter's Tale* and Desdemona (whose heart is won by storytelling) are anything to go by, however, women's love affair with fiction was indeed already well-established in the Elizabethan and Jacobean world. Yet, there is not much to connect the lower-class, rustic Mopsa with the Italian urbanite, Desdemona, except that during the ritual of courtship both characters enjoy stories of marvels and monsters and both receive traditional tokens of affection and commitment: 'ribbons and gloves' in the case of Mopsa (4.4.234) and 'a handkerchief / Spotted with strawberries' (3.3.437–8) in the case of Desdemona. Mopsa's 'Is't true?' occurs in response to Autolycus's narrative of an ostensibly new, true story (now printed as a ballad) of the usurer's wife who gave birth to bags of money and developed an unnatural appetite for toads. Desdemona's life is closer to that of the ballad's wife than to Mopsa's.[5] The wife's fate is arguably punishment for a transgressive match, a point intimated by her rustic friend Dorcas's response to the story: 'Bless me from marrying a usurer' (4.4.268).

While the fictionality of Autolycus's ballad is undeniable, the veracity of the story of the origins and provenance of the handkerchief is far more problematic. Othello advances truth claims about this 'antique token' (5.2.214) and since they are made within the context of tragedy, the audience must take them seriously. In his first account, the handkerchief has maternal and entirely female origins having been given to Othello's mother by an Egyptian 'charmer'. Because it is part of his attempt to wrest evidence of adultery from Desdemona, this account possesses the moral agenda of a fable: '[W]hile she kept it, / 'Twould make her amiable and subdue my father ... / ... but if she lost it / ... my father's eye / Should hold her loathed' (3.4.59–64).Yet, at the end of the play, when Othello claims that it was a keepsake 'my father gave my mother' (5.2.215), the napkin has become a patriarchal object. From the vantage point of these contradictory histories of the handkerchief, this essay briefly considers the relationship between tragedy, complete with its complex gender coding, and fictionality itself.

* * *

Female susceptibility to fiction – which amounts to gulli-bility in the case of Mopsa, 'I love a ballad in print, a-life, for then we are sure they are true' (4.4.260–1) is typically adduced as evidence of inferior intellectual capacity, a failure to grasp reality in a rational and objective manner. Othello's potent narrative has worked upon Desdemona's 'delicate youth' (1.2.74) and enervated her senses, making her physi-cally, sexually vulnerable to that which 'weakens motion' (1.2.75). Telling stories, in other words, is the early modern equivalent of Rophynol, 'drugs or minerals' (1.2.74). A story 'Hath thus *beguiled* your daughter of herself' (1.3.67, my emphasis), and the power of fiction to evacuate agency (both male and female) is one of its most dangerous characteristics. Fiction is a form of pleasure and a form of abuse: 'She is abused' (1.3.61).Yet Brabantio arrives at this conviction about

Othello's 'mighty magic' (1.3.93) only because of his own susceptibility to reading: 'Have you not read ... / Of some such thing?' (1.1.171–2).[6]

Othello's story is, however, ostensibly not just 'made up'. That is, it purports to be a 'travailous history' (1.3.140).[7] The adjective here indicates not only Othello's past hardships but also that this is not some light, frivolous or fanciful tale. It is not fiction but autobiography – that is, if we can accept (as the play encourages us to do) that Desdemona 'seriously inclines' to believe that stories about 'men whose heads / Do grow beneath their shoulders' (1.3.145–6) are indeed a factually verifiable aspect of Othello's experience. This is a different although very much thematically related form of information from the estimations of the number of ships in the Turkish fleet, which preface Othello's great autobiographical speech. The reckonings about the fleet are contradictory, but Montano's is the report that wins out in part because: 'Your trusty and most valiant servitor / Prays you to *believe him*' (1.3.41–3).[8] Similarly, *history* is a respectable category of fiction, a story that is dignified by its assertion of veracity and facticity.[9] When in the seventeenth and eighteenth centuries women became completely identified with those 'bad' kinds of fictions called 'novels' and 'romances', Defoe, Richardson and Fielding called their fictions 'histories' precisely in order to exempt themselves from the taint of femininity.

The forms of attention that attach to listening to a story are, here and elsewhere in Shakespeare, also marked by gender difference. There is more than a hint of unsophisticated credulity in Desdemona's 'greedy ear':

> This to hear
> Would Desdemona seriously incline,
> But still the house affairs would draw her thence,
> Which ever as she could with haste dispatch
> She'd come again, and with a greedy ear
> Devour up my discourse.
>
> (1.3.146–51)

This act of listening is reminiscent of the young princes Guiderius and Arviragus who attend to the war stories in *Cymbeline*.[10] Whereas Desdemona is characterized as a 'pliant' (1.3.152) consumer, the boys immediately transform what they hear into action: 'in posture / That acts my words' (3.3.94–5).[11] Desdemona's greedy ears, her voracious consumption of the story, are arguably mitigated by her serious inclination – that is, her careful, curious, eager attention and the physical posture 'serious inclination' suggests. Desdemona attends the story in 'a pliant hour', the time when she has the leisure to listen. 'Pliant' also connotes yielding and succumbing to Othello's sexual advances.[12] There is no such pliability in the princes who do not absorb the story so much as immediately *express* it. The princes' agency is never in question, whereas Othello admits that he 'often did *beguile* her [Desdemona] of her tears' (1.3.157, my emphasis). 'Beguile' has connotations both of fraud, cunning (guile) and magical deceit.[13] However, the boys in *Cymbeline* are incapable of the kind of sympathy exhibited by Desdemona's 'world of sighs' (1.3.160) – or, according to the Folio, a 'world of kisses':

> 'Twas pitiful, 'twas wondrous pitiful!
>
> (1.3.162)

It is her seriousness and empathy that separates Desdemona from the entertainingly dizzy-headed frivolity of Mopsa and Dorcas. They, of course, want to believe what they hear is true, and Autolycus is happy to oblige with comic verification: 'Here's the midwife's name to't, one Mistress Tale-Porter' (4.4.269–70). In contrast, when Desdemona hears the story of the handkerchief, she believes it, even while wishing it to be a fabrication. Importantly, her interrogatives, 'I'faith, is't true?' and 'Is't possible?' do not follow the narratives performed in the rites of courtship but rather serve as the sequel to the macabre yet lyrical post-nuptial tale of the origin and provenance of the handkerchief. It is only at this critical moment, and importantly not before, that Desdemona shares Mopsa's admixture of credulity and doubt about tall tales. This incipient, new-found scepticism represents a *volte face* from her earlier trustful attention to Othello's (literally) outlandish accounts of his exotic adventures.[14]

Barbara Hardy has demonstrated that *Othello*, which begins with Othello's life story and ends with Emilia's revelations, is 'a play about the ethics of narrative'[15] and a 'performance of telling'.[16] The intimation of duplicity inherent in Othello's double story of the handkerchief plays out the Puritan commonplace that all fictions are lies. Further, the first napkin story potentially undermines Othello's assertion in 1.3 that he used no enchantments to win Desdemona's heart.[17] Othello's use of the object wrought by an enchantress, a 'charmer' who 'could almost read / The thoughts of people' (3.4.59–60), is precisely one of the 'indirect ... courses' that he is initially charged with using to 'subdue' (a word first uttered in the Senate's charges against him) Desdemona's affections (1.3.113). Clearly, if the handkerchief is meant to have the power to 'subdue'[18] husbands, it has failed miserably because Desdemona dropped it in the process of trying to quell the headache induced by Othello's belief that his brow now bears the cuckold's horns: 'Your napkin is too little, / Let it alone' (3.3.291–2). There is more at play here than sheer inconsistency in these narratives about the handkerchief. This is at a point in the play *after* Othello has sworn on his knees with Iago to kill his wife. Thus, far from being a neutral, objective narrative, this is a story intended to terrify her – just as the jealous husband, Harebrain, in Middleton's comedy *A Mad World My Masters* seeks to control his wife with horrific stores of damnation: 'Terrify her, terrify her!' (1.2).

Many commentators have assumed that Shakespeare simply made an error in the double napkin narrative, one that is inconspicuous in performance.[19] In so doing, such readings trivialize the handkerchief along the lines of that entertaining but nonetheless undeniably obtuse early commentator on the play, Thomas Rymer. For it is not the ontological status of the handkerchief itself that is momentous, but rather its discursive function. That is to say, what accords an object symbolic significance as talisman or fetish, is the story that attaches to it. Audiences tend not to notice the discrepancy in Othello's mythmaking around the handkerchief, in part because he unequivocally asserts its truth in response to Desdemona's horrified question: 'Is't possible?' (3.4.70): ''Tis true ... / And it was dyed in mummy, which the skillful / Conserved of maidens' hearts' (3.4.71–7).

The myth does not tell us *how* the maidens' hearts were procured or whether they died of natural causes, or whether they were butchered specifically for the purpose of making the dye, black mummy, which denotes Othello's alienation from all that is Venetian.[20] There are ominous, indeed grisly, intimations here that resonate with Othello's later promise to dispatch Desdemona by violent means: 'I will chop her into messes!' (4.1.197). In a recursive gesture characteristic of Ovidian myth, these violently dismembered 'messes' ('portions of meat; pulpy or semi-liquid food')[21], bring us back to the spectre of 'the cannibals that each other eat' at the start of the play. While for her father, Desdemona is the victim of Othello's potent narrative, here *she* is one of the greedy Anthropophagi, a devouring man-eater. Yet, Desdemona, who earlier listened to far-fetched stories of cannibalism, 'the cannibals that each other eat, / The Anthropophagi' (1.3.144–5), and would 'with a greedy ear / Devour up my discourse' (1.3.150–1), has by Act IV herself become, so to speak, a serving portion. E. A. J. Honigmann's note on the somatically confused image of the 'greedy ear' that substitutes the ear for the mouth while intimating and foreshadowing the randomly butchered body parts of 'messes', shows that it has stronger implications than the sense that Desdemona has been hanging on Othello's every word. In *Macbeth* what is being ingested is toxic but is devoured with indiscriminate animal appetite: 'greedily devour the treacherous bait' (3.1.128). Similarly, in Sonnet 129, the poet's post-coital condition is described as 'hated as a swallowed bayt, On purpose layd to make the taker mad'. Desdemona's greed connotes the voracity of Erysichthon, who was punished by the gods with insatiable hunger, and who finally eats himself. He thus reached what Leonard Barkan calls 'the outer limits of metamorphosis'.[22] Indeed, the connection between this first story and the subsequent stories about the handkerchief is specifically Ovidian. The *Metamorphosis* is replete with images of cannibalism, and at the poem's conclusion, the Pythagorean defence of vegetarianism argues that carnivores *are* cannibals.[23] Leonard Barkan observes: 'Cannibalism is the ultimate extension of metamorphosis and its ultimate crime. If transformation bridges organisms and the universe via a corporeal metaphor, then it can all be reduced to a terrible kind of eating.'[24]

In the double story of the handkerchief, then, we enter the complex and mysterious etiology of myth that undermines what Kenneth Gross calls 'the artifactual status of the handkerchief'. This is a story not of beginnings, which belong to human history, but of origins, which belong to the quasi-divine territory of myth where there is no requirement either for linearity or consistency and where the story of human culture to be told over and over again is that of the necessity of exogamy and the fears that attend it.[25]

In *Othello*, both men and women are susceptible to the power of fiction, to the plausibility of misrepresentation. A further terrible suspicion looms, however, that the world is invented rather than known. By this I mean that inherent in Shakespeare's tragic scepticism here is the fear that truth is not simply hidden and obfuscated in the slippery exchanges between appearance and reality and the world is not there waiting to be known, but is being variously created, wrought, remodelled, built, imagined, invented, demolished, desecrated or distorted by language and narrative strategy. Far from being the harmless entertainment for women that it is in *The Winter's Tale*, in *Othello* there is a terrifying tragic apprehension of the power of fiction: to kill those who consume it.

Notes

1   William Shakespeare, *Othello*, ed. E. A. J. Honigmann, 3rd
    edn. Arden Shakespeare, 1996.

2   William Shakespeare, *The Winter's Tale*, ed. John A. Pitcher,
    3rd edn. Arden Shakespeare, 2010.

3   For critical accounts of this phenomenon, see Nancy
    Armstrong, *Desire and Domestic Fiction: A Political History of
    the Novel* (New York, 1987). Janet M. Todd, *Feminist Literary
    History* (New York, 1988). Ian Watt, *The Rise of the Novel:
    Studies in Defoe, Richardson And Fielding* (Whitefish, MT,
    2010). Jane Spencer, *The Rise of the Woman Novelist: From
    Aphra Behn to Jane Austen* (Oxford and New York, 1986).

4   Franco Moretti, *Graphs, Maps, Trees: Abstract Models for a
    Literary History* (London and New York, 2005), pp. 26–7.

5   Lena Cowen Orlin points out that Desdemona's disposition
    comports with another genre poised between the fictive
    ideal and the social real, namely that of the conduct book,
    'Desdemona's Disposition' in Shirley Nelson Garner and
    Madelon Sprengnether, *Shakespearean Tragedy and Gender*
    (Bloomington, IN, 1996), pp. 171–92.

6   I am grateful to Deanne Williams for this point.

7   James A. Knapp, '"Ocular Proof": Archival Revelations and
    Aesthetic Response', *Poetics Today*, 24, 4 (Winter 2003),
    695–727, 715.

8   Despite the editorial emendation of 'believe' to 'relieve' by
    Honigmann among others on grounds of military strategy,
    the juxtaposition of belief with truth and of appearance with
    reality in the Ottomans' attempt to distract the Venetians with
    a 'pageant' of ships towards Rhodes rehearse what will be the
    crucial terms of this tragedy.

9   Two important examinations of evidentiary standards are
    Frances E. Dolan, *True Relations: Reading, Literature,
    and Evidence in Seventeenth-Century England*, 1st edn
    (Philadelphia, 2013) and Holger Schott Syme, *Theatre and
    Testimony in Shakespeare's England: A Culture of Mediation*
    (Cambridge and New York, 2012).

10   Dympna Callaghan, *Who Was William Shakespeare?
     An Introduction to the Life and Works*, 1st edn (Oxford,
     2013), pp. 215–16.

11   William Shakespeare, *Cymbeline*, ed. Roger Warren (Oxford,
     1998).

12   William Shakespeare, *Othello*, ed. Michael Neill (New York,
     2006), p. 224.

13   Ibid.

14   Iago also succumbs to storytelling in the form of gossip about
     Emilia's alleged infidelity.

15   Barbara Nathan Hardy, *Shakespeare's Storytellers: Dramatic
     Narration* (London and Chester Springs, PA, 1997), p. 58.

16   Ibid, p. 62.

17   William Shakespeare, *Othello: Texts and Contexts* ed. Kim
     Hall (New York, 2006), p. 12. On the wider significance of
     witchcraft here, see Lena Cowen Orlin, *Private Matters and
     Public Culture in Post-Reformation England* (Ithaca, NY,
     1994), pp. 207–15.

18   There is a connection here between the handkerchief and
     Sidney's *Old Arcadia* where the recipe for the potion that
     makes Basileus appear dead is initially said to belong to
     the Kings of Cyprus but is subsequently discovered to have
     been manufactured by Gynacia's grandmother to 'subdue' a
     young nobleman into marrying her. As David Houston Wood
     points out, both Sidney and Shakespeare's stories involve
     the 'representation of female autonomy and power,' *Time,
     Narrative, and Emotion in Early Modern England* (Farnham,
     2009), p. 62.

19   Michael C. Andrews, 'Honest Othello: The Handkerchief Once
     More', *Studies in English Literature, 1500–1900* 13, 2 (1 April
     1973), 273–84 (283).

20   Virginia Mason Vaughan, *Othello: A Contextual History*
     (Cambridge and New York, 1994), p. 33.

21   Neill, p. 336.

22   Leonard Barkan, *The Gods Made Flesh: Metamorphosis and
     the Pursuit of Paganism* (New Haven, CT, 1990), p. 92.

23 Ibid.

24 Ibid.

25 Knapp, p.716.

26 'Metamorphosis is a figure for all the fears and necessities
    of exogamy, and so stories of metamorphosis are stories of
    pursuit, of travel, or unfamiliar and alien loves', Barkan, p. 14.

3

'Bride-habited, but maiden-hearted': Language and Gender in *The Two Noble Kinsmen*

Hannah Crawforth

King's College London

The Two Noble Kinsmen (1613–14) is a play fundamentally concerned with questions of sameness and difference; the two eponymous knights are troublingly alike, to the extent that Emilia struggles to choose between them when forced to do so. Their identities are treated as interchangeable by Shakespeare and Fletcher; 'a husband I have 'pointed, / But do not know him,' Emilia says, knowing only that she will marry either Palamon or Arcite, and apparently caring little (or beyond caring) as to which (5.1.151–2).[1] The play's collaborative authorship, and evidence suggesting that its two playwrights deliberately set out to imitate one another's style, has long since placed the issue of likeness at the heart of critical discussions of this tragicomedy.[2] More recently *The*

Two Noble Kinsmen's treatment of gender politics has been
the focus of such conversations, with the play's examination
of same-sex friendship – and desire – providing a nexus for
the considerations of difference that have dominated readings
of the play. In this essay I take up this debate, shifting its
terms whilst keeping the key issue of gender firmly in mind.
I will argue that the playwrights consciously attempt to
play out ideas of sameness and difference through language
itself, and that their unusually close engagement with the
play's Chaucerian source, in an edition published by Thomas
Speght in 1602, permits them to draw upon the contrasting
etymological origins of English vocabulary in order to cast
light upon the congruities and disparities that underpin the
vernacular in which they write.[3]

As Ann Thompson notes, Speght's 1598 and 1602 volumes
of Chaucer's *Workes* produced a flurry of drama inspired by
the medieval poet.[4] Notably, Speght appends a list of 'The
hard words of Chaucer, explained', using a series of abbre-
viations to demarcate derivations from Latin, Arabic, Greek,
Italian, French, Dutch and 'the Saxon tongue'.[5] Speght's
identification of the etymological origins of the Chaucerian
vocabulary he glosses is important because it allows us to
begin to address a question that has been little considered
in relation to early modern dramatists' work: where did
they think their words came from? In the wake of polem-
ically-motivated attempts to recover the origins of English
in Anglo-Saxon led by Archbishop Matthew Parker in the
mid-sixteenth century, writers were forced to acknowledge
for the first time that their own vernacular was not predominantly classical but rather had more in common with so-called
Teutonic languages including German and Dutch.[6] Looking at
Speght's glosses, which highlight the often equally unfamiliar
roots of borrowed words and those held to be ostensibly
'native', one is forced to ask whether all English vocabulary
might in fact be regarded as alien in its origins. The wordlist
reveals the tension between sameness and difference that was
beginning to emerge in early modern understanding of the

history of the vernacular, bringing into focus the question of how far even Old English is 'English'. The perplexing 'strange likeness' this unfamiliar form bears to our own language would both trouble and inspire scholars and literary authors throughout the period.[7]

In introducing the Arden Third Series edition of *The Two Noble Kinsmen*, Lois Potter describes the 'mixed' genre and setting of the play, as well as its more obviously mixed authorship: 'a Jacobean dramatization of a medieval English tale based on an Italian romance version of a Latin epic about one of the oldest and most tragic Greek legends; it has two authors and two heroes' (1). We might add to this list the play's reimagining of gender categories and sexual identities as themselves 'mixed'. Encountering Chaucer's English in an edition that makes the diverse origins of his language explicit, Shakespeare and Fletcher can have been in little doubt that they were writing this conspicuously hybrid play in a language that is itself a hybrid. This impetus may account for the numerous compounds that we find in the play, which often juxtapose terms drawn from contrasting roots (as emphasized by hyphenation in modern editions). Emilia's lament (from which my title derives), 'I am bride-habited / But maiden-hearted' (5.1.150–1) is just one notable example of this tendency to combine words in a way that draws attention to the disparate roots of English, compounding terms of Old English, Latin, High German and again Old English derivation, respectively. Shakespeare and Fletcher choose to have Emilia express the ambiguities of her sexuality, and specifically her attitude to marriage, in a phrase that foregrounds the awkwardness arising from attempts to reconcile the contradictory and estranged origins of our language.

Speght's 1602 glossary offers unique insight not only into how the playwrights might have expected their audience to respond to the vocabulary of this tragicomedy, but also as to the way they themselves understood the history of the language out of which *The Two Noble Kinsmen* is constructed. Where an entry in Speght's list corresponds to a word's usage in the play we can legitimately ask whether the dramatist employs a particular term in a self-consciously archaizing way. At the beginning of the fifth act, for instance, Arcite and Palamon prepare to encounter one another in the combat upon which the outcome of the drama's events will seemingly depend. Each addresses his prayers to the gods, entreating their assistance in securing victory against the other and thus winning the hand of Emilia. Arcite prostrates himself at the altar first, addressing:

> Thou mighty one, that with thy power hast turned
> Green Neptune into purple; whose approach
> Comets preward; whose havoc in vast field
> Unearthed skulls proclaim; whose breath blows down
> The teeming Ceres' foison; who dost pluck
> With hand armipotent from forth blue clouds
> The masoned turrets

(5.1.49–55)

The curious word 'armipotent', which might seem at first glance to be a compositor's error, or at first hearing to be a malapropism committed by actor or author, is in fact the pivotal term in Arcite's speech. His god is not 'omnipotent', all-powerful, but 'armipotent', a Latin term meaning 'mightie in armes', Speght tells us. Arcite's misplaced faith in the gods of war will ultimately destroy him, his own skill in horsemanship helping to bring about his tragic fate. The choice of this adjective is not a slip on the dramatists' part, but a carefully selected term that anticipates Arcite's downfall whilst at the same time looking back to the source of his tale. As Potter notes, Shakespeare and Fletcher seem to have borrowed this word directly from Chaucer's *The Knight's Tale* (l.1982); Chaucer, in turn, derives the term from Boccaccio's *Teseida* (7.32); its ultimate source appears to be Statius' *Thebiad* (7.78). The entire history of the story of Palamon and Arcite is encapsulated in this single word, an ostentatious borrowing from Latin that mirrors the borrowing of the play's key narrative from these diverse sources. The moment causes the listener or reader to reconsider their own awareness of the English language, casting doubt over both the concept of an omnipotent god, which is evoked only to be rejected here, and also towards any notion of masculinity that is over-reliant on military might. Just as the word 'armipotent' has strayed far enough from its Latin root as to be unrecognizable to early modern readers, as its presence in Speght's glossary suggests, so one should ask whether any notion of masculinity that depends on placing trust in the power of arms could lead one similarly astray.

Speght's list expounds meanings in the playwrights' words that have since been lost to us, and which would have been at least partly unfamiliar to his first audiences, owing to the processes of language change between Chaucer's time and his own. In the passage quoted above we find two additional terms that Speght thought worthy of further explanation. The sense of the word 'foison, *f.* plenty' is amplified by the etymological note provided by Speght, looking beyond the word's primary early modern sense of 'harvest', which had come into being relatively recently, and back to the earlier medieval origins of the noun, meaning 'abundance' (*OED*, 'foison, *n*'). The French roots of the word contrast with the Anglo-Saxon adjective Shakespeare and Fletcher pair it with here, 'teeming' (*OED*, 'teem, *v*'), and using Speght's list to reconnect the term to its etymology allows us to see it as a characteristic juxtaposition of two terms of different derivations. The other word from Arcite's prayer that Speght glosses is 'laude, *l.* praise', another borrowing into English from Latin. The presence of this lemma in Speght's list, despite the fact that it appears to have been in current usage, seems designed to highlight the slight change in spelling by which 'laude' (like numerous other Chaucerian words) has lost its final '-e', an important metrical feature of the earlier poet's work (and one that was notoriously misunderstood in the Renaissance). Whilst neither 'foison' nor 'laud' would be considered archaisms at the moment the play was written, each of these terms has deviated from its original meaning or spelling as it was first borrowed into Middle English, and as it is listed in Speght's wordlist. As such, reading this speech with Speght as a guide prompts the reader of the play to consider from a linguistic viewpoint the issue of divergence from these origins, articulating at the level of diction precisely those questions of similarity and difference that concern the playwrights throughout the drama by drawing attention to the issue of how far the language of the past is contiguous with that of the present.

In other cases, the distance between a word's origin and its usage in *The Two Noble Kinsmen* is greater. When the First Queen describes the lips of a suppliant woman as 'twinning cherries' (1.1.178), the quarto spelling 'twyning' recalls Chaucer's etymological use of the word: 'twynned, *b*., parted,' Speght glosses. The evolution of 'twin' into the dual senses of 'twofold, double' and 'sunder, sever, part' is complex, and they remain intertwined (*OED*, 'twin, *a* and *n*, 4'; 'twin, v^1').[8] The line is enriched by the residual history of meaning within this word; the image depicts not just a pair of lips but the additional sensuous information that they are parting, moving to speak, to beg, to entreat, and even to kiss, hinting at a sexuality informing the suppliant's gesture. When Palamon asks 'What canon is there / That does command my rapier from my hip' in the service of his hateful uncle Creon (1.2.55–6), a similar etymological echo adds a secondary meaning to what he says: 'canon, *g*., a rule' observes Speght. It is not just the report of a gun that might drive him to act, but rather a complex legal system in which he owes fealty to his ruler.

In both of these instances, Speght's list can help us to recover additional meanings of the verse, from which we ourselves have been distanced by linguistic change across time. In fact, as the necessary obsolescence of any term appearing in Speght's list implies, these meanings were already on the verge of disappearing as Shakespeare and Fletcher wrote. But it is worth considering the possibility that having read Chaucer in Speght's edition the dramatists might have discovered for themselves these semantic echoes in the appended glossaries, and might have chosen to use these terms in such a way as to subordinate their older medieval, and pre-medieval, senses to the service of their own verse. The supplementary significances Speght's list helps us to extract from such words both amplify and undercut the primary senses the playwrights' vocabulary evokes (and I have selected here only a few representative examples amongst many instances in the drama). They prompt consideration at a linguistic level of the issues of sameness and difference, convergence and divergence, which are the keynote of the play's treatment of gender. The audience, in either theatre or print, is forced to re-examine the stability of their most basic assumptions in the light of a new understanding that even aspects of their own vernacular might in fact be alien to them. As such, this richly ambivalent diction is also entirely in keeping with the dramatists' treatment of other aspects of their Chaucerian source here and elsewhere. The play 'enters into a continuing and detailed dialogue with its original', argues Helen Cooper, which not only carries over the complex moral problems of *The Knight's Tale*, 'but makes them sharper; the untied thematic ends of Chaucer's original are not just left loose but rendered jagged'. This reflects the ways in which Shakespeare and Fletcher produce a version of the tale that problematizes the portrayal of 'rationality, affection, and passion in both men and women', Cooper continues, destabilizing gender identities in a way absent from *The Canterbury Tales*.[9]

In utilizing Chaucer's words in such a way as to substantiate, extend, and even challenge the gender assumptions of their source text, Shakespeare and Fletcher also question the status of their primary material and assert their own capacity to make literary history. By thus evoking the history of their language and at the same time reforming their Chaucerian linguistic inheritance in their own image, the collaborators negotiate what Kathryn L. Lynch has called a 'complicated relationship to poetic authority', contesting Harold Bloom's claim that the medieval poet was sufficiently 'remote in time' as to be unproblematic for the early modern writers who followed him.[10] In fact, Chaucer's literary reputation was in flux at the time Shakespeare and Fletcher wrote, having not yet attained the status as 'father' of English poetry that would be confirmed by Dryden at the start of the eighteenth century, but instead 'most frequently known simply as 'master' or as the inventor, the 'finder' of the English tongue', Lynch and others have shown; 'Chaucer was a comparatively recent memory, and an overshadowing native one at that'.[11] In yet another iteration of the problem of sameness and difference underwriting *The Two Noble Kinsmen*, the dramatists must find a way of articulating their own distinctive identities in the shadow of their predecessor. And in responding to Chaucer, they must first answer to his language.

One hint as to the way that Shakespeare and Fletcher go about this lies in Speght's wordlist, I have argued. By demonstrating the extent to which Chaucerian English not only derives from other tongues, both 'native' and foreign, but also the degree to which it has since become obsolete, Speght challenges the common perception that the Middle English poet perfected the vernacular, revealing instead that his diction represents just one stage in the ongoing development of the language over time. The playwrights take their lead from this approach, treating their precursor's vocabulary as flexibly as they treat other aspects of his source material, including its portrayal of gender. Furthermore, by handling English freely and irreverently, coining new terms and reworking existing ones throughout the play, the authors of *The Two Noble Kinsmen* stage the incompletion of the English language itself, and thus, by implication, challenge the sufficiency of any accompanying notions of sexual identity. They frequently deploy nouns as verbs here, for example, 'graves' (1.1.149), 'scissored' (1.2.54); recast existing nouns as adverbs, 'futurely' (1.1.74); make adjectives into verbs, 'thirds' (1.2.96); and coin new words out of old ('terrene' (1.2.14), 'importment' (1.3.80). Such inventiveness – in the early modern sense of the word – typifies the playwrights' attitude towards their linguistic inheritance; by dramatizing the incompletion of English and its continuing capacity for development they are able to make the language, plots and characters of the Chaucerian original their own. It is not insignificant that they choose to do so in a play fundamentally concerned with the politics of sameness and difference, an issue that I have suggested is embodied as much in the drama's language as in its treatment of gender. By showing their familiarity with the roots of the Chaucerian vernacular, and by drawing upon the sense of the historicity of his own language gained from Speght's glossary, Shakespeare and Fletcher are able to remake English itself, and thus to remake the sexual politics of their source.

Notes

1   All references are to William Shakespeare [and John Fletcher], *The Two Noble Kinsmen*, ed. Lois Potter, Arden Shakespeare, Third Series (London, 1997, repr. 2007).

2   See Ann Thompson, *Shakespeare's Chaucer: A Study in Literary Origins* (Liverpool, 1978), p. 167, and Potter, Introduction, pp. 19–34, for the generally agreed division of authorial labour in the play.

3   Geoffrey Chaucer, *The workes of our ancient and learned English poet, Geffrey Chaucer, newly printed*, ed. Thomas Speght (London, 1602).

4   Thompson, *Shakespeare's Chaucer*, p. 30.

5   Derek Pearsall, 'Thomas Speght', in *Editing Chaucer: The Great Tradition*, ed. Paul G. Ruggiers (Norman, OK, 1984), pp. 71–92, and Robert K. Turner, '*The Two Noble Kinsmen* and Speght's Chaucer', *Notes and Queries* 27 (1980), 175–6.

6   See Eleanor N. Adams, *Old English Scholarship in England from 1566–1800* (New Haven, CT, 1917); Carl T. Berkhout and Milton McC. Gatch (eds), *Anglo-Saxon Scholarship: The*

First Three Centuries (Boston, MA, 1982); Timothy Graham, ed. *The Recovery of Old English: Anglo-Saxon Studies in the Sixteenth and Seventeenth Centuries* (Kalamazoo, MI, 2000).

7   The phrase is Geoffrey Hill's: 'Not strangeness, but strange likeness', *Mercian Hymns* (London, 1971), 133; see also Chris Jones, *Strange Likeness: The Use of Old English in Twentieth-Century Poetry* (Oxford, 2006), pp. 4–5, and Allen J. Frantzen, *Desire for Origins: New Language, Old English, and Teaching the Tradition* (New Brunswick, NJ, 1990), p. xi.

8   *Oxford English Dictionary*, ed. John Simpson, 2nd edn (Oxford, 1989). Compare *Twelfth Night*: 'An apple cleft in two, is not more twin / Than these two creatures' (5.1.230).

9   Helen Cooper, 'Jacobean Chaucer: *The Two Noble Kinsmen* and Other Chaucerian Plays' in Theresa M. Krier ed., *Refiguring Chaucer in the Renaissance* (Gainesville, FL, 1998), pp. 189–208, 189.

10   Kathryn L. Lynch, 'The Three Noble Kinsmen: Chaucer, Shakespeare, Fletcher', in Yvonne Bruce ed., *Images of Matter: Essays on British Literature of the Middle Ages and Renaissance* (Newark, DE, 2005), p. 72; Harold Bloom, *The Anxiety of Influence: A Theory of Poetry*, 2nd edn (Oxford, 1997), p. xlvi.

11   Lynch, 'The Three Noble Kinsmen,' 73. See also David Matthews and Gordon McMullan, 'Introduction' to *Reading the Medieval in Early Modern England* (Cambridge, 2007), p. 1.

4

Gender, the False Universal and Shakespeare's Comedies

Hilda L. Smith

University of Cincinnati

This essay explores common themes among three of Shakespeare's comedies, including *As You Like It, The Merry Wives of Windsor* and *Twelfth Night*, as they relate to the conflation of age, condition and sex. Here, and elsewhere, Shakespeare employed the common epitaphs and characteristics used by his contemporaries considering the intellectual and moral limitations of the young, women and the lower classes. He employed concepts associated with the 'false universal', a phrase I coined to bring attention to terms that conflated the qualities of adult men with those considered essentially human. The principle is laid down most clearly in the verse outlining 'the seven ages of man' as it appears in *As You Like It*. While it famously begins with the lines, 'All the world's a stage, / And all the men and women merely players,' Shakespeare shifts immediately to a single man standing for the aging of all mankind. He begins with the phrase, 'And one man in his time plays many parts, / His acts being seven ages.' He then enumerates those ages: infant, school-boy, lover, soldier, justice, pantaloon and old age, with the last 'sans teeth, sans eyes, sans taste, sans everything.'[1]

Within the concept of the false universal, what differs from an independent adult man is distinct, and almost always negatively distinct, from the human norm. Shakespeare clarifies the conflation of children and youths with all women later when he advises through Rosalind as Ganymede: 'be effeminate, changeable, longing and liking, proud, fantastical, apish, shallow, inconstant, [and] full of tears, ... as boys and women are for the most part cattle of this color' (3.2.399–404). Shakespeare employs the typical antiwoman tropes of garrulousness and a desperation to wed in the lines (from Rosalind), 'Do you not know that I am a woman / When I think, I must speak', and time 'trots hard with a young maid, between the contract of her marriage and the day it is solemnized' (3.2.246–7, 308–10). Women's maturing to dependence within the nuclear family contrasts fundamentally with men's advancing through training and education to an independent adulthood; thus aging, as we think of it broadly for human beings, exists only in the lives of men. While few scholars have conflated men with humans, they have treated women in Shakespeare's comedies; this scholarship recognizes their need to confront men: as R. W. Maslen notes, this is 'hardly surprising, since their lives and livelihoods are most at risk from men's failure to keep faith.'[2]

The false universal also offers the central framework for my own scholarship on skilled women workers (which I will discuss later in the essay). It posits that the reason these skilled women are considered outside the crafts they pursue and the businesses they operate is because early modern society deems them incapable of fulfilling the role and responsibilities of adult, independent males. Women are thus consigned to perpetual dependency. This false universal has also contributed to contemporary scholarship, which fails to recognize and credit skilled women artisans and shopkeepers, thereby neglecting to lift these women from the historical oblivion in which they largely remain.

Shakespeare's portrayal of his women characters assumes that perpetual dependency is their sex's natural state. In the three plays under discussion the women may be exceedingly clever and manipulative but only in response to men's efforts at courtship. Essentially, men act; women react. Thus Shakespeare shares the false universal view that women's very nature restricts them from being fully formed human beings. In contrast, fully formed males are capable of independent thought (if not always smart) and action unrestricted by gender assignment.

And this independence is tied just as clearly to class, where those who are servants or from the lower classes never emerge from a status dependent upon, and required to serve, someone else. Shakespeare's treatment of the lower classes, often equated with country naiveté, conforms to tropes of early modern humour, which identify those outside an educated, or cultured male elite as legitimate targets of ridicule. In *As You Like*, unlike in other dramatic instances, Shakespeare does acknowledge that qualities associated with class and rural/urban differences often reside in the eye of the beholder rather than in the inherent superiority or inferiority of one or the other, even while finding greater flaws in the former. In describing Corin, the shepherd, Shakespeare displays his simple mind: 'that the property of rain is to wet and fire to burn; that good pasture makes fat sheep' (3.1.24–6). But after Corin reveals his similarity to a fool, Shakespeare then posits the shepherd's possible familiarity with the Court and follows it with an explicit comparison of the two. 'Such a one is a natural philosopher. Wast ever in court, shepherd?' (3.1.30–1). And Corin contends: 'Those that are good manners at the court are as ridiculous in the country as the behaviour of the country is most mockable at the court' (3.1.43–6).

The Merry Wives of Windsor dismisses those lacking standing and knowledge, in this instance the use of flawed

Latin. Shallow (a justice of the peace) and Slender (Shallow's young relative) have the following exchange:

> Shallow: Ay, cousin Slender, and Cust-a-lorum.
> Slender: Ay, and Rato lorum too, and a gentleman born, master parson, who writes himself *Armigero*, in any bill, warrant, quittance, or obligation – *Armigero*.[3]

Here, and throughout the comedies, Shakespeare satirizes the deficiencies of the young and of those subservient to others, characteristic of these two characters.[4] He highlights those who claim status, but in language and imagery clarifying that they do not, as with Shallow describing himself thus: 'Robert Shallow esquire saith he is wronged' (1.1.99–100). While women, the young and poorer relatives, or those from the working classes, are often characterized in similar terms, each has particular qualities separating them from the independent gentleman. The qualities of the groups not defined by gender are more transitory and associated with ill breeding, rural habits and limited cultural opportunities. The young have the greatest chance to change when they attain accomplished maturity, those from the lower classes and countryside a lesser chance, but women are incapable of, and discouraged from, changing their essential nature. For women, their qualities are more intrinsic and less open to alteration; to be essentially female, one must not seek advanced learning or personal accomplishment and independence, and thus a woman has little opportunity to pursue a life open to basic human fulfilment.

Shakespeare, though, while expressing typical early modern misogynist comments, does allow the audience to question their veracity by placing the following words in Rosalind's cross-dressed persona: 'I thank God that I am not a woman, to be touched with so many giddy offences as he has generally taxed their whole sex withal' (3.2.340–43). How do we read these lines knowing that they are spoken by a woman? Yet the false universal broadly characterizes the play in that both men and women accept male behaviour as the norm and acknowledge women's incapacity to attain such qualities.

The Merry Wives of Windsor's focus on Falstaff's foibles, and the efforts to ensnare him in his efforts to seduce married women while gaining a financial reward, uses the bluster of husbands against their wives' ignorance and susceptibility to sexual advances and foolish blandishments. Mrs Ford and Mrs Page cannot be trusted to protect themselves, and the feared outcome is cuckoldry and men's ridicule of any man who cannot control his wife and allows her to besmirch his reputation. Servants plot with masters and mistresses to pursue each person's interest, such as the distinct goals of each of the Pages for their daughter's marriage, and the play integrates the values associated with men's ego and wealth as dictating their behaviour at women's expense, although in the comedy the wives, and especially the daughter Ann Page, ultimately triumph. But their victories emerge in the context of men's need to be seen in control of their household and free from any suspicion that they do not wear the breeches. Clearly, Falstaff is the antithesis of such a man, and Ford and Page lose their way when they and their compatriots buy into the values associated with men's need for dominance and sexual control of the women about them. And the women's recognizing and exploiting men's belief that their nature and needs are supreme is central to the comedy's plot.

Twelfth Night employs cross dressing and confused identities even more effectively to pinpoint and satirize English society's sexual, social and age distinctions when assessing the legitimacy and importance of an individual's needs and desires. Over-reaching one's proper class, age and gendered status offered Shakespeare, as well as other authors of comedy, endless opportunities to pinpoint human peccadilloes and to judge a person's choices as legitimate or not based on their standing in early modern society. As in *As You Like It*, *Twelfth Night* also used ill education to reveal one's nature beyond the qualities of an educated gentleman exemplifying the apex in human attainment. Sir Andrew, portrayed as an unacceptable suitor, is told by Sir Toby Belch to pursue Maria, and he responds: 'By my troth, I would not undertake her in this company.' He asks, 'is that the meaning of accost?' following Sir Toby's urging him to 'front her'.[5] Shakespeare regularly links uncouth or ill-informed social behaviour with limited education and culture. And he employs languages to document ignorance, in this instance French. Sir Toby: '*Pourquoi*, my dear knight?' Sir Andrew: 'What is *pourquoi*? Do, or not do? I would I had bestowed that time in the tongues that I have in fencing, dancing, and bear-baiting. O, had I but followed the arts!' (1.3.89–93). Women, of course, are not so castigated because of their exclusion from grammar school or university, but their immersion in music, dancing and the social graces is very much the female equivalent of Sir Andrew's anti-intellectual training except it was the established path for gentlewomen, not a deviation from superior, proper standards.

The qualities associated with Duke Orsino in *Twelfth Night* exemplify the best characteristics of human beings as described by Olivia while explaining to Viola/Cesario why she cannot wed him; he is 'In voices well divulg'd, free, learn'd, and valiant' (1.5.254).While valiant is a term normally reserved to men, the other descriptors are admirable qualities in either sex, and they embody the man/human at the heart of the false universal. They represent the independence and competence of an adult who has developed his innate abilities to speak well and act authoritatively. Nothing prevents a woman from embodying those qualities except the conflation of man and human in the supposed qualities of an accomplished adult. His appearance is described as 'the shape of nature, a gracious person' (1.5.255–6), again, a phrase not normally applied to women's beauty or appearance.

After reiterating her negative response to the duke's romantic overtures, Olivia asks Viola disguised as Cesario to not have the duke pursue his offer, but that she would return to let her know his reaction to her rejection. And she states:

> Methinks I feel this youth's perfections
> With an invisible and subtle stealth
> To creep in at mine eyes. Well, let it be (1.5.290–2).

Here, as with Rosalind in *As You Like It*, cross dressing undermines a reading of Shakespeare as assuming only men stand for the best in humanity. And, of course, the all-male casts of his day also complicate the application of the false universal to his works. Even so, verbally there is no recognition of women's broad representation of mankind in these comedies, simply the confused identities of men as female characters imitating men. When Olivia speaks to Sebastian, she urges him: 'Let thy fair wisdom, not thy passion, sway / In this uncivil and unjust extent / Against thy peace' (4.1.52–4). While clearly seeking similar goals for her, and likely other women, would she employ wisdom as the path they should pursue?

In my own research on skilled women workers in early modern art, the false universal is obvious in both the limited range of women's work portrayed in art and their small role in contemporary scholarship. Even so, women are clearly listed in sixteenth and seventeenth century guild charters; yet, there are few illustrations of their presence, such as in Henry VIII's founding of the barber surgeons' guild. The charters make clear women's presence in this quintessential role of urban citizenship, but their artistic imagery is minuscule, and the accounts of historians also tend to ignore them, except for the recent work of women's historians. The false universal gave contemporaries and later historians a sense that women could not master, or were not present, in a range of crafts or settings where they clearly existed.

Recent scholarship has undercut the long-held assumption that early modern women only produced domestic products or were involved in unskilled labour, assisting skilled men in craft shops, but early modern art did not reflect this reality. In looking at guild charters from the sixteenth century the equal presence of women is clear. For instance, when Henry VIII combined the fullers and shear men into one guild, he termed it the 'Cloth Workers' guild of the City of London and determined that the guild 'make and have among the Citizens of the same City, being then Brethren and Sisters of the same Fraternity of Cloathworkers ... one Livery or Robe'. An 1890 account of barber-surgeons verified as well women's long-term admission to the guild; 'from the earliest times the custom has prevailed to admit women to the freedom, mostly by apprenticeship but also by patrimony, and these freewomen bound their apprentices, both boys and girls, at the Hall.' A 1637 guild document noted that 'if any brother or sister' falls into poverty they will qualify for aid', or if 'any brother or sister ... shall not come when he be summoned' he or she shall be fined. Finally, we find evidence of women conferring status on dependents, not just men doing so. The merchant guild charter of Exeter granted by Queen Elizabeth in 1560 has the following language: 'that the eldest son of every Freeman and Freewoman of this Company shall be admitted to the freedom'. But here, as elsewhere, the visual, as well as the later scholarly record, does not reflect this reality, as exemplified in this image of Henry VIII granting a charter for the barber surgeons' guild.[6]

Finally, in my research on women in early modern guilds, perhaps most surprising was the variety of trades women pursued, and how that pursuit led to their being termed citizens.[7] It is still strange to our ears to hear the following petition from Ann Beverly in 1699 stating that she 'was bound to Joyce Warren Citizen and shipwright of London for the terme of seven years & served her said Mistress five Years and six months.' The rights of the 'Freeborn Englishman' was the rallying cry for those seeking first restrictions against, and later the execution of, Charles I based on his high church policies and his subversion of parliamentary authority. One could argue, though, that

FIGURE 1 *Henry VIII granting charter to Barber Surgeons*

this democratization of the national electorate was at odds with women's standing as urban citizens based on their economic achievements. And, it led to so many later linguistic omissions of women from central principles of political equality; the freeborn Englishman led to the first insertion of the word male into a British Constitutional document with the Reform Act of 1832 granting suffrage to middle-class men, up to contemporary phrases such as 'one man, one vote' and 'universal brotherhood'.

It is above all this little-examined linking of basic human qualities, democratic rights, and personal independence to adult men that has led us to unthinkingly omit women from economic and social roles they clearly held. It led Shakespeare and other authors to treat male and female characters in quite different ways, to judge their behaviours differently, and to select distinct actions and qualities when assessing male and female characters. While both men and women sought romantic ties, which drove plot development, these comedies concerned themselves with different actions on the part of the two sexes. Women were more concerned with virtue and with not appearing at odds with husbands or the wishes of male family members. Men were more concerned with their social standing and their egos to ensure they were not belittled or cuckolded by the women around them. But these realities simply involved broad-based schema which allowed individual exceptions for men to forget their pride to pursue the women they loved and for women to take an aggressive stance to gain control over their personal destiny. Yet, in setting the stage of early modern gender values, the false universal influenced Shakespeare's judgements about the distinct life choices open to men and women. And these values also apply to those writing about, and illustrating, women's work and political standing in the early modern period and among scholars today.

Notes

1   William Shakespeare, *As You Like It*, in Richard Proudfoot, Ann Thompson and David Scott Kastan eds, *The Arden Shakespeare Complete Works*, revised edn (London, 2011), 3.1.139–66.

2   R. W. Maslen, *Shakespeare and Comedy*, The Arden Critical Companions (London, 2005), pp. 111–12.

3   William Shakespeare, *The Merry Wives of Windsor*, ed. Giorgio Melchiori, 'The Arden Shakespeare', 3rd edn (London, 2000).

4   But in 1 *Henry IV*, those open to sport by their betters such as the 'drawer' come from an urban setting. And the hostess, in a scurrilous conversation with Falstaff in defending herself against charges of pickpocket and bawdy house claims 'I am an honest man's wife,' perpetuating women's purity and standing as confirmed through male qualities and ties (see *Henry IV, Part 1*, in *Arden Complete Works*, 3.3.120).

5   (see *Twelfth Night*, in *Arden Complete Works*, 1.3.57–8, 55)

6   For a fuller discussion of this topic see Hilda L. Smith, *All Men and Both Sexes: Gender, Politics, and the False Universal in England, 1640–1832* (University Park, PA, 2002), pp. 73–88, 93–8.

7   This engraving by AB Baron from 1736, based on a Holbein portrait, is owned by the Wellcome Library, London.

5

In Plain Sight: Visible Women and Early Modern Plays

Yale University

It is a cliché of literary history that the extraordinary drama professionally produced in early-modern England was exclusively the achievement of men. No female playwrights wrote for the commercial stage, and, of course, no actresses played the female roles that male playwrights imagined. The cliché has, of course, been qualified by recent scholarship that has begun to recover not only what Ann Thompson has called 'the relatively hidden tradition of female performance',[1] but also the only slightly less hidden traditions of female playwrights, patrons, spectators, and readers, who did create, support, attend, read, and collect plays. But the *professional* theatre was a bastion of male activity, with the exception of the labour of women who certainly made up part of the ancillary work force that a theatre company depended upon to mount a play.[2] Their names for the most part are lost to history, as the names of such subsidiary workers in every field inevitably are. Yet there is one place within the collaborative activities defining the early modern theatre where women are regularly named – indeed where they were themselves often responsible for their naming: the world of print.

Women were involved in the normal activities of the book trade, and their names regularly appear on title pages as printers, publishers, or booksellers,[3] although in the book trade too their role has sometimes been misrepresented, in part because the extant records inevitably serve only as imperfect snapshots of the complex realities of early-modern book trade practices, but also because gender-based assumptions have sometimes led to misunderstandings of the records that do exist. For example, Edward Arber, who was responsible for the magisterial edition of *The Registers of the Company of Stationers*, transcribed an entry of 25 September 1605, when William Cotton 'Entred for his copy by assignement from Nathanael Butter. A booke called *The Resolued Christian* ... which was entered to **Nathanael mother**.'[4] Arber, however, 'corrects' the transcription with his addition '[or rather **Butter**]'. Yet, as Helen Smith has shown, an entry for 9 March 1604 'indicates that the copy *was* entered by Nathaniel Butter's mother, the widow Joan Newbery, who purchased the copy from Thomas Busshell but appears to have entrusted its further transmission to her business partner: her son from her first marriage'.[5] Although it is unquestionably odd to have an entry referring to Joan Newbery in terms of her relationship to her son, the proper correction would seem to have been to add an 's' after '**Nathanael**' rather than to emend '**mother**'.

But, even if Smith is right in this case, usefully calling attention to what would be only one of several places where Arber has seemingly assumed male agency in his reading of the registers, the effort to uncover and rectify the errors stemming from unconscious gender bias ironically can produce its own. For example, Smith herself, cataloguing the activities of women stationers, says that Joan Broome published four plays by John Lyly: one printed by Thomas Scarlett 'for I.B.', two printed by John Charlewood 'for the widdowe Broome' and one, *Sappho and Phao*, printed by 'T. Orwin for W. Broome'.[6] Smith seemingly has taken the publisher's first initial in the imprint to indicate 'widdowe', thus adding to Joan Broome's accomplishments, but it refers, in fact, as the actual title page makes clear in spelling out both names of the stationers, to her husband William.[7]

If, then, it is difficult, even with the best of scholarly will and enterprise, fully to recover the role of women in the print trade, nonetheless, it is true that Joan Broome on her own did publish *three* plays by Lyly, editions of *Endymion* (1591), *Gallatea* (1592), and *Midas* (1592). She inherited the rights to *Sapho and Phao*, though she never published an edition of it, as was true also of *Campaspe*; and the Stationers Company records the transfer to George Potter of the rights to the five Lyly plays as well as eight other titles 'whiche belonged to mystris **Brome** Lately Deceased' on 23 August 1601 (Arber, III, 191). Perhaps she was indeed, as Tara Lyons suggestively hints, the first person to imagine a collection of an English playwright's work any more substantial than the few editions of two-part plays like *1 and 2 Tamburlaine* published by Richard Jones in 1590.[8]

Joan Broome was only one of a number of women involved in the printing and publication of playbooks. Among the seventy-four women whose names appear on imprints of early printed books are thirteen women involved in the publication of over forty playbooks, which included, in addition to the three plays by Lyly published by 'the Widdowe Brome', editions of *Dido, Queen of Carthage* (printed by Joan Orwin in 1594), *Arden of Faversham* (printed and published by Elizabeth Allde in 1633), *Bussy D'Ambois* (printed by Alice Norton [A.N.] in 1641), and Fanshawe's translation of *Il Pastor Fido* (printed and published by Ruth Raworth in 1647) – although as we inevitably want to know, only one of these was a play by Shakespeare, Q3 of *King Lear*, printed, published, and sold by Jane Bell in 1655 (of which, more later).[9]

Virtually all of these women were like Joan Broome: wives who inherited a business in which they had no doubt worked alongside their husband while he still lived and who took control of the business upon his death. Although as women they were not eligible for full membership in the Company, they functioned formally as stationers, assuming the responsibilities and properties of the inherited business, including the rights to titles, like those established in 1597 as belonging to Joan Broome 'To enioy Duringe her widowe[hood] or that shalbe a free Stationers wife of this companye' (Arber, III, 82).

Joan Broome did not remarry a free stationer, or anyone else for that matter, although many women who inherited businesses did. Henry Overton entered thirteen titles on 13 May 1630, 'which were the Copies of Master **Sheffard** whose wydow the [said] Overton lately married' (Arber, IV, 235). John Kingston's widow, Joan, remarried twice, first George Robinson, who had been their apprentice, and then, upon Robinson's death, Thomas Orwin. Orwin's entry of various books in 1593 confirms the way in which a widow's inheritance was used to establish rights to copy, recording these as titles 'which were first **kingstons** and after **George Robinsons** whose widowe the said **Orwin** hath married' (Arber, II, 630). A widow might also lease titles to a member of the Company if she did not want to continue in the business herself, though such transfers were inevitably conditional, as in the case of Elizabeth Winnington's transfer of three copies inherited from her late husband John to John Wright in 1595, where the transfer depended upon the copies actually having belonged to Winnington and also 'Provyded alwaies that yf the said **Elizabeth** marrie againe to any of the Companie. That then she shall haue their copies againe as in her former estate' (Arber, III, 51). The rights to copy inherited by a widow who then remarried someone who was not a Stationer would revert to the Company and were eligible to be reassigned.

The rights of widows were vigorously protected by the Company, if only to preserve them for a liveried member who might marry their owner. An interesting case with bearing on the theatre world was William Jaggard's effort in 1593 to secure the monopoly on printing playbills, which had belonged to John Charlewood. The Court of Assistant offered only provisional approval of his claim: 'Whereas William Iagger hath made request to haue the printinge of the billes for players as Iohn Charlwood had[,] yt is graunted: that if he can gett the said Charlwood his Wydowes consent hereunto or if she die, or marry out of the company. That then the company will haue considerac[i]on to prefer him in this sute before another.'[10] But Charlewood's widow did not give her consent and soon married James Roberts, who assumed the useful monopoly worth about £3 a year with little work involved and no risk.[11] In 1602, when Jaggard pursued these rights again, the claim was again 'found to be the right of the said James Robertes in the right of his wife', though Roberts did allow Jaggard to assume the printing of playbills for the Earl of Worcester's men for a fee of four shillings a month.[12]

But perhaps it is the one example of a Shakespeare play published by a woman that provides the most notable example of how women worked within the densely interrelated familial and commercial world of early print, as well as an extraordinary case of confusion about a title. In 1655 Jane Bell printed and published an edition of *King Lear*, though the rights to Shakespeare's play had originally belonged Nathaniel Butter (Arber, III, 366), who must have leased them (unrecorded) to Jaggard and Edward Blount to allow them to appear in the first and second Shakespeare folios in 1623 and 1632. Butter's rights to the play were preserved, however, and were assigned along with twenty-five other titles to Miles Fletcher in 1639 (Arber, IV, 466). At first glance, we might guess that there was an unrecorded arrangement of Fletcher with Bell to allow her to publish the play, but the truth is more interesting and more useful for a reconstruction of the role women stationers played in the transmission of playbooks. And the actual circumstances reveal something surprising about how the system of entrance on the basis of title might complicate rather than clarify the question of what we have come to think of as copyright, or, put more simply, what it might mean to own a text.[13]

In 1594 the anonymous 'most famous Chronicle historye of Liere kinge of England and his Three Daughters' was entered to Edward White (Arber, II, 649). Seemingly White never published an edition, and on 8 May 1605, Simon Stafford entered 'for his copye *The Tragicall history of King LEIRE and his Three Daughters &c*', a title that was immediately reassigned to John Wright, reserving for Stafford the right to print the play (Arber, III, 289). Wright's edition of *King Leir*, widely known as one of the sources of Shakespeare's play, appeared later that year, printed by Stafford as specified. Nonetheless, in 1624, the rights to the play were again reassigned when the widow of Edward White transferred 'Leire and his daughters' to Edward Allde (Arber, IV, 120). Almost certainly by reasserting her late husband's original claim from 1594, White's widow successfully transferred the rights to *King Leir* to Allde, establishing his rights to the title.

Allde died in 1627, survived by his second wife, Elizabeth, who took over the business and continued working until her death in 1637. The title to *King Leir* would then have belonged to her. Her career looks much like that of most of the women who worked as printers and publishers. She was active in the trade, and worked according to the rules of the Company, eligible for its protections and liable to its regulations, even though she had not been formally admitted. In a list of Master Printers dated 8 October 1634, the 'Widdow Aldee' appears as having 'succeeded her husband who was a Master Printer' (Arber, III, 700), but another list written sometime after 'the fall of 1635' states that now 'she keepes her trade by her sonne' (Arber, III, 701), Richard Oulton (her son from a previous marriage, misnamed 'Robert' on the previous page in Arber), probably an indication that her health was failing. By the end of 1636, she was dead. Four years later, Oulton entered twenty-one titles (immediately assigning one to John Benson), including *Lear and his 3. Daughters*, all titles that 'lately did belong to Mistris Aldee his mother in Law deceased' (Arber, IV, 507), although this *Lear*, as the convoluted history makes clear, was really *Leir*.

Oulton never published an edition of either play. But Jane Bell did. Although there is no record of the transaction,[14] it is clear that his titles were acquired by Bell sometime before her edition of *King Lear* appeared in 1655. In the back of her edition of Q3 *Lear* is an advertisement of 'Books Printed: And are to be Sold by Jane Bell at the East-end of Christ Church.' Bell's list contains the nineteen titles (other than *King Lear*, which of course is the title in which the advertisement appears)[15] that Oulton had entered and kept for himself and prints them in the exact order in which they appear in the Stationers Register, although she adds two new titles to her list at the end. Although she printed and published Shakespeare's *King Lear*, basing it closely on a copy of Pavier's falsely dated Q2 (1608 for 1619), it seems therefore certain, as Kirschbaum claims, that she did so on the basis of a right to copy that in fact was of the anonymous *King Leir* – but it seems almost equally certain that she did not know this to be the case.

What is also certain, as the convoluted story of the publication of Q3 of *King Lear* makes clear, is that printed plays, like printed books of all sorts, often demanded and recorded the activity of women, here as the rights to the anonymous *King Leir* were transferred to and by women stationers, until one of them unwittingly vested them in an edition of the 'other' *King Lear*, the only quarto of a Shakespeare play to be printed and published by a woman. Even, then, if it is accurate to say of the professional English stage, as Thomas Nashe wrote in his characteristically fervid idiom, that 'Our Players are not as the players beyond [the] Sea, a sort of squirting baudie Comedians, that haue whores and Common Curtizens to playe womens parts',[16] and similarly true that the words these 'Players' spoke on stage were written by men, it is no less the case that many professionally proficient and respected women[17] did appear among the actors in the world of early print, which enabled the achievement of the early modern theatre to be shaped and preserved for the future.

Notes

1   'Women / 'Women' and the Stage,' in Helen Wilcox ed.,
    Women and Literature in Britain 1500–1700 (Cambridge,
    1996), p. 103.

2   See Natasha Korda's *Labors Lost: Women's Work and the
    Early Modern Stage* (Philadelphia, 2011).

3   Helen Smith's *'Grossly Material Things': Women and Book
    Production in Early Modern England* (Oxford, 2012) is the
    first extended and much welcome treatment of women's
    involvement in the making of early modern books. See also
    Maureen Bell, 'Women in the English Book Trade 1557–1700,'
    Leipziger Jahrbuch zur Buchgeschichte, 6 (1996), pp. 13–45.

4   Edward Arber, *A Transcript of the Registers of the
    Company of Stationers of London; 1554–1640 A.D.*
    (London: n. p. 1875–9), III, 301.

5   Smith, p. 105.

6   Smith, p. 89, fn. 8.

7   Smith seems here to have relied on the *STC*, which represents
    the imprint as 'T. Orwin f. W. Broome' rather than accurately
    reproducing what reads on the title page: '*Thomas Orwin*, for
    William Broome.' Although Joan was certainly working with
    her husband, and, as he neared his death, probably taking on
    the majority of the responsibilities, the two 1591 Lyly imprints
    attributed to him must be considered his own. Joan's solo
    career seems to have begun with her publication of *Endymion*,
    one of the three Lyly plays that she did publish, as she remarks
    in her 'Note to the Reader' that 'There are certain Commedies
    come into my hands by chaunce … This is the first, and if in
    any place it shall displease I will take more paines to perfect
    the next' (sig. A2^r).

8   Joan Broome never did publish such a collection, but she
    seemingly published her three plays by Lyly as a series and
    at very least must have imagined these bound together by
    owners. See Tara Lyons's remarkable dissertation, 'English
    Printed Drama in Collection before Jonson and Shakespeare',
    University of Illinois, 2011.

9   The *STC* lists 74 women among the 1,367 stationers it names
        in the Index, which no doubt under-represents the number of
        woman active in the trade given how much is inaccurate or
        occluded in imprints and how many editions of books have
        not survived (see Smith, pp. 100–1). By 1700, according to
        Maureen Bell, over 300 women can be identified as being
        active in the print trade. The figures on women involved with
        playbook publication come from *DEEP: Database of Early
        English Playbooks*, Alan B. Farmer and Zachary Lesser (eds).
        Created 2007. http://deep.sas.upenn.edu. I am grateful to both
        Alan Farmer and Zach Lesser, as well as to Aaron Pratt, for
        reading and commenting on various drafts of this essay.

10   Smith, p. 102.

11   *Records of the Court of the Stationers' Company 1576–1602*,
        W. W. Greg and E. Boswell (eds) (London, 1930), p. 46.

12   See Tiffany Stern, *Documents of Performance in Early Modern
        England* (Cambridge, 2009), p. 42.

13   *Records of the Court of the Stationers' Company 1602–1640*,
        ed. William A. Jackson (London, 1957), pp. 1–2.

14   Copyright in early modern England, of course, belonged to
        publishers not to authors. On this particular case, see Leo
        Kirschbaum's brillant reconstruction of the history, 'How Jane
        Bell came to print the Third Quarto of Shakespeare's *King
        Lear*,' *Philological Quarterly* 17 (1938), 308–11.

15   Jane Bell's business was inherited in 1649 from her husband,
        Moses Bell, and was located, like Oulton's, 'near Christ-
        Church.' Presumably, as working neighbours, they reached an
        agreement for a fee for Oulton's titles, which, like many others,
        was never recorded in the Company's register.

16   *Pierce Pennilesse his Supplication to the Diuill* (London, 1592),
        sig. H3^r.

17   On 7 February 1624/5, Nathaniel Butter was fined 6s. 8d.
        by the Stationers' Court for 'vnfitting Speaches' to Hannah
        Barrett, including calling her a 'durtye slutt.' See Jackson ed.,
        Records of the Court of the Stationers' Company 1602–1640,
        p. 173.

6

Remaking the Texts: Women Editors of Shakespeare, Past and Present

Valerie Wayne

University of Hawai'i

Few endeavours in the humanities have been so consistently exercised by men to the exclusion of women as editing the texts of Shakespeare. Yet much has changed since Gary Taylor remarked in 1988 that '[w]omen may read Shakespeare, but men edit him',[1] and this essay will assess those changes by weighing the current contributions of women as editors of early modern drama. I begin, however, with a look back at the progenitors of those editors, a topic that Ann Thompson briefly addressed in her essay, 'Feminist Theory and the Editing of Shakespeare', and that is treated in more detail in entries from her anthology with Sasha Roberts, *Women Reading Shakespeare 1660–1900*. Since the publication of both works in 1997, women editors have been the subject of more research by Gail Marshall and Ann Thompson, Jeanne Addison Roberts, and Laurie Maguire. What we now know offers something of a lineage for the work that more women are currently doing, although any reconstruction of that history is advised to heed Phyllis Rackin's warning that 'overestimating past repression can easily slip into a dangerous complacency about present progress'.[2]

The tradition of Shakespearean editing began in 1709 with the publication of Nicholas Rowe's first edition, and the eighteenth-century editors who followed him developed a presentation of the plays that we have now come to expect: with *dramatis personae*, consistent stage directions, notes with variant readings and critical commentary, and introductions. All the editors of that century were men, and their relationships with one another were often adversarial, sometimes aggressively hostile. When Henrietta Maria Bowdler published her own edition of the plays nearly a hundred years later, then, it is understandable that she did not identify herself within this contentious community. If the Brontës obscured their identities as authors and even as forceful an intellect as Mary Anne Evans assumed a male pseudonym in the century's second half, it is not surprising that Henrietta preferred not to be known, although she had already been discovered as the author of the much-reprinted *Sermons on the Doctrines and Duties of Christianity*. Her *Family Shakespeare* of 1807 appeared anonymously in a four-volume edition published in Bath that included twenty plays. Its preface says it is directed to 'young persons of both sexes' and expurgated to remove 'everything that could give just offence to the religious and virtuous mind'.[3] In 1818 a second edition by her brother Thomas was published in London, and it was his text, with thirty-six plays and many cuts restored, that became a best-seller after the *Edinburgh Review* said it made all other editions of Shakespeare obsolete.[4] Henrietta's editorial method of making cuts concerning 'religion and sex' is more extreme than others', but her predecessors and contemporaries also softened Shakespeare's obscenities, avoided some sexual language, and made many changes and excisions in their performance texts.[5] Discretion and propriety have influenced the editorial tradition more than is sometimes recognized,[6] and the popularity of Thomas' edition suggests that Henrietta had recognized what some of her contemporaries most wanted and did not want in their bard. Shakespeare's texts vary considerably over time as editors meet and construct the needs of their changing audiences.

Mary Cowden Clarke's accomplishments are somewhat more akin to later sensibilities. Marshall and Thompson claim she may be 'the first woman, other than actresses, to make a living out of Shakespeare'. She was prolific as writer and editor, 'achieved significant renown both in Britain and in the United States', and exhibited 'a proto-feminist line' throughout her work.[7] Her major achievement was the first complete concordance to Shakespeare's plays, sixteen years in the making, that was published in eighteen monthly instalments in 1844–5 and reprinted in ten editions through 1875. In 1860 her *Shakespeare's Works, Edited with a Scrupulous Revision of the Text* was published without commentary notes because she saw them as 'mere vehicles for abuse, spite and arrogance'. Understandably unaware of her predecessor, she announced herself in the preface as 'the first of [Shakespeare's] female subjects who has been selected to edit his works', and her husband Charles disclaimed responsibility for the Glossary after a reviewer assumed it was his. Five years later Mary and Charles collaborated on an annotated, expurgated, and illustrated Shakespeare, and this time a reviewer objected to '"the lady editor"' for '"tampering with our great poet's language"'.[8] Cowden Clarke is best known today for her *Girlhood of Shakespeare's Heroines* (1850–2), which creates back stories for the characters' lives, accounts full of 'romance and melodrama' that offer 'a form of moral pedagogy' to young readers. Mary and Charles also prepared an 800-page book called *The Shakespeare Key* (1879) that addresses a range of topics including style and dramatic time. Mary's life and work were permeated by 'the worship of Shakespeare ...

of a curiously intimate kind', but she lived when reverence was highly valued, and she was sufficiently revered for her own work that she was presented with a Testimonial Chair carved of rosewood with Shakespeare's head on it in 1852. Among the 64 subscribers to this gift were Washington Irving and Henry Wadsworth Longfellow, together with professors, judges, and state officials.[9]

One of Cowden Clarke's correspondents was the American scholar Horace Howard Furness, who would launch the Variorum Shakespeare in the 1890s. In 1883 Furness persuaded Charlotte Porter to edit a new periodical called *Shakespeariana* that 'claimed to be "the only Shakespearian Magazine in the world"',[10] to which Cowden Clarke contributed several pieces. When Porter resigned as editor in 1887, she began working with Helen A. Clarke to produce the *Pembroke Shakespeare* of 1903 in twelve volumes, with several plays to each volume. Over the next ten years they published forty single-volume editions of the plays and poems, the first complete edition to be based entirely on the First Folio, with extensive, strong-minded commentary. Jeanne Addison Roberts commends their 'examples of early feminist criticism, … their rejection of didactic intention in Shakespeare's works, and their application of principles of revolutionary change in the perception of literary productions'.[11] Their accomplishments during the first wave of feminism were overlooked by later editors until Roberts' 2006 essay, but their preference for the First Folio has brought them attention from Jonathan Bate, whose 'Case for the Folio' justifying editorial procedures in the 2006 *RSC Collected Works* notes that their 'attention to the *theatrical* origins of most of the Folio texts was … nearly a hundred years before its time'.[12] Porter and Clarke may finally have found their audience.

In the twentieth century women began to take a larger role in establishing Shakespeare's texts. Grace R. Trenery edited *Much Ado About Nothing* (1924) for the first series of the Arden Shakespeare (1899–1944). During the second Arden series (1946–82), Una Ellis-Fermor served as general editor for the first twelve years and Agnes Latham edited *As You Like It* (1975) after publishing editions of Walter Ralegh's poems and letters. Alice Walker was an especially important figure in mid-century, succeeding R. B. McKerrow as editor of the Old-Spelling Oxford Shakespeare in 1940 because he 'considered her accurate beyond his own standards'.[13] That edition was never finished, perhaps, as Laurie Maguire conjectures, because Walker came increasingly to doubt that an old-spelling text recorded an author's spelling.[14] What she produced instead was an influential book on compositors, called *Textual Problems of the First Folio*. For T. H. Howard-Hill, that 1953 volume together with her reviews of Arden and New Variorum editions and textual articles for Fredson Bowers' *Studies in Bibliography* 'revealed her as the most acute and challenging textual critic of the decade'.[15] She edited *Troilus and Cressida* and, with J. D. Wilson, *Othello* for the New Cambridge Shakespeare. Maguire characterizes Walker's hallmark as 'textual heterogeneity – compositor study, stage history, literary criticism, humour, verve, and idiom'.[16]

Katharine F. Pantzer did not edit any of the plays but had a major role in completing the second edition of *The Short-Title Catalogue*, first published in 1926. F. S. Ferguson and William A. Jackson began a full revision, and when the project moved to Harvard, Jackson recruited Pantzer in 1962. Then he died unexpectedly two years later, leaving her with much to do on the first half of the alphabet as well as decoding his marginalia on I to Z. The second half was published in 1976 and the first half in 1986. The information we now take for granted on *Early English Books Online* would not exist without the *STC*. Jeffrey Masten calls it 'the reference tool with which all work on Renaissance printed texts must begin'; David McKitterick says 'no other country can boast such a detailed or full bibliographical record'.[17] Pantzer's sense of humour about the frustrations of dealing with long, complicated entries is recorded in one running head for Henry Smith, Minister, where an intentional typo identifies him as 'Monster'.[18]

Anne Barton and Molly M. Mahood were two important women editors from the second half of the century. In addition to their other distinguished work, Barton wrote introductions to the comedies for *The Riverside Shakespeare*; Mahood edited *Twelfth Night* for New Penguin and *The Merchant of Venice* for New Cambridge. Yet it was not until the last decade of the twentieth century that women became significantly more visible in editorial roles. One mark of that transition is the difference between the general editorial teams of two collected works: the *Oxford Shakespeare* and the *Norton Shakespeare*. The former, under general editors Stanley Wells and Gary Taylor working with John Jowett and William Montgomery, focused on textual scholarship. They produced a revisionary text of the plays in 1986, but it was published without introductions and commentary notes, making it unsuitable for the lucrative college market. In 1997 the *Norton Shakespeare* was published using the *Oxford* text along with critical introductions, glosses, and bibliographies of criticism. These were prepared under the general editorship of Stephen Greenblatt together with Walter Cohen, Jean E. Howard, and Katharine Eisaman Maus, editors valued for their cutting-edge critical expertise. The presence of two women on this team signalled the edition's attention to gender as well as theatricality, history, and culture. By 1997 feminist criticism of Shakespeare had established its credentials. The editing of early modern women writers was creating a substantial body of work, and essays clarifying the contributions of feminist editing had begun to appear.[19]

The appointment of women as general editors began as early as 1992, when Ann Thompson joined Richard Proudfoot as a general editor of the Arden 3 Shakespeare, making her the first contemporary woman editor of a single-volume, scholarly series. Two men were later added to the team. The first instance of full gender parity among general editors was the Folger Shakespeare Library's complete revision of its single-volume series for general readers, launched in 1992 and recently completed by Barbara A. Mowat and Paul

Werstine. As the decade continued, women became increasingly active as editors and general editors. In 1994 I became an associate general editor of *The Oxford Middleton*, joining two general editors and three associate general editors. The edition recruited twenty-three women and was published in 2007. Suzanne Gossett became one of three general editors for Arden Early Modern Drama, which published its first texts in 2009, and she is one of two general textual editors for the forthcoming Norton Shakespeare 3. A New Oxford Shakespeare is also in preparation, and Terri Bourus serves as general editor along with two others. Tiffany Stern is one of three editors of the current New Mermaids series, which focuses on non-Shakespearean drama. The other major single-volume Shakespeare series (New Cambridge, New Variorum, Oxford, Penguin, Signet) and the collected works (Bevington, Pelican, Riverside, RSC and *The Cambridge Works of Ben Jonson*) have no women in general editorial roles. Jean E. Howard is sole general editor for the Bedford Shakespeare contextual series, which uses previously published texts. Women's increasing presence as general editors matters in part because, as the first readers of an edition, they are in the best possible position to encourage or redirect an editor's perceptions and can also recruit others.

The presence of women as contributing editors for complete works or volume editors for single-volume series has increased more significantly, and a table is a concise way to convey this information. Listed below, according to data available as of January, 2013, are the numbers of women who serve as contributing editors on fully re-edited editions and their percentage of the total number of editors for collected works or editions in single-volume series.[20] The editions listed are already published except where 'commissioned' signals that some volumes are still in progress and editors are under contract. Dates given are for the publication of the first volume in the series or collected works.

Series or collected works	Women editors	% of total
Cambridge Ben Jonson (2012)	9 out of 33	27%
Arden Early Modern Drama (2009)	5 out of 8 as editors 1 more as co-editor	68 %
Oxford Middleton (2007)	10 out of 57 as editors 13 more as partial editors	29%
Norton Critical Ed. of Shakespeare (2003)	6 out of 12	50%
Arden 3 Shakespeare (1995) 79% published; 21% commissioned	9 out of 42 as editors 4 more as co-editors	26%
Folger Shakespeare Library (1992)	1 out of 2	50%
New Mermaids (1987)	15 out of 53 as editors 1 more as co-editor	29%
New Cambridge Shakespeare (1984)	5 out of 42 as editors 9 more as co-editors	23%
Oxford Shakespeare (1982)	2 out of 39	5%
New Variorum Shakespeare (1977)	0 out of 5 as editors 1 as co-editor	10%

The highest proportions of women editors appear in non-Shakespearean editions and two Shakespeare series for general or undergraduate readers. The more scholarly series directed to specialists and graduate/postgraduate students have fewer women, although more recent series in this category have higher percentages. Taken as a whole, the data show women have made quite remarkable progress over the past two decades in editing Shakespeare and early modern texts, especially if their work is viewed in the context of the last three centuries. All women editors are not feminists, of course: the texts that women produce are diverse in ideology and editorial choices, and those recently edited by men can be very attentive to gender and sexuality. On the other hand, earlier editions reveal that gender-neutrality among editors, even if it were possible or desirable, has rarely been aimed for much less achieved.[21] A consideration of some ways in which women's editions do and do not differ from their predecessors' appears in Suzanne Gossett's essay in this volume.[22] Beyond the numbers, women have earned serious respect for their editorial and scholarly work and have repeatedly demonstrated the value of their contributions. There is more to be done, but women are well underway in rethinking and remaking the texts of Shakespeare.

Notes

I am grateful to Suzanne Gossett, Ann Thompson, and to members of the Early Modern Forum at the University of Hawai'i at Mānoa, including Urvashi Chakravarty and Elizabeth McCutcheon, for their readings and suggested revisions of this essay.

1   Gary Taylor, 'Textual and Sexual Criticism: A Crux in *The Comedy of Errors*', *Renaissance Drama* 19 (1988), 195–225, quote at 195.

2   Phyllis Rackin, *Shakespeare and Women* (Oxford, 2005), p. 2.

3   Ann Thompson and Sasha Roberts (eds) *Women Reading Shakespeare, 1660–1900: An Anthology of Criticism* (Manchester, 1997), pp. 46–8. Henrietta's *Sermons* went through fifty editions from 1801 to 1853.

4   Noel Perrin, *Dr. Bowdler's Legacy: A History of Expurgated Books in England and America* (Boston, 1992), pp. 83–4.

5   Perrin, *Dr. Bowdler's Legacy*, p. 80, pp. 87–96.

6   See Valerie Wayne, 'The Gendered Text and its Labour', in

Valerie Traub ed., *The Oxford Handbook of Shakespeare and Embodiment: Gender, Sexuality, Race* (Oxford, forthcoming).

7   Gail Marshall and Ann Thompson, 'Mary Cowden Clarke', in Gail Marshall ed., *Jameson, Cowden Clarke, Kemble, Cushman* (London, 2011), vol. 7, Great Shakespeareans, pp. 58–91, quotes at p. 59, p. 73, p. 90.

8   Marshall and Thompson, pp. 60–2, pp. 69–71.

9   Marshall and Thompson, p. 63, p. 72, pp. 86–9.

10 Thompson and Roberts (eds) *Women Reading*, pp. 160–2.

11 Jeanne Addison Roberts, 'Women Edit Shakespeare', *Shakespeare Survey* 59 (2006), 136–46, quote at 145–6.

12 Jonathan Bate, 'The Case for the Folio' (2007), 1–69, quote at 67, www.rscshakespeare.co.uk/pdfs/Case_for_the_Folio.pdf

13 T. H. Howard-Hill, 'Alice Walker', in H. C. G. Matthew and Brian Harrison (eds), *Oxford Dictionary of National Biography*, 61 vols. (Oxford, 2004), vol. 56, p. 812.

14 Laurie Maguire, 'How Many Children Had Alice Walker?' in Douglas A. Brooks ed., *Printing and Parenting in Early Modern England* (Aldershot, 2005), pp. 327–50, information at p. 331.

15 Howard-Hill, 'Alice Walker', *ODNB,* vol. 56, p. 812.

16 Maguire, 'How Many Children?', p. 345.

17 Jeffrey Masten, *Textual Intercourse: Collaboration, Authorship, and Sexualities in Renaissance Drama* (Cambridge, 1997), p. 11. David McKitterick, 'Obituary: Katharine F. Pantzer, 1930–2005', *The Library* 7, 1 (March 2006), 87–9, quote at 87.

18 McKitterick, 'Obituary', 87–9. See A. W. Pollard and G. R. Redgrave, 2nd edn rev. W. A. Jackson, F. S. Ferguson, Katharine F. Pantzer, *Short-Title Catalogue of Books Printed in England, Scotland, and Ireland, 1475–1640*, 2 vols. (London, 1976), vol. 2, 340.

19 Ann Thompson, 'Feminist Theory and the Editing of Shakespeare: *The Taming of the Shrew* Revisited', in D. C. Greetham ed., *The Margins of the Text* (Ann Arbor, 1997), 83–103; Valerie Wayne, 'The Sexual Politics of Textual

Transmission', in Laurie E. Maguire and Thomas L. Berger (eds), *Textual Formations and Reformations* (Newark, 1998), pp. 179–210; Laurie E. Maguire, 'Feminist Editing and the Body of the Text', in Dympna Callaghan ed., *A Feminist Companion to Shakespeare* (Oxford, 2000), 59–79.

20 The Pelican, Penguin, and Bedford Shakespeare series are excluded from this table because their most recent texts have not been completely re-edited, and the focus here is on textual editing. Norton Critical Editions are included because editors are responsible for developing a text. I am grateful to Bill Carroll, a general editor of New Mermaids, for information on that series and its procedures. Other information is taken primarily from publishers' websites. The contributions of 'partial editors' on the Middleton range from preparing introductions, annotations, or both, to co-editing a text.

21 See Wayne, 'The Gendered Text', forthcoming.

22 Suzanne Gossett, 'Women making Shakespeare – and Middleton and Jonson', in this volume.

7

'To be acknowledged, madam, is o'erpaid': Woman's Role in the Production of Scholarly Editions of Shakespeare

Neil Taylor

University of Roehampton

In 1946 Una Ellis-Fermor became General Editor of the New Arden Shakespeare (hereinafter 'Ard2'). When she died in 1958 Harold Brooks wrote eloquently and movingly of her life and work, including her importance as the person who had established the principles of the series. He noted that she was held in honour and affection 'for her service in countless personal ways to the international brotherhood of scholars.'[1]

That final phrase was telling. Editing Shakespeare was indeed the province of brothers rather than of sisters.

In 1992, Ann Thompson was appointed a general editor
of the third Arden Shakespeare ('Ard3'). Five years later,
she noted that still only eight women had edited plays in the
Oxford, New Cambridge, Penguin or Ard2 series.[2] Since then,
as Valerie Wayne observes elsewhere in this volume, women
have begun to edit more frequently. But if one analyses the
history of the 1,004 major British and American editions
of Shakespeare texts which have been published since the
original Arden Shakespeare was launched in 1899,[3] one finds
that 216 of the 262 editors have been men. That means that
men have outnumbered women five to one. And only thirty
women have ever edited a text on their own. Even in the
eighteen years since Ard3 launched in 1995, the gender ratio
has only moved to three to one.

If one looks back at the whole period of 114 years, one
finds that, while there have been forty-three general editors or
sole editors of a series, only two of them have been women.[4]
And only one of these women has ever been in sole charge.
That was Una Ellis-Fermor.

This male-dominated culture extends into other related
areas. *Shakespeare Survey* (founded 1948) has had four
editors, all male. Each time an editor has retired he has then
joined the advisory board and served on it for at least eleven
years. While the board began with eight men and one woman,
Ellis-Fermor, after her death it waited until 1973 to appoint
another woman. Since then the number of women members
has steadily grown to seven, but they are still well outnumbered by the other members – the male editor and ten other
men. *Shakespeare Quarterly* (founded in 1950) has a man as
chair of an editorial board consisting of four men and one
woman, and an advisory board (chaired by a man) consisting
of nineteen men and two women. At the time of submitting
this essay for publication the editor is a man.[5] He is currently
assisted by two female consulting editors, two male and one
female associate editors, and an editorial board of eleven
men and seven women. Finally, *Shakespeare* (founded in
2005) has five editors (three men and two women), and an

editorial board consisting of 28 men and six women. While
these figures indicate that, in the cases of *Shakespeare Survey*
and *Shakespeare Quarterly* at least, the gender imbalance
has lessened, if one puts the current numbers of editors and
editorial board members from each journal together, men still
outnumber women by more than two to one.

What about Shakespeare conferences? To take an
arbitrary example, attendance at the biennial International
Shakespeare Conference in Stratford-upon-Avon is restricted
to invited delegates (and until recently at least only repeated
non-attendance removes the invitation). The conference's
advisory committee in 1994 (the first conference I attended)
consisted of nine men and three women; in 2012 it was
nine men and four women. In 1994 there were 147 male,
as opposed to seventy-six female, delegates; in 2012 male
attendance had dropped to 123 while female attendance had
risen to 92. A marked change, but still the men outnumber
the women.[6]

Ellis-Fermor went to Oxford. By 1918 she was teaching
in the University of London. But that was two years before
Oxford fully admitted women to the University and thirty
before Oxford appointed its first female professor. Indeed, in
1939 women still made up less than twenty-five per cent of the
university student population.[7] Yet, by 1992, that figure had
risen to 50 per cent and, at the time of composing this essay,
the most recent UK figures reveal that women undergraduates
now make up fifty-seven per cent of the undergraduate
population.[8] Furthermore, while the majority of academic
staff in UK institutions of higher education in 2010–11 were
male,[9] my own calculations of academic staff teaching and/or
researching in UK English departments suggest that, in 2012,
women just outnumbered men (1,193 to 1,157).[10]

So, while the history of education clearly provides reasons
why women for many years found it difficult to break into
the male preserve of scholarly editing, one might expect the
problem to have resolved itself by now. Why is it, then, that
female editors are still such a minority? It's not as if English

departments are short of female students or female staff. But since almost all general editors are men, when it comes to appointing the editors of individual texts, I can only assume that they turn first (unconsciously, I have no doubt) to other men.

* * *

Books are not made by one man. Or, indeed, by one woman. Acknowledging this fact has become increasingly widespread. Glancing along the fiction shelves of my local bookshop, I find that these days even novelists include a section labelled 'Acknowledgements'. Among those doing it are names as diverse as Jeffrey Archer, Margaret Atwood, Dan Brown, Peter Carey, J. M. Coetzee, Geoff Dyer, Ken Follett, Andrea Levy, Hilary Mantel, Tom McCarthy, Ian McEwan, D. B. C. Pierre, Alice Sebald, Ali Smith, Zadie Smith, Sarah Waters, Irvine Welsh and Jeanette Winterson. Perhaps under the influence of Oscars ceremonies, the extent of some novelists' thanks would seem to know no bounds. For example, in her most recent book, Jilly Cooper not only devotes as many as fourteen pages to acknowledging the help of 152 men, 124 women, three dogs and a cat, but bemoans the fact that she has mislaid the names and contact details of many others (*Jump!*, London, 2010, pp. 909–22, 920).

However, in respect of more academic writing, David Scott Kastan has written that '[n]o form of scholarly work more obviously reveals itself less as an individual labour and more as a collective activity than an edition of a Shakespeare play.'[11] He spreads the net wide, for he sees himself as collaborating with the dead as well as with the living: 'not only is this edition an effort to commune with Shakespeare, to attempt to recover his intentions from the Ouija board of the surviving texts, but it is also a series of vigorous conversations through the medium of print with all previous editors'.[12]

My interest here, however, is in those living collaborators who help make Shakespeare editions. The original Arden

Shakespeare and Cambridge New Shakespeare editors rarely thanked anyone other than the occasional fellow scholar. But as the century wore on the number of acknowledgements grew steadily and the 36 Ard3 titles so far published have amassed 1,079. (Indeed, one Ard3 editor has alone accounted for eighty-one.) Most thanks still go to fellow scholars, and here the gender imbalance is again apparent. Between them, the male scholars acknowledged by the editors of the editions mentioned in this essay have outnumbered their female counterparts by more than two to one.

Most editors, even the most unprofligate, have dutifully thanked their general editors: for obvious reasons the men once again outnumber the women – this time by more than five to one. And many editors have mentioned the help they have received in libraries. But for long what appeared in the Acknowledgements were the names of the libraries rather than those of individual staff members. In recent years, however, individuals have begun to be singled out for thanks and praise. As a result women have begun to come into their own: Ard2 editors mentioned by name twelve men and six women librarians, but Oxford mentioned fourteen men and twenty-eight women and New Cambridge nine men and thirty-three women. Ard3 mentions 20 men and 58 women.

Who else gets thanked? Very occasionally, but not very recently, a male editor has thanked a female secretary or administrator for typing up his manuscript. Much more frequently, and always right at the end of the Acknowledgements, loved ones are thanked for their forbearance. Usually that loved one is a woman, and usually she has no name. Often her love and support have been needed because her man has found editing almost unbearable. One reads of the editor 'lost in the dark room of the editing process', and of wives enduring their husbands' 'groans', and even 'despair', on 'the long ascent'. If editing is such hell, perhaps women are better off out of it?[13]

Some wives, however, seem to have been operating as editors themselves. One editor confessed that his wife had worked with him on 'every aspect of the volume'. Another drew on his wife's 'intimate and wide-ranging knowledge of things Elizabethan'. One thanked his wife for 'diligently revising the commentary and amplifying the notes', while another felt that his wife had done 'more proof-reading than any wife should be asked to undertake.' (How much *should* that be?) And one editor of a Complete Works told how his wife 'with truly Spartan endurance read aloud to me the complete text (including all the punctuation marks).'[14]

* * *

One group is still missing from my analysis of those whose contribution editors have learnt to acknowledge – the staff of the publishing house. The earliest of these to be mentioned was Mrs Margaret Pearce, who copy-edited the 1975 *Twelfth Night* for Ard2. Two more Ard2 editors also acknowledged their copy-editors by name, one in 1979 and one in 1982. In that last year, Oxford editors took up the practice, and by the time the series was complete, had thanked members of OUP staff fifty-one times. The earliest New Cambridge editors had refrained from mentioning such people, but they began in 1984 and eventually thanked individuals sixty-two times.

The prize, however, goes to Ard3, whose editors have so far thanked individual publishers, editors, copy-editors and proof-readers 128 times. And 'prize' seems not be an inappropriate word since, not only is their praise often fulsome, and sometimes more than fulsome, but there is a competitive edge to what many of them have written. Copy-editors are often commended for being 'eagle-eyed', but one pair of co-editors write that 'If there is a bird with sight even sharper than that of an eagle, it is to this that we liken our brilliant copy-editor' (*The Poems*, 2007, p. xviii). One editor thanks his 'meticulous, self-effacing' copy-editor, for having 'sharpened my logic and clarified cloudy sentences, and ... not infrequently bettered the substance as well as the accidents of this book' (*Richard II*, 2002, p. xviii). Another writes at length of how his copy-editor's 'encyclopedic editorial experience', 'formidable critical faculty', and 'unwavering commitment to the strictest accuracy and to the very highest standards of clarity', have transformed his manuscript (*The Merchant of Venice*, 2010, p. xix). Indeed, one editor admits that his copy-editor has served as 'virtually another co-editor' (*The Two Gentlemen of Verona*, 2004, p. xviii), while another goes further and abandons the concept of virtuality: 'I don't exaggerate when I say that in places ... [she] has become my co-editor.' He describes her 'quizzing, correcting, and gently nudging me towards what she's sure I meant to say' (*The Winter's Tale*, 2010, p. xx). Finally, one editor goes for broke and claims that the expertise of the Ard3 publishing team 'puts all other publishing houses to shame' (*Much Ado About Nothing*, 2006, p. xix).

The last-mentioned editor refers to the publishing team as 'all these women' (idem). Just as men dominate textual editing, so women dominate publishing,[15] and the acknowledgements pages, now that they have begun to include the publishers, reflect this fact. The New Cambridge editors, for example, have thanked men twenty-two times and women forty times; the Oxford editors have thanked men four times and women forty-seven times. And once again the Ard3 figures are the most dramatic. Its textual editors have so far thanked men five times, but women 123 times.

In *The Shakespeare Wars* (New York, 2006), Ron Rosenbaum reported that Ann Thompson had told him that her rapid rise to become a general editor of Ard3 'may in part have been a response to her critique of the male-dominated textual-editing establishment' (p. 78). While the numbers of women editors may still disappoint her, it is possible that she will be heartened by my last statistic. Her own editors, the majority of whom are men, have shown themselves to be more prepared than most to acknowledge not only that '[e]diting a play, like staging a play, is a collaborative exercise' (Keir Elam, Preface to Ard3 *Twelfth Night*, 2008, p. xviii), but that the exercise normally involves a good number of women collaborators – above all when it comes to ensuring that their editions are presented to readers, and presentable.

Notes

1   In G. K. Hunter ed., *All's Well That Ends Well*, New Arden Shakespeare (London, 1959), p. 7.

2   'Feminist theory and the Editing of Shakespeare: *The Taming of the Shrew Revisited*', in D. C. Greetham ed., *The Margins of the Text* (Ann Arbor, 1997), pp. 83–103, p. 85.

3   I am including series (three Arden, two Cambridge, two Folger Library, and two Pelican, along with Oxford, Penguin, Shakespeare Originals and Signet) and complete works (Arden, Norton, Oxford, Riverside and RSC, along with those edited by Peter Alexander, David Bevington, Hardin Craig, Wilbur L. Cross and C. F. Tucker Brooke, G. B. Harrison, G. L. Kittredge and C. J. Sisson).

4   Virginia A. Lamar co-edited the Folger Library General Readers Shakespeare and Barbara Mowat co-edited the Folger Library Shakespeare.

5   I am informed, however, that by the time the essay is published he will have been replaced by a woman.

6   By contrast, at the 2013 Shakespeare Association of America conference, women represented fifty-three per cent of the delegates. Membership of SAA is open and not restricted to invitees or previous attendees.

7   See Stijn Broecke and Joseph Hamed, *Gender Gaps in Higher Education Participation: An Analysis of the Relationship between Prior Attainment and Young Participation by Gender, Socio-Economic Class and Ethnicity*, DIUS Research Report 08–14 (2008), para. 1.

8   Enrolments and qualifications figures for 2011/12, published on the Higher Education Statistics Agency website, SFR 183, Table 5.

9   Ibid., SFR 185, Table 1. The numbers are 100,610 males out of 181,385 (55.34 per cent).

10 My figures are based on the English departments listed on the CCUE (Council for College and University English) website at the time of submitting this essay, and trying as far as possible to be consistent in disentangling English staff from staff in

other disciplines where there is a department or school or other unit which mixes English staff with others.

11   Preface to the Ard3 *Henry IV Part One* (2002, p. xv).

12   Idem.

13   The phrases quoted in this paragraph come from Prefaces in the Ard3 *Twelfth Night* (2008, p. xx), Oxford *King John* (1989, p. ix), Oxford *A Midummer Night's Dream* (1994, p. vi) and Oxford *Julius Caesar* (1984, p. v).

14   The phrases quoted in this paragraph come from Prefaces and Acknowledgements in the New Cambridge *Othello* (1984, p. x), Ard2 *Hamlet* (1982, p. ix), Ard2 *2 Henry IV* (1966, p. ix), Oxford *Othello* (2006, p. vi), and *The Riverside Shakespeare* (1974, p. vi).

15   See, for example, Sue Ledwith and Frances Tomlinson, 'Women in Book Publishing – A "Feminised" Sector?', in Sue Ledwith and Fiona Colgan eds, *Women in Organisations: Challenging Gender Politics* (Basingstoke, 1996), pp. 44–77, p. 48.

8

Some Women Editors of Shakespeare: A Preliminary Sketch

H. R. Woudhuysen

Lincoln College, Oxford

Through her own precept and practice, few scholars have done as much as Ann Thompson to challenge and dispel that dangerous but too commonly received notion that women have not played a significant role in the editing of Shakespeare. Her own editions – *The Taming of the Shrew* (1984, revised 2003) for Cambridge and the three-text *Hamlet* with Neil Taylor (2006) for Arden 3 – her explorations, especially with Sasha Roberts, of women reading and writing on Shakespeare, her theorizing of the relations between editing and feminist practice have all shown that editing is not and has not always been man's work alone. As one of the General Editors of the Arden 3 series, she has also helped to promote the precept as practice.

A full scale history of the involvement of women in the editing of Shakespeare would be a major project engaging with a number of related fields, including publishing history, the history of scholarship, of literary societies and of women's education and their position in society. What follows is a brief outline that might suggest some avenues of enquiry for future researchers. If it is no more than in the nature of literary gossip, then that is more or less inevitable: editions are complicated negotiations between editors, publishers and readers, subject to different demands, not least the endless compromises necessary between the individual editor and the requirements of the series and between the ideal edition and the publisher's much more pragmatic business – to publish successful books.

* * *

In the spring of 1924, with the publication of *Much Ado About Nothing*, Methuen were able to complete the Arden Shakespeare series, an undertaking begun in 1899 with Edward Dowden's *Hamlet*. The final play was the work of Grace R. Trenery, the only woman to edit an Arden volume until Agnes Latham produced *As You Like It* in 1975. Trenery's edition has a relatively brief introduction and a very full commentary (one page in classic Arden style has only two lines of text on it). The only personal acknowledgement that she makes is to the series' General Editor, Robert Hope Case (1857–1944), thanking him 'for advice and sympathy in difficulties, and for encouragement which has extended over many years'. Beyond a few further references to his assistance in the commentary ('Professor Case notes ... Professor Case suggests ...') nothing more is revealed about who Grace Trenery was or the nature of those 'difficulties'.[1] The reviewer of her edition in *The Times Literary Supplement* (the ineffable John Middleton Murry) reported that 'Miss Trenery enjoys and admires the play, and sets herself to all the work of elucidating it with an admirable quickness and subtlety of apprehension'.[2]

Like so many women editors, Trenery's life is regrettably obscure. Born in 1887 in Stoneycroft, Liverpool, she seems to have spent most of her life in or around the city. At Wallasey High School, she was successful in the Oxford Local Examinations of 1900 and graduated from Liverpool University with a scholarship in English Literature in 1912.[3] In 1915, she contributed an article on 'Ballad Collections of the Eighteenth Century' to the journal *Modern Language Review*:[4] at this time, one of *MLR*'s three editors, James Fitzmaurice-Kelly (1858–1923), was Professor of Spanish at Liverpool. Her article surveys the various collections, discriminating between genuine ballads and those that had been fabricated or rewritten for publication in print. Her help in the preparation of William Thomas Young's edition of Keats's poems, published at Cambridge in 1917, is acknowledged by Oliver Elton: Young (1881–1917) had been educated at Liverpool where Elton (1861–1945), the King Alfred Professor, would have taught him. The edition shows that Trenery had been awarded an MA. *Much Ado* was published when she was about 37. During the Second World War, part of Liverpool University was evacuated to Coleg Harlech on the Cambrian coast. Trenery and Alexander James Dow Porteous (1896–1981), Professor of Education, were in charge of the College and, remembering her presence there, a student recalled that 'one of her asides was "there are streaks in Bacon"'.[5] Her later history is unknown.

* * *

Grace Trenery was not Shakespeare's earliest female editor, and the story of her predecessors – Henrietta Bowdler (1754–1830), Mary Cowden Clarke (1809–98) and the ardent American Shakespeareans Charlotte Endymion Porter (1859–1942) and Helen Archibald Clarke (1860–1926) – is sufficiently well known not to need rehearsing again.

Ann Thompson has told the less happy narrative of Teena Rochfort Smith (1861–83) and her parallel-text edition of *Hamlet*.[6] It was to have presented the texts of the two quartos and the Folio, along with a 'Revized Text' of the play

for the New Shakspere Society. Frederick James Furnivall
(1825–1910) encouraged the project, but although a thirty-
six-page sample text was published by Nicholas Trübner, the
full edition never appeared because of Smith's tragic death
in 1883. If it had been issued, it 'would have been the most
complex presentation of the texts of *Hamlet* ever attempted'.[7]
It would also perhaps have represented the most ambitious
piece of Shakespearean textual scholarship undertaken by a
woman until well into the next century. It is likely that the
intensity of Smith's friendship with Furnivall broke up his
marriage or, at least, contributed to its break up, but his role
in promoting literary scholarship by women is characteristic.

* * *

These early editors represent one path of scholarly work
by women. Another might be opened up by looking at
editions and translations of the plays and the poems published
elsewhere than in the United Kingdom and North America. To
take just one example, annotated editions of *Macbeth* and of
The Taming of the Shrew were published at Copenhagen in
1885 and 1886, respectively, edited by A. Stewart MacGregor
and Mrs Selma S. Kinney, the second in collaboration with
H. C. Damm. In 1898, Mrs Kinney arrived in the US and
went on to teach French and German in Hawai'i. Her work
in Denmark shows how towards the end of the nineteenth
century another direction for women editors was opening up.

The growth in popular education and in English literature
as a suitable subject for study created a need for school
editions of Shakespeare's works. These might be abridged
in addition to being annotated, as were the editions that the
novelist Charlotte Mary Yonge (1823–1901) prepared for the
National Society's Depository in the mid-1880s.[8] Some of the
earliest and more professional classroom editions of the plays
were produced by Katharine Lee Bates (1859–1929), who
edited *The Merchant of Venice* (1894), *A Midsummer Night's
Dream* (1895) and *As You Like It* (1896) for The Students'

Series of English Classics.[9] Bates, a graduate of and professor at Wellesley College, had published a study of the English religious drama (1893): she is perhaps best remembered as the author of the lyrics of 'America the Beautiful'. The Shakespeare editions were published by Leach, Shewell, and Sanborn at thirty-five cents, and had cloth bindings, attractively lettered and decorated on their upper covers. The extensive notes for each play were divided into three categories:

> textual, for the use of more advanced classes, that are interested in seeing how far the play they read is the play originally printed; grammatical, for the use of students who would familiarize themselves with Elizabethan idiom; and literary; this third group of notes being, in the judgment of the editor, more fruitful and appropriate, especially for beginners, than the two technical divisions. In classes where textual and grammatical work is done, it is believed better to separate these special lines of investigation from the essential study of the play.[10]

In England, Elizabeth Lee (1857/8–1920), the translator of Jean Jules Jusserand's *The English Novel in the Time of Shakespeare* (1890) and the sister of Sidney Lee (1859–1926), was responsible for editions of *The Tempest* (1894 and of *Twelfth Night* (1895) for Blackie's Junior School Shakespeare.[11]

The plays that Bates and Lee chose or were asked to edit are largely characteristic of the publishing practices of the next century: comedies and some histories for women, tragedies for men. This was not always the case, and one of the first editions of a play produced by a woman in Britain for a school series was Phoebe Sheavyn's *King Lear* of 1898.[12] Sheavyn (1865–1968) was then in her second year as a tutor at Somerville College, Oxford, having studied at Aberystwyth and Bryn Mawr; her famous monograph *The Literary Profession in the Elizabethan Age* was not to be published until 1909. The *Lear* edition, published by Adam and Charles Black as part of Black's School Shakespeare, cost a shilling and was attractively presented in green cloth with dark blue lettering. The series General Editor was the prolific Lionel William Lyde (1863–1947), then of Glasgow Academy. Sheavyn's edition is a conventional school one, with an introduction dealing with such subjects as the play's sources, date, characters, and construction. The twenty pages of notes in double columns concentrate on the play's vocabulary; they are followed by a brief index which allows the reader to locate examples of 'Prothesis' and of 'Abstract for concrete' nouns.

More school editions by women may well exist; some may lurk unidentified behind editors' chaste initials and others are hard to locate since even major libraries acquired copies only sporadically. The demand from schools led publishers to embark on a number of series, and women editors were commissioned to edit volumes for them. For example, the University Tutorial Series, whose General Editor was William Briggs (1861–1932), Principal of University Correspondence College, London, had the rather interesting novelist Agnes Russell Weekes edit *As You Like It* and *The Tempest* in 1909 and *Cymbeline* a decade later.[13] In 1924, Magdalene Marie Weale edited *Love's Labour's Lost*, and in 1929, Gertrude Eleanor Hollingworth produced *Henry VIII* for the same series.[14] The blue-grey cloth, blocked with black lettering, of these books is unattractive and the format of the introductions allowed their writers little space for their own views or ideas as characters, metre, rhyme and prose were all analysed. The notes to the editions are, however, quite generous and are well indexed.

None of these school series employed editors who had or later established reputations as Shakespeare scholars. The same is not true for the Heath or Arden Shakespeare, published by D. C. Heath in London. Lilian Winstanley (1875–1960), who had a first in English from what became Manchester University, was a lecturer at Aberystwyth and later wrote critical-historical studies of the major tragedies, edited *2 Henry IV* in about 1918 for this series which also included editions by such familiar male scholars as J. C. Smith, E. K. Chambers, A. J. Wyatt, G. C. Moore Smith, F. S. Boas, and David Nichol Smith.[15] Similarly, the Tudor Shakespeare, whose general editors were William A. Neilson and Ashley H. Thorndike, and which was published at New York by Macmillan, commissioned several women to edit plays for it: *As You Like It* (1911) from Martha Hale Shackford (1875–1963); *1 Henry VI* (1911) from Louise Pound (1872–1958); *The Winter's Tale* (1912) from Laura Johnson Wylie (1855–1932); *2 Henry IV* (1914) from Elizabeth Deering Hanscom (1865–1960); *King Lear* (1914) from Virginia Crocheron Gildersleeve (b. 1877).[16] Among the male editors of plays in this series were W. W. Lawrence, F. M. Padelford, J. W. Cunliffe, J. S. P. Tatlock, E. E. Stoll and Carleton Brown.

For many of these editors, the plays of Shakespeare were not their first editorial projects. Katharine Lee Bates, for example, had already prepared Coleridge's *Rime of the Ancient Mariner* (1889) and a *Ballad Book* (1890) for the same school series as the Shakespeare volumes she produced. Similarly, before turning to Shakespeare Lilian Winstanley had taken on the task of editing some of Chaucer's *Canterbury Tales*, Spenser's *Fowre Hymnes* (1907) and the first two books of *The Faerie Queene* (1914–15) for Cambridge's Pitt Press series. A similar path from Book I of *The Faerie Queene* (1905) to Shakespeare was followed by Martha Hale Shackford. For others, such as Agnes Russell Weekes and Gertrude Eleanor Hollingworth, the Shakespeare editions seem to have been among their earliest publications in the form of books.

* * *

The fact that these women were commissioned as editors of school and more scholarly editions shows that publishers or general editors were ready to make use of the new generation of university-educated women to produce the works they wanted to sell. 'The names of Shakespeare's editors are legion', Andrew Murphy wrote and went on to ask mournfully, 'who now remembers H. Bellyse Baildon, Henry Ten Eyck Perry, N. Burton Paradise, Thomas M. Parrott or Virginia Gildersleeve?'[17] In fact, Gildersleeve, the editor of *King Lear* for the Tudor Shakespeare, had a doctorate from Columbia University for a thesis on *Government Regulation of Elizabethan Drama* (1908) and is also remembered – at least in *ODNB* – as the founder in 1919, with her companion the Chaucer and Shakespeare scholar Caroline Spurgeon (1869–1942), of the International Federation of University Women.

If, in the end, commercial demands drove the production of these Shakespeare editions and the employment of women editors, it is interesting to see female scholars before Grace Trenery being commissioned in their own right to produce distinctive editions. One example of this is the volume of the Sonnets that Charlotte Carmichael Brown Stopes (1840–1929) produced for Alexander Moring's De La More Press in 1904. This was part of his attractive series called the King's Classics and described itself as the King's Shakespeare, although no other plays or poems were issued. The feminist Stopes wrote extensively on Shakespeare and Elizabethan history: the edition of the poems (quarter-bound antique grey boards for 1*s*. 6*d*.), her only Shakespeare edition, is characteristically idiosyncratic ('I have been unable through lack of space to give reasons for my difference of opinion on so many points from all previous editors').[18]

Presumably Moring commissioned the edition but, although publishers evidently had the final say as to who was given a contract, the role of the general editor of the series should not be forgotten. Learned societies provide an early model for this; for example, women edited volumes or parts of volumes for the Camden Society from as early as 1847 when Charlotte Augusta Sneyd (1800–82) translated and annotated Andrea Trevisano's *A Relation, or rather a True Account, of the Isle of England*. In 1856, Mary Everett Green (1818–95), recently appointed an editor of the calendars of state papers, edited the diary of John Rous for the Society. Furnivall's role in promoting Teena Rochfort Smith's work on *Hamlet* has already been referred to; it may be possible to detect his influence in the employment of women editors for the publications of the Early English Text Society that he founded in 1864. Lucy Toulmin Smith (1838–1911) completed her father's work on English gilds for the Society in 1870 and Octavia Richardson generously acknowledged Furnivall's encouragement in her edition of *The right plesaunt and goodly historie of the foure sonnes of Aymon* for the Society in 1885: many other women subsequently edited volumes for the Main and the Extra Series.

Similarly, it is possible that W. W. Greg (1875–1959) encouraged Willy Bang (1869–1934) to commission Evelyn Mary Spearing's edition of *Studley's Translations of Seneca's Agamemnon and Medea* (1913) for Bang's Materialen zur Kunde des älteren englischen Dramas. Spearing is more immediately recognizable as Evelyn Simpson (1885–1963), the great editor of Jonson and of Donne's sermons. By the time her edition came out ('the second volume of her endeavours was lost when the Louvain University Press was destroyed' during the First World War),[19] the Malone Society had been in existence for six years, but it was not until the 1920s that, with Greg as General Editor, women began to edit volumes for the Society. The first was Anthony Munday's *John a Kent and John a Cumber* (1923) edited by Muriel St Clare Byrne (1895–1983), followed by *Edmond Ironside* (1927) by Eleanore Boswell (b. 1897), Philip Massinger's *The Parliament of Love* (1928) by Kathleen Marguerite Lea (1903–95) and *Thomas of Woodstock* (1929) by the Dutch scholar Wilhelmina Paulina Frijlinck (1880–1965).

In this context of school and scholarly editions of Shakespeare, of volumes for learned societies, Grace Trenery's *Much Ado* seems less of a phoenix and more of a sign of what was still to come. During the next sixty or so years, the work of women editors and of women general editors, like Ann Thompson, was increasingly to be recognized by the publishing and scholarly worlds.

Notes

1 *Much Ado About Nothing*, ed. Grace R. Trenery, The Arden Shakespeare (London, 1924), pp. xxvii, 116, 134, 135.

2 *TLS*, 15 May 1924, p. 293.

3 1901 Census; *Liverpool Mercury*, 21 August 1900; *Manchester Guardian*, 8 July 1912.

4 'Ballad Collections of the Eighteenth Century', *Modern Language Review* 10 (1915), 283–303.

5 P. E. H. Hair, ed., *Arts, Letters, Society: A Miscellany Commemorating the Faculty of Arts at the University of Liverpool* (Liverpool, 1996), p. 54; *Manchester Guardian*, 28 December 1940.

6 Ann Thompson, 'Teena Rochfort Smith, Frederick Furnivall, and the New Shakspere Society's Four-Text Edition of Hamlet', *Shakespeare Quarterly* 49 (1998), 125–39; not in Andrew Murphy, *Shakespeare in Print: A Hisory and Chronology of Shakespeare Publishing* (Cambridge, 2003).

7 Thompson, 'Smith', p. 131.

8 Not in Murphy.

9 Thompson and Roberts, *Women Reading*, p. 225; not in Murphy.

10 *Shakespeare's Comedy of As You Like It*, ed. Katharine Lee Bates (1896), pp. iii–iv.

11 Not in Murphy; for Elizabeth Lee, see *ODNB*.

12 Not in Murphy.

13 Murphy, nos. 943, 963, 966. Weekes gained a first in English and French in 1907 and an MA in English in 1910 from London University.

14 Murphy, nos. 949, 968; the first edition of *Henry VIII* may be considerably earlier. Hollingworth also edited *Coriolanus* (1924), *Hamlet* (1926), *Macbeth* with Stephen Edwardes Goggin (1927) and *1 Henry IV* (1929) for The Matriculation Shakespeare which is not in Murphy.

15 Murphy, nos. 842, 865.

16 Murphy, nos. 1058, 1059, 1062, 1070, 1074, 1084.

17 Murphy, p. 13.

18 *Sonnets* (1904), p. lv; not in Murphy.

19 *ODNB*.

9

Bernice Kliman's *Enfolded Hamlet*

John Lavagnino
King's College London

If you have read Ann Thompson's essay about Teena Rochfort Smith, you will always remember the story of this gifted Shakespearean who died tragically at the age of twenty-one in 1883, after making a start on an edition of *Hamlet* and a relationship with the most colourful literary scholar of the age, Frederick J. Furnivall.[1] Her edition used six different styles of type, along with stars, daggers, and vertical bars, to mark many kinds of differences among the three early texts of the play; they highlight variations in the spelling of speech-headings, for example, and not just by marking the words but by indicating the *letters* that differ. I'd like to pay tribute to Ann by looking at another strikingly innovative edition of *Hamlet* in the same tradition of analytic presentation, one that both builds on and counters the editorial and scholarly trends of its time.

That edition is *The Enfolded Hamlet* by Bernice Kliman, who fortunately saw it to completion (and indeed to publication in three different forms), and whose death in 2011 came after a long and productive scholarly career. It was originally only intended as one component of a far larger project, still underway – the New Variorum edition of *Hamlet* that Kliman initiated and directed – but it had its own value and rationale. Though well known among Shakespeareans, its innovations are not much publicized in the wider scholarly world; in the history of textual scholarship more generally, and particularly that of digital scholarly editions, it is a far more important contribution than has been recognized.

In its earliest published form, as a forty-four page special issue of *The Shakespeare Newsletter* in 1996, *The Enfolded Hamlet* was designed to show at once both the original-spelling text of Q2 and all significant differences in the First Folio text.[2] Q2 material that is different or absent in F1 is marked by curly braces; F1 material is similarly supplied in angle brackets. As an example, for TLN 1233 the edition prints:

> *Pol.* I meane the matter {that} you {reade}<meane,> my
>   Lord.

Only Q2 prints 'that' and 'reade'; only F1 prints 'meane,'. In this line the spelling and punctuation of the rest of the line happen to be the same in Q2 and F1, but when there is no significant variation what you get is Q2 and no indication of what F1 might be doing. 'Significant' variation includes some differences in spelling and punctuation, based on Kliman's judgment. There is no reference at all to readings in Q1. There are no notes, only a 2,400 word introduction.

This edition does only a few things, not everything. According to Kliman's introduction, it arose in 1989 as a byproduct of the New Variorum Edition, as a way to solve the problem of choosing one base text as the series required; the enfolded text keeps all the significant variants from Q2 and F1 visible as part of the main text, without requiring a look at the notes. Though it later turned into an online publication, its origins are in the world of scholarly editing for the printed page, with considerations of space and compression always in mind. And it continues the sequence of editions that included Teena Rochfort Smith's: Smith was not the first editor to create an analytic presentation of textual variation in early *Hamlet* texts, but hers is certainly one of the most ambitious.

Among scholarly editions of English texts from the 1980s and 1990s, *The Enfolded Hamlet* is unusual: there are few parallels in its era to the choices it makes. Though there was a continuing tradition of interventionist editing, in such editions as the Oxford Shakespeare, the Northwestern–Newberry edition of *Moby-Dick*, and Hans Walter Gabler's edition of *Ulysses*, the increasing trend in the field was towards non-intervention and attempts at mediation-free transmission. That trend produced a number of editions focused on manuscripts rather than printed versions, such as the Cornell Wordsworth, the Cornell Yeats, and R.W. Franklin's *Poems of Emily Dickinson: Variorum Edition*. In all of these editions, the primary aim is to print complete transcriptions of manuscripts rather than to construct a single text from them. Another approach in this line was the large-scale facsimile edition of manuscripts, as in the numerous series of printed facsimiles published by Garland, of materials by Byron, Shelley, Tennyson, Whitman, Shaw, Joyce, and many others. An editor's role had once been to select and to reconstruct, building the proper text out of a study of the evidence and with some judicious emendation, and in print presenting a smooth surface backed up by unobtrusive notes. But the taste was increasingly for things not so smoothed out, for preservation of the details in full. Michael Warren's *Complete King Lear, 1608–1623* in 1989, with its facsimiles of the play's early publications as well as an analytic parallel text, was a significant manifestation of this textual attitude. Teena Rochfort Smith's edition had a similar ambition of completeness but before facsimiles became so common.

Digital publications in the humanities in that era were also often projects in diplomatic or facsimile reproduction;

by the 1990s the practicality of large-scale publication of digital images on CD-ROM led to the idea that an edition might simply publish everything, without mediation, so that readers would be freed from the interfering figure of the editor. Jay David Bolter and Richard Grusin have shown how, over and over again in the history of publishing, new technology that was obtrusive and hard to use was still seen as offering transparent access without the undesirable mediation of older methods.[3] One curious belief about digital editions in the 1990s was that it was not merely good for them to be transparent channels without editorial intervention, it was impossible for them to be anything else. Creators of serious digital editions of the time, such as the Blake Archive, knew very well that these ideas were naive, but the completeness of Warren's *Lear* was still the dominant idea.

But *The Enfolded Hamlet* is not complete, and Kliman's introductions to its various editions made that very clear. The 1996 publication omitted most F1 spelling and punctuation variants, all Q1 readings, and all press variants. Writing in 2006 about this and other secondary products of the New Variorum *Hamlet*, Kliman observed 'Modern marketers try to suggest that every edition has to suit all purposes: general reading, study, scholarship and performance. Our *Enfolded* edition is in this respect distinctly retrograde: a text for a specific audience – which as it turns out is not as narrow as one would think: relatively little of the text's peculiarity, compared to modern editions, is unfathomable'.[4] Indeed, one common claim in plans for complete digital editions in the 1990s was that they would do everything for everybody and you'd never need to do it again – adapting a claim that used to be made within Fredson Bowers's sphere of influence about scholarly editions, that the work would be done once and for all if it was really done right. Bowers himself was more judicious than that, and usually said only that fundamental bibliographical research wouldn't need to be redone; he knew that there were always further possibilities in editing.

Smith's work would have answered far better to the spirit of the 1990s, in its ambition to provide a complete guide to the textual evidence for *Hamlet*; Ann Thompson commented on the increased interest in such analytic presentations in the digital era. But Kliman was obviously right about the context, in which there are huge numbers of *Hamlet* editions constructed on many other principles readily available, and more value in doing something different rather than something total.

Kliman's *Enfolded Hamlet*, then, was unusual for its time in offering a view of a selection of evidence, rather than completeness. In another respect, it is very much of its time, in its attention to the effective presentation of that evidence using a newly-developed system. Presentation was a topic that Kliman addressed on other occasions: as in her work on *The Three-Text Hamlet*, a parallel-text presentation of all three *Hamlet* sources, or her essay about Charles Jennens, whose neglected editions of Shakespeare plays had new design features intended to assist analysis rather than reading. *The Three-Text Hamlet* was possible in part because of the rise of desktop publishing in the 1980s: it would have been far more difficult to produce through the traditional sort of collaboration with compositors.

New technology in the 1980s and 1990s tended to be enlisted for works with complex textual situations, and until the late 1990s led to printed books rather than online publications. Most famous is Hans Walter Gabler's edition of *Ulysses*, with a 'synoptic' presentation showing the later stages of the development of Joyce's text, as he revised and expanded it through a series of manuscripts, typescripts, and proofs. It manages to describe the symbols and conventions it uses for this in only two pages, and the really crucial symbols are actually only four in number: paired brackets to indicate additions and deletions, with superscripts to indicate the document in which it happened. Some later editions that didn't need to handle quite as much variation were able to use vertical alignment of variants on the page to do this:

that was the approach of J. C. C. Mays in his edition of Coleridge's poems, and Jesús Tronch-Pérez in his own Q2/ F1 edition of *Hamlet*. The series of Chaucer editions by Peter Robinson and his collaborators has been the most advanced of this kind, with a system for presenting variants from dozens of manuscripts that makes it very clear what's in each manuscript and how it compares with the rest – it is far easier to work with than the edition of John M. Manly and Edith Rickert from 1940 that had tried to be similarly comprehensive. Robinson's editions moved into a realm where only digital publication was practical, in view of the vast amount of information that was included.

At first encounter, the editions of Gabler, Mays, Tronch-Pérez, and Robinson look very complex, but their systems are not difficult to learn and are more usable than traditional apparatus notation. Ten to 20 years on, though, few literary scholars are making extensive use of editions of this sort, and one reason is that things in the wider digital world we inhabit have moved in a different direction. That direction is exemplified by the transformation of online library catalogues in the same period. When these first began to be widely available in the 1980s and 1990s, they offered interfaces based on the traditional structure of cataloguing records, with separate searches on author, title, and subject indexes. In the twenty-first century this approach has receded into the background: though it is usually still available, it has been supplanted for most purposes by a Google-style interface in which you don't bother to choose an index, but just type some words. That minimalism arose from the circumstances of web searching, in which there was very little structured data available, and from the practical discovery that you usually got something about as usable even in searching a library catalogue if you just looked for words and didn't worry about where they were.

Many areas of computer use, such as engineering, still involve complex software that requires significant effort to learn; the idea persists that editions of literary works ought to have a broader public, though, and by the twenty-first century the usual assumption was that software for the general public should be as simple as possible and require no awareness that one was learning to use it. The restricted interfaces of mobile phones have made simplicity even more imperative, so *The Enfolded Hamlet* has only looked more and more up-to-date. Kliman published a new version in book form in 2004, which is the only scholarly edition ever published that has a distinctive form of apparatus and manages to explain what all its symbols do within its title: *The Enfolded Hamlets: Parallel Texts of <F1> and {Q2} Each With Unique Elements Bracketed.* Sadly, though, many library catalogues and citations garble or omit the symbols.

That publication actually represented a drift away from simplicity: it added a version based on F1 and displayed it in parallel with the older Q2-based version, so that it was now possible to see details of F1 spelling and punctuation, but in a larger, more expensive, and more complex book. The (somewhat earlier) online publication was also more complex; it offered the same choice of base text, backed up the symbols with colour highlighting of the variant passages, and included a search interface. It is the 1996 publication that shows the idea of enfolding with the fewest accretions, and with the strongest suggestion that you might *read* the play in this form, rather than checking a passage here and there. Ron Rosenbaum, in his account of Shakespeare scholarship written for a non-academic audience, describes the initial difficulties even of Kliman's system for a reader, and also his appreciation of its value for helping him to think about the texts of *Hamlet*; the apparatus symbols became familiar enough that he could read the enfolded text while keeping both versions in mind at once.[5] This simultaneous reading of several versions is only possible when the usual process of consciously decoding the apparatus is overcome: when the symbols are just another kind of punctuation.

Why is *The Enfolded Hamlet* so successful? One key is that its design is exactly attuned to the textual situation it presents, in which two versions are very close and the great majority of the variants involve a difference within a line, rather than entirely different lines. Though a parallel-text edition is useful, it also leaves much of the work undone, at least in the common form of parallel presentation that *The Three-Text Hamlet* uses: a reader is left to do the work of finding the variants within lines. The material is also in the same sequence in Q2 and F1, so no provision is needed to indicate the migration of blocks of text. In all of these respects, Q1 would be difficult to integrate into the enfolded text: the level of variation is higher and the order is different.

Because the differences between Q2 and F1 are not enormous, as Shakespeareans have long known, a very minimal apparatus suffices. As Kliman herself pointed out, the approach starts to become a problem in some passages that happen to have greater variation. It is not that the symbols become impossible to understand, but that too much is happening at once and the possibility of simultaneous reading of both versions, as Rosenbaum described it, becomes much less available. When there are two or three variants in a line you can keep them in your head at once; beyond that it starts to be a problem. In my experience, repetition of phrases can also block reading and require a halt to decode the symbols, which are no longer quite so easy to work through. For example, a passage at TLN 3368–9 reads 'this same skull sir, <this same Scull sir,> was {sir} *Yoricks* skull'. That is indeed an F1 repetition, and an added 'sir' in Q2; the repetition can feel like an error or a variant of the Q2 version, in part because of the change from 'skull' to 'Scull' as we move from Q2's spelling to F1's. F1 actually says 'Scull' both times; this is one instance where the mixture of spellings is a distraction from what matters.

These occasional failures of the edition make clear its success most of the time in conveying an idea of both versions at once: and it's the compression that makes this work. *The Three-Text Hamlet* and other editions that pursue completeness make a great deal of information available, but they are best for textual analysis and construction, and not extensive reading. Another feature of *The Enfolded Hamlet* that supports reading is the avoidance of the kind of font changes that Teena Rochfort Smith used – because it is difficult for readers to avoid seeing font and colour changes as indicating emphasis. The most familiar instance of this problem is the King James Bible's use of italics: though italicized words are usually ones added by the translators, modern readers are often heard trying to emphasize these insignificant words. It's true, though, that the online version of *The Enfolded Hamlet* does use colour as well as symbols: in the 1990s this was an almost obligatory feature of web pages.

Since then, attention in Shakespearean circles to the multiple versions of works like *Hamlet* has only grown, and editions such as Ann Thompson and Neil Taylor's give even Q1 a new prominence. Their decision to treat the three texts as independent is a step beyond the work of editors who focused on juxtaposing and comparing them, from Teena Rochfort Smith and other nineteenth-century scholars through to Bernice Kliman. But Kliman when comparing *Hamlet*s was already thinking about the distinctive value of each version. She wrote appreciatively of the differences in pace, tone, delivery, characterization, and philosophy that Q2/F1 variants suggested; she only conceded with evident reluctance that sometimes one or the other was just wrong. This, of course, is the final way in which her edition is characteristic of its age: it sees the multiplication of versions as multiplying possibilities for readers and performers, rather than needing reduction to one text.

Notes

1   'Teena Rochfort Smith, Frederick Furnivall, and the New
     Shakspere Society's Four-Text Edition of *Hamlet*', *Shakespeare
     Quarterly* 49 (1998), 125–39. Photographs of the Folger
     Shakespeare Library copy of Smith's edition are online at:
     http://luna.folger.edu/luna/servlet/s/dg3447

2   *Shakespeare Newsletter* 46, extra issue (1996).

3   'Remediation', *Configurations* 4 (1996), 311–58.

4   'Print and Electronic Editions Inspired by the New Variorum *Hamlet* Project', *Shakespeare Survey* 59 (2006), 157–67.

5   *The Shakespeare Wars: Clashing Scholars, Public Fiascoes, Palace Coups* (New York, 2006), pp. 86–90, 96–8.

10

Women Making Shakespeare – and Middleton and Jonson

Suzanne Gossett

Loyola University Chicago

About fifteen years ago, in an essay called 'Feminist Theory and the Editing of Shakespeare: *The Taming of the Shrew Revisited*', Ann Thompson briefly traced the history of women editing – or mostly not editing – Shakespeare. As Valerie Wayne's essay in this volume demonstrates, in the interim this situation has changed.[1] Some of the change is ideological. Feminism is now engrained in the profession, and, as I argued in 'Why should a Woman Edit a Man?' feminist editors cannot be confined to texts by women.[2] And some of the change is institutional. Because most editions are undertaken on commission, the attitude of the publisher becomes particularly important. It's hard to ascertain cause and effect, but currently the editors and publishers at Cambridge, Oxford, Norton, and Bloomsbury who are responsible for many of the important editions of early modern drama, are all women. In their view, presumably, women teach, write, publish, interpret; why would they not also edit?

A similar change can be found in the largest professional organization of Shakespeareans, the Shakespeare Association of America, now forty years old, which also 'makes' Shakespeare institutionally. In its first ten years the SAA had one female president; in the next ten there were four; after that, the proportions reversed, and in each of the next decades there were six female presidents to four male presidents. We begin the fifth decade with yet another female president. The profession has for a long time been predominantly female, but now women are accepted in positions of authority.

Editing is one form of that authority, but does female authority actually lead to editions that look different? Thompson foresaw possible feminist impact on text, intro-duction, and commentary notes. In this brief paper I will consider the *genre* of play feminist editors choose or accept; the *topics* they cover in notes and introductions; and finally, some textual *cruxes* and editorial responses to them.

Almost invariably, men edit Shakespeare's tragedies, histories, and comedies; women edit Shakespeare's comedies (including, occasionally, the late 'romances'). This division of labor has long endured: Agnes Latham, editing *As You Like It*, was the only Arden 2 female volume editor; even in Arden 3 women have edited almost exclusively comedies. In fact, the two tragedies that have so far emerged with a woman's name on the cover have both been co-edited by a man and woman, *Hamlet* by Ann Thompson and Neil Taylor and *Timon of Athens* by Anthony Dawson and Gretchen Minton. In the single-volume Oxford World Classics and the New Cambridge Shakespeare there are a few exceptions, but the pattern tends to hold. Even more remarkably, across these three series so far, only one Shakespeare history play has been edited by a woman.

Since scholarly editions take time, one possible expla-nation is that these editors were commissioned when quite different professional conditions obtained. For certain general editors assigning volumes, the tragedies were unquestionably more important than the comedies, and hence needed 'more important' (read 'male') editors. Amusingly, in the new *Cambridge Works of Ben Jonson*, despite a good number of women editors, the hierarchy of genre reverses but not the pattern of assignment by significance: Jonson's four most popular/frequently taught plays, all comedies, are edited by men. The pattern began to break down in the Oxford *Middleton*, which under Gary Taylor's leadership deliberately included many women editors from the beginning.

But perhaps this division is self – rather than externally – imposed. Are the comedies assigned to women because, with their female protagonists and domestic concerns, they are less important than the tragedies, with their heroic protagonists and national ramifications? Or are women editors attracted to the comedies for that very content? Either way, editions of the comedies are now frequently as dense as earlier editions of the tragedies and histories, and they have feminist introductions. Juliet Dusinberre begins her Arden 3 introduction to *As You Like It* with 'Fictions of gender'.[3] Agnes Latham, in contrast, began conventionally, with a discussion of the text.

Any generalization about women editors must recognize that gender and sexuality studies have been absorbed into mainstream scholarship by men as well as women. It is dangerous to attribute the differences between Harold Jenkins' Arden 2 *Hamlet* and the Thompson-Taylor Arden 3 *Hamlet* only to Thompson – though her name does appear first, out of alphabetical order.[4] Nevertheless the reader is struck by differences that seem related to traditionally female interests. For example, although Jenkins (p. 75) says his text is based primarily on Q2, he adopts without comment F's reading of Hamlet's address to Gertrude, ''Tis not alone my inky cloak, good mother', where Arden 3 not only retains 'cold mother' but analyses the implications of the phrase. Similarly, Laertes' claim that 'That drop of blood that's calm proclaims me bastard, / Cries 'Cuckold!' to my father, brands the harlot /

Even here between the chaste unsmirched brow / Of my true mother' (4.5.117–20) elicits from Jenkins a vague note that 'the solitary reference to the mother of Laertes reinforces the contrast between him and Hamlet, for whom such simple asseverations are not possible' with a considerably longer note on the grammar of 'between the … brow'. Thompson and Taylor instead describe the history of branding harlots, as well as the implications of 'true mother'.

Conventionally women are assumed to be more interested in fabric and clothes than men are; I have found it so. Editing *Pericles* 3.2, I pointed out that modernizing Cerimon's call for 'the fire and clothes' reveals the ambiguity of cloths/clothes – words not differentiated until the nineteenth century, a difficulty unmentioned by previous editors – and considered the different implications if the physician merely wants to rewrap Thaisa or to replace her shroud with more ordinary dress.[5] Similarly, for the line 'A little month, or e'er those shoes were old' (1.2.147), Jenkins' *Hamlet* glosses only 'or e'er'; Thompson and Taylor discuss the material of which the delicate shoes must have been made and their difference from the 'more substantial shoes worn outdoors by ordinary people'. For 'My father in his habit' (3.4.133), Jenkins glosses 'habit'; Thompson and Taylor consider what 'actual clothing' this might be.

The feminism of editors has also affected the editing of Shakespeare's contemporaries, where, Wayne writes, 'the highest proportion of women editors appear', possibly again signalling lower valuation. Compare, for example, Andrew Gurr's edition of Beaumont and Fletcher's *Philaster* from 1969 and my own, published forty years later. This complex play survives in two versions. It contains a notorious scene in which a 'Country Fellow' enters as the Hamlet-like hero stabs the heroine, who nevertheless objects to this intrusion 'upon our private sports'. The Country Fellow, understandably horrified, fights and wounds Philaster, who flees. Then the apparently heroic Fellow turns to Arethusa and demands, 'I prithee, wench, come and kiss me now'. To none of this does

Gurr, presumably constrained by the scholarly prudery of the period, offer any commentary note, while my edition mentions the sexual harassment and argues that 'Arethusa's phrases suggest that her interaction with Philaster is sexual; that the furious passion, abjection, and violence is a form of play; and that her wounding substitutes metaphorically and physically for sexual penetration'.[6]

Sometimes merely the tone of notes varies. Gurr and I both describe the different endings of the two versions of *Philaster*: in the 'good' quarto, the young woman who has been disguised as a page for love of Philaster refuses the King's offer of a dowry for any match she chooses: instead, she announces, she will never marry but be content to 'serve the princess, / To see the virtues of her lord and her', to which Arethusa replies that she 'cannot be jealous ... nor will I suspect her living here'. Gurr simply points out that in the 'bad' quarto Bellario does marry,[7] while my edition describes how 'Euphrasia's refusal to accede to a heteronormative marriage violates the usual comic conclusion, which requires the neat pairing-off of all unmarried females.... . Q1 reimposes the standard ending, keeping Euphrasia silent while her father agrees to 'surrender of all the right a father has' and gives her to the courtier indicated by Philaster'. A second note contrasts this ending to the triangles at the conclusions of *Twelfth Night* and *Merchant of Venice*, where the participants are two men and a woman (pp. 269–70).

When we turn to cruxes, it is critical to avoid the essentialism that equates only female editors with a feminist point of view. What does seem to happen is a different valuation of proposed emendations. Editing *Pericles* I twice found that the best solutions to famous cruxes – both related to female anatomy – were proposed by men but rejected by subsequent editors. The first was Dionyza's hypothetical explanation of Marina's death. Q has, 'Nurses are not the fates to foster it, not ever to preserve'. The bibliographically convincing emendation, 'Nurses are not the fates. To foster is not ever to preserve' was proposed by the nineteenth-century scholar

H. H. Vaughan, reported by J. C. Maxwell in a second issue of his New Cambridge edition, but not accepted into any edition before mine.

Similarly, in the first brothel scene of that play, after the Bawd sends Bolt into town to stir up 'the lewdly inclined' and he promises to 'bring home some tonight', Marina vows:

> If fires be hote, kniues sharpe, or waters deepe,
> Vntide I still my virgin knot will keepe.
> *Diana* ayde my purpose.

The Bawd's reply, 'What haue we to do with *Diana*?' does not explain Marina's apparently illogical promise to keep her virgin knot, her maidenhead, *untied*. Clearly she intends to keep that knot *tied*, even at the cost of suicide or murder. I accepted Richard Proudfoot's suggestion that the problem arose from graphic error, the scribe or Compositor having omitted one letter (Vntide> Vntride), and wrote a feminist commentary note – 'Marina's line, and editors' failure to notice Q's illogic, may reflect the complex of contradictions, real and semantic, surrounding virginity'. In fact, Stephen Orgel had noticed the illogic, but still chose to retain the original.[8]

The most famous crux in *All's Well that Ends Well* occurs in 4.2. Bertram urges Diana to sleep with him, and she appears to yield:

He says,

> Stand no more off,
> But give thyself unto my sick desires,
> Who then recovers. Say thou art mine, and ever
> My love, as it begins, shall so persever.

And she replies,

> I see that men make rope's in such a scarre
> That we'll forsake ourselves. Give me that ring.

For 'I see that men make rope's in such a scarre', Gary
Taylor reports over twenty-five conjectural emendations, and
after twenty closely argued pages concludes that the best
solution is 'I see that men make toys e'en such a surance'.
This incomprehensible reading is adopted in the Oxford
and consequently the Norton 2 text. Taylor glosses it as
follows: 'Diana sees that men make [sexual play; antics, tricks;
fantastic frivolous speeches; idle fancies; trifles; playthings]
appear to be such [a formal betrothal; a guarantee; a legal
transfer of property; something trustworthy and dependable]
that women, tempted, forsake their own integrity'.[9] Norton 2
simplifies to 'Men treat trifles as if they were such guarantees
of good faith.'

Here again a persuasive emendation was first suggested by a
male editor, P. A. Daniel, and adopted by some mid-twentieth-
century editors. The emendation, 'that men may rope's in such
a snare' – *make* an error for *may*, *rope's* a standard elision
of *rope us*, *scarre* a misreading, easy in secretary hand, of c
for *n* – is convincing: it requires the least radical emendation
and it makes sense in the situation. Diana is trying to lead
Bertram to give her his ring in exchange for a promise to
come to his bed: she is resisting him although she intends to
yield (and send Helen in her place). At this point she makes a
general statement about the power of men to entrap women
in such a way that they 'forsake' themselves, that is, abandon
their principles. Taylor objects that 'Daniel's conjecture does
not explain Diana's sudden demand for the ring', but it does.
Because Diana – like other women, '*us*' – has been ensnared,
and consequently (*that*=so that) has forsaken herself, precisely
as Bertram directs she 'stand[s] no more off' and begins to
negotiate with him. Even Bertram's invented 'backstory' in
5.3, that the ring was thrown to him by a woman who consequently 'thought I stood ingag'ed', confirms that treating of
the ring signals being in some way 'engaged'. Earlier Diana
has spoken of the position of women, '*us*', generally – 'so you
serve us Till we serve you'. At the moment of the crux – 'I
see that men may rope's in such a snare' – she pretends to

yield. For a similar moment compare *Troilus and Cressida*
5.2.115–16. Having yielded to Diomedes, Cressida laments,
'Ah, poor our sex! This fault in us I find; the error of our
eye directs our mind' and, in a reversal of Diana's asking for
the ring, Cressida hands over the sleeve, the love token she
received from Troilus.

In this changed intellectual climate one challenge is to
decide how far it is appropriate for feminist editors to
impose their preferences. In *Merry Wives of Windsor* there
are a number of places where both texts seem inaccurate.
The two wives are not distinguished, and textual corruption
is suggested by the immediate repetition of a speech prefix.
In 4.2, as the women warn Falstaff that the men are
coming, the 'good' Folio text has [italics indicate problem
areas]:

> Falstaff: What shall I do? I'll creep up into the chimney.
> *Mistress Ford*: *There they always use to discharge their*
>   *birding-pieces. Creep into the kiln-hole.*
> Falstaff: Where is it?
> Mistress Ford: He will seek there, on my word! Neither
>   press, coffer, chest, trunk, well, vault, but he hath an
>   abstract for the remembrance of such places, and goes
>   to them by his note. There is no hiding you in the
>   house.
> Falstaff: I'll go out then.
> *Mistress Ford*: If you go out in your own semblance, you
>   die, Sir John – unless you go out disguised.
> *Mistress Ford*: How might we disguise him?
> *Mistress Page*: Alas the day, I know not. There is no
>   woman's gown big enough for him. Otherwise he might
>   put on a hat, a muffler, and a kerchief, and so escape.

To clarify, editors have reassigned whole or partial speeches.
Giorgio Melchiori, following Malone and Dyce, has:

> Falstaff: What shall I do? I'll creep up into the chimney.

Mistress Ford: *There they always use to discharge their birding-pieces.*
Mistress Page: *Creep into the kiln-hole.*
Falstaff: Where is it?
Mistress Ford: He will seek there, on my word! Neither press, coffer, chest, trunk, well, vault, but he hath an abstract for the remembrance of such places, and goes to them by his note. There is no hiding you in the house.
Falstaff: I'll go out then.
Mistress Ford: If you go out in your own semblance, you die, Sir John – unless you go out disguised.
Mistress Page: How might we disguise him?
Mistress Ford: Alas the day, I know not. There is no woman's gown big enough for him. Otherwise he might put on a hat, a muffler, and a kerchief, and so escape.[10]

Melchiori does not explain his reassignments. But for her Norton 3 edition, Helen Ostovich offers a specifically feminist justification for similar choices: 'in terms of the scene's showing Mrs Ford's active seizing of the chance to humiliate both Falstaff and her husband, thus ending unwanted solicitations from the one, and unwanted suspicions from the other, *it is better* for Mrs Ford to have the imaginative lines solving the problem of Falstaff, because she grows in authority and self-confidence as a result. Mrs Page already has these traits, and is 'coaching' Mrs Ford out of her tendency to be 'womanly' and propitiating' [italics added]. Furthermore, Ostovich argues, the assignment of the final speech beginning 'Alas' to Mistress Page is inappropriate, 'as she is the sharp-witted one, who never plays the helpless female'.[11]

Is this explanation, based on close reading of action and character, the traditional purview of the literary critic, a sufficient foundation for editorial decisions? What, exactly, does 'it is better' imply about how Shakespeare is 'made'? In 1997 Thompson concluded by noting the 'ongoing debate within feminist criticism itself between what one might call 'apologist' critics, who want to 'save' Shakespeare or even co-opt him as a protofeminist, and the more negative, or pessimistic critics, who see him as quite irredeemably patriarchal' (p. 65). In 15 years the debate has softened, but the issue of how much female or feminist editorial authority will lead to editions that look different remains open. Even a feminist editor must respect the actual words of a text. Nevertheless, in solving a crux, writing a note, or structuring an introduction, she (or he) will 'make' a slightly different Shakespeare.

Notes

1   Valerie Wayne, 'Remaking the Texts: Women Editors of Shakespeare, Past and Present'.

2   *Text* 9 (1996), 111–18.

3   *As You Like It*, ed. Juliet Dusinberre (London, 2006), pp. 9–36.

4   *Hamlet*, ed. Harold Jenkins (London, 1982), was the last volume to appear in the Arden 2 series. *Hamlet*, ed. Ann Thompson and Neil Taylor (London, 2006).

5   *Pericles,* ed. Suzanne Gossett (London, 2004), 300, note to 3.2.86.

6   Francis Beaumont and John Fletcher, *Philaster*, ed. Suzanne Gossett (London, 2009), pp. 219–20.

7   Francis Beaumont and John Fletcher, *Philaster or Love Lies a-Bleeding*, ed. Andrew Gurr (Manchester, 1969), p. 121.

8   I discuss this crux more fully in 'Emendations, Reconstructions, and the Uses of the Past', *TEXT* 17 (2005), 50–2.

9   Gary Taylor, 'Textual Double Knots: 'Make Rope's in Such a Scarre", in Ronald Dotterer ed., *Shakespeare Text, Subtext, and Context* (Selingsgrove, PA, 1989), p. 177.

10 Giorgio Melchiori ed. *The Merry Wives of Windsor*, The Arden Shakespeare, 3rd edn (London, 2000).

11 Helen Ostovich, private communication.

PART TWO

Reception

PART TWO

Reception

11

Juliet and the Vicissitudes of Gender

Catherine Belsey
Swansea University

Ann Thompson is an international treasure. I need hardly
detail what she has done for Shakespeare studies and for
feminism in a succession of books, editions, anthologies, and
articles, not to mention her work as General Editor of the
Arden Shakespeare. Ann pursues intellectual questions because
they cry out to be solved, and is generous with her knowledge.
I have myself been a beneficiary of that generosity, as have the
many younger scholars she has supported. At the same time,
as a feminist, she has been, has had to be, strong-minded. For
this occasion I have thought about her antecedents among
Shakespeare's resolute women and, from the many available
options, I have chosen Juliet as a precursor. At the risk of
disappointing readers, I perceive the parallel not so much in
terms of a history of forbidden romances and secret marriages
as of an independence of mind, a forthrightness, and a built-in
resistance to irascible patriarchs. *Romeo and Juliet* ascribes a
remarkable degree of autonomy to its heroine and establishes
an exceptional parity between the protagonists.

Since imitation is the sincerest form of flattery, I offer in tribute a venture into Ann's own territory, the Shakespearean text and its subsequent appropriations from the perspective of gender. Ann Radcliffe's *The Italian* was published in 1797, exactly 200 years, as luck would have it, after the appearance of the first quarto of *Romeo and Juliet*. The novel records the love between Vincentio di Vivaldi and Ellena Rosalba, divided by parental opposition to their relationship. When Vivaldi finds his way to the garden of her house by night, 'a light issuing from among the bowery foliage of a clematis led him to a lattice, and showed him Ellena'. Hearing his beloved sigh at her window and then pronounce his name, he is unable to command himself and makes his presence evident. Ellena's response is pained but decisive: 'She stood fixed for an instant, while her countenance changed to an ashy paleness; and then, with trembling haste closing the lattice, quitted the apartment', not to return.[1]

Ellena is by no means indifferent to Vivaldi's love but, when it comes to midnight conversations with her admirer, propriety prevails over passion. Mrs Radcliffe's reinscription of Shakespeare's play throws into relief the difference of the original text. There is no ashy paleness for Juliet, no hasty closing of the window. But then Juliet has already gone considerably further than her eighteenth-century successor: 'Romeo, doff thy name, / And for thy name, which is no part of thee, / Take all myself' (2.2.47–9).[2] This is when Romeo reveals himself: 'I take thee at thy word' (1.49). If the contract in the garden stands in for the marriage we do not witness, when *I, Romeo, take thee, Juliet*, the play reverses the order specified by the Book of Common Prayer: it is the woman's injunction that, however unwittingly, prompts the hero's declaration.

Romeo and Juliet does not retreat from this establishment of equality between the lovers. In place of the conventional Petrarchan monologue uttered by a male lover, the orchard scene presents a dialogue between the couple, where Juliet is allowed more lines – and more initiatives – than Romeo. This impression of symmetry was surely fostered by Elizabethan stage practice: played by a boy, Juliet would look and sound more like her lover's equal. The parity between the lovers is intensified, however, by love's effect on Romeo. If it makes Juliet bold (brave enough, for example, to take the potion and face waking up in the vault), it correspondingly renders Romeo 'effeminate', he complains, when it comes to fighting Tybalt (3.1.115–16). In due course, the Friar will try to induce Romeo to take his banishment like a man: 'Thy tears are womanish', he insists (3.3.108–12). Love brings about a convergence between the sexes and it is not clear that 'effeminacy' is altogether disgraceful, since it impels Romeo towards peace. In the end, it is love that puts an end to the recurring violence, but not before masculinity has brought about much bloodshed.

In the course of the play Juliet will be called on for a number of minor acts of defiance. She not only puts up a stout resistance to her father's marriage plan, but in a series of double entendres she declares her fidelity to Romeo, while seeming to go along with her mother's threat to kill him (3.5.94–5). And she deftly fends off the proprietary attentions of Paris at the Friar's cell without giving outright offence (4.1). The play's most audacious affirmation of gender equality, however, must be the ascription to a woman of the account of their wedding night. This extraordinary speech, unique even in Shakespeare, succeeds in being at once lyrical and explicit in its declared impatience for the 'amorous rites' to be performed in darkness. 'Hood my unmanned blood', Juliet enjoins the night, 'till strange love grow bold', as the initially unfamiliar sexual act becomes increasingly confident, daring.

The emphasis throughout the speech is on reciprocity. Juliet will learn 'to lose a winning match, / Played for a pair of stainless maidenhoods'. The maidenhoods are both equivalent and interchangeable: loss is gain.

> O, I have bought the mansion of a love
> But not possessed it, and though I am sold,
> Not yet enjoyed.

(3.2.1–31)

Juliet identifies herself as both purchaser and property, eager to take ownership and in the process surrender it. And as if to confirm the homology it establishes between the lovers, the play's final couplet reverses the order of their names as these are given in the title: 'For never was a story of more woe / Than this of Juliet and her Romeo' (5.3.309–10).

How, then, did Ann Radcliffe derive Ellena's ashy paleness and abrupt flight from Juliet's readiness to exchange vows with Romeo? The history of the relations between men and women indicates that Shakespeare's vision of parity was too good to last. Faramerz Dabhoiwala traces the polarization of gender roles that took place in the course of the Enlightenment: in 1600 it was assumed that women were equally capable of enjoying sex; by 1800, however, it was just as widely believed that, while men were passionate and impetuous, women, or at least respectable women, exemplified restraint.[3]

The descent Dabhoiwala describes was precipitate. *Romeo and Juliet* resurfaces as a component of Thomas Otway's historical play *Caius Marius* in 1679, where substantial quantities of Shakespeare's text are ascribed to Young Marius and Lavinia, with adjustments to fit changing tastes, as well as the reduced textual space now available. Although Lavinia resists arranged marriage – 'lawful Rape', she calls it (2.1) – Juliet's other small acts of defiance are erased.[4] Deep cuts are imposed on the wedding-night speech: the amorous rites, the stainless maidenhoods and strange love grown bold have all gone, and in case we suppose that this was designed purely to save time, a further tell-tale elision occurs in the metaphor of the purchased mansion, deleting the reference to Juliet sold but not yet enjoyed (3.2). Lavinia revives before Marius dies, allowing a moment of rhapsodic dialogue between them and, since the waking Lavinia is for the moment not quite in her right mind, more Ophelia than Juliet, this does little to enhance her stature. Meanwhile, Otway's heroine has shown herself suitably nurturing: finding Marius Senior starving in the wilderness outside Rome, she supplies him, as a good woman should, with food and water.

A corresponding change occurs in the depiction of Young Marius, removing what was by now the slur of effeminacy. Otway's hero defers his projected wedding night with Lavinia until he has earned his father's approval in the wars. All ambivalence towards the capacity for violence has disappeared: in this play the readiness to fight defines heroism. While Lavinia displays a decorous sexual reticence, along with a proper maternal potential, Marius has become a real man. Out of Shakespeare's resemblances between the lovers, Otway has succeeded in plucking opposite sexes.

His modifications were to prove influential when Romeo and Juliet returned to the stage under their own names in the mid-eighteenth century. Theophilus Cibber, who abridged Shakespeare's play for performance in 1744, keeps the reference to arranged marriage as 'lawful Rape' (1.3) but his version radically curtails Juliet's epithalamion on much the same lines as Otway's.[5] Moreover, an interpolation casts an anticipatory light on Radcliffe's Ellena. Cibber's Lady Capulet, her suspicions aroused by her daughter's immediate resistance to an arranged marriage, demands accusingly, 'What sensual, lewd Companion of the Night / Have you been holding Conversation with, / From open Window, at a Midnight hour?' (1.3). Evidently Ellena is wise to forestall the imputation of such unseemly behaviour.

Cibber's Romeo is no Marius but he briefly shows a heroic disregard of death: awaiting the Prince's sentence, the protagonist declares, 'He can but doom me dead, and I'm prepar'd' (3.3). Shakespeare's reversal of the title names in the final couplet was evidently unacceptable: Cibber's version substitutes, 'Never true Lovers Story did impart / More real Anguish to a humane Heart'.

In 1750 David Garrick, too, rewrote the closing couplet, while perversely keeping the rhyme, as if to draw attention to the change: 'From private feuds, what dire misfortunes flow; / Whate'er the cause, the sure effect is WOE'.[6] Garrick reproduced for Juliet Lavinia's Ophelia-like response to waking in the tomb. If in his version a little more of Shakespeare survives, there is no hint that Juliet knows anything about sex, and when it comes to the reference to sale and enjoyment, Garrick follows Otway's elision. In consequence, by the time the Bowdlers came to prepare *The Family Shakespeare* early in the nineteenth century, their work on this play had mostly been done for them, although they opted in addition to delete all reference to the mansion, bought and sold, possessed or to be enjoyed.

It would be many years before Juliet was once again allowed a significant degree of independence but in Romeo's case adapters were more conservative. Both Cibber and Garrick retain the self-reproach for his effeminacy in letting Mercutio die; both include an abridged version of the Friar's reproaches for Romeo's womanish tears. We may assume that Garrick, who played Romeo for many years, relished the opportunity this scene offered for the display of intense emotion. But there was a price to pay for this indulgence. While it was Garrick's version of the play that held the stage until the mid-nineteenth century, in due course the number of productions decreased: the part of Romeo held less and less appeal for male actors, who were particularly embarrassed by his prostration in the Friar's cell.

In the end it was a woman who rescued Romeo for the nineteenth century, when the American Charlotte Cushman dazzled London by her performance in 1845–6. Rather than evade the hero's fervour, Cushman gave it full rein and the reviews were rapturous. The anguish that had proved so problematic for male actors was now accorded special praise. Evidently intensity was acceptable in a Romeo played by a woman: the ambiguity surrounding the hero's gender was able to preserve both Shakespeare's play and Victorian masculinity.

Unfortunately, however, Romeo's rehabilitation did not entail Juliet's. Although Cushman reintroduced Shakespeare's text, the play was cut to observe Victorian standards of decorum. She chose her sister Susan as Juliet, but the family likeness between two female leading figures did little to restore the symmetry that had disappeared from the adaptations. This may have been partly because the younger sister was a less confident performer: where *The Times* praised Charlotte unreservedly, it patronized Susan. A picture of the production in *The Illustrated London News* speaks volumes: it shows Juliet looking upwards at a gallant Romeo, as if imploring reassurance.[7] Meanwhile, an image of the Cushmans in the parting scene also portrays a Juliet who gazes up at a much taller Romeo. His right hand supports her arm and his left cradles her head protectively, while his face is turned away as if to confront his destiny.[8] *The Times* confirms in words the impression created by the illustrations, commenting that Susan played the orchard scene with a 'beautifully confiding and truly feminine air'.[9]

In a motif that would recur during the period, it sometimes seemed that Juliet was not fully capable of rational thought. Here, *The Times* records, she listened to the Friar's plan for her to take the potion as if she could barely follow it. Is it possible that her momentary madness in the tomb, invented by Otway, reproduced by Garrick, and thus a feature of early nineteenth-century productions, was now influencing the epoch's perception of Juliet in her entirety? Henry James would go on to note 'the frenzy of Juliet with her potion'.[10] Was that how they saw her?

Either way, on the stage an ambiguously feminized Romeo seems to have pushed Juliet towards greater helplessness, preserving a contrast between the sexes, as if the parity Shakespeare depicted was simply unintelligible in a culture that perceived gender difference as opposition. But misogyny also promotes resistance as its unintended consequence. All this time Shakespeare's own text had been available to be read in full and in 1817 William Hazlitt notably reprinted the whole of the Juliet's epithalamion as an affirmation of freedom.[11] A number of women, too, spoke up for Juliet. Anna Jameson was reading Shakespeare, not Garrick, when she praised the heroine's 'truth', 'intensity of passion', and 'singleness of purpose'. In *Characteristics of Women* Mrs

Jameson defends what she calls Juliet's 'Hymn to the Night', declaring herself outraged by those who find it offensive.[12]

At the same time, there is disapproval. Jameson's book as a whole is arguing for an education of women that goes beyond mere accomplishments to inculcate habits of thoughtfulness and ethical sensibility. Juliet, for all her virtues, is ultimately disappointing. She is prone to petulance, Jameson notes, bewildered by the speed of events, too given over to self-will. What is to be expected, after all, of a young woman whose father was himself wilful and tyrannical and whose mother was ready to poison Romeo to avenge the death of Tybalt? Their daughter's education has sadly been left to the Nurse and it is a miracle, in view of her background, that Juliet remains so honourable, so loyal, capable of such delicacy. Even so, Jameson concludes, 'With all this immense capacity of affection and imagination, there is a deficiency of reflection and of moral energy'.[13]

Juliet is judged and found ultimately wanting. Mary Cowden Clarke had evidently read Jameson when she composed *The Girlhood of Shakespeare's Heroines* (1850–2). Clarke shared Jameson's values, as well as her assessment of Juliet's upbringing. In her version, Juliet's father, a recovering voluptuary, inadvertently incites Lady Capulet's jealousy to the point where she procures a murderer and then succumbs to blackmail. Juliet grows up neglected, and in consequence susceptible, affectionate, but governed by nature, not morality, impulse, not reason. While these women are drawn to her fidelity and commitment, they are unhappy about her rashness: as one of her defining qualities, their Juliet lacks discretion. Precipitate passion, secret marriages are not to be endorsed; independence should always be tempered by deliberation. According to nineteenth-century standards of propriety, any well-brought-up Juliet would have closed her window just as firmly as Radcliffe's Ellena.

Helena Faucit Martin, who played Juliet many times, praises her artless generosity, her constancy and, surprisingly in the period, her clear intellect. Treating the lovers as sacrificial victims of the feud, Faucit Martin restores something of the symmetry between them, both 'pure, beautiful, generous, devoted'. She also quotes Shakespeare's own final couplet as a fitting conclusion to the story. Even so, the familiar difference between the lovers reasserts itself: we need to understand that Romeo has been luckier in his background than his beloved. 'To judge Juliet rightly', Faucit Martin concludes, 'we must have clear ideas of Romeo, of her parents, and of all the circumstances that determined her conduct'.[14]

Despite their good intentions, none of these nineteenth-century women escapes the obligation to *judge*. In Jameson's case, it was the project: Juliet perfectly illustrates her thesis that a bad education has unfortunate consequences. But the same pressure to arrive at a moral assessment informs the other readings I have quoted. As far as it concerns young women, morality in this period is first and foremost sexual morality, and in these terms Juliet's behaviour is foolish, if not worse. Sympathy fights a battle with censure and does not easily prevail.

It was not until the following century that Juliet would once again be able to claim her just deserts, and then inconsistently, on the screen as well as on the stage. The history of gender shows that gains can be reversed – and that even our best allies have not always been able to stand entirely clear of the influence of an anti-feminist culture. As Ann Thompson and I contemplate retirement, I believe we both count on the next generation to be vigilant in defence of hard-won liberties.

Notes

1   Ann Radcliffe, *The Italian* (Oxford, 1998), pp. 11–12.

2   Shakespeare references are to René Weis ed., *Romeo and Juliet,* The Arden Shakespeare, 3rd edn. (London, 2012).

3   Faramerz Dabhoiwala, *The Origins of Sex: A History of the First Sexual Revolution* (London, 2012).

4   Thomas Otway, *The History of the Fall of Caius Marius*
     (London, 1680).

5   Theophilus Cibber, *Romeo and Juliet, A Tragedy* (London,
     1748).

6   *Romeo and Juliet. By Shakespear* (London, 1750).

7   *The Illustrated London News*, 3 January 1846, 9.

8   Reproduced in *Romeo and Juliet*, p. 68.

9   *The Times*, 30 December 1845, 5.

10   Henry James, *The Tragic Muse* (London, 1995), p. 129.

11   *The Complete Works of William Hazlitt*, ed. P. P. Howe
     (London, 1930–34), 21 vols, vol. 4, 253.

12   Anna Jameson, *Characteristics of Women*, 3rd edn (London,
     1836), pp. 156–7, p. 193.

13   Jameson, *Characteristics of Women*, 203.

14   Helena Faucit Martin, *On Some of Shakespeare's Female
     Characters* (Edinburgh, 1885), pp. 136, 192.

12

Women Painting Shakespeare: Angelica Kauffman's Text-images

Keir Elam

University of Bologna

Histories of the paintings, engravings, and illustrations of Shakespeare's plays have been almost exclusively devoted to male artists,[1] despite the considerable number of women painters who have portrayed Shakespearian subjects over the centuries.[2] This is partly due to the fact that female artists received scarce critical (as opposed to popular) attention in their own time. Probably the most significant woman painter of Shakespeare – and the only one to attract considerable critical discussion in her own day – is the Swiss-German artist Angelica Kauffman (1741–1897). Kauffman enjoyed enormous popularity and prestige in Georgian England, where she lived and worked from 1766 to 1781, and where she was effectively elected to the ranks of British artists, as Richard Samuel's celebrated group portrait *The Nine Living Muses of Great Britain* (1778) suggests, placing her emblematically in the company of the eight leading Blue Stockings of the day, including such writers as Charlotte Lennox, Elizabeth Montagu, and Elizabeth Griffith, all of whom were known, among other things, for their essays on Shakespeare.[3] Samuel thus elevates Kauffman to the order not only of British women artists and intellectuals but, more specifically, of British women Shakespearians. Particularly pertinent in the context of the group portrait is Kauffman's vicinity to Montagu, whose 1769 *Essay* in defence of Shakespeare against Voltaire, a key text in the canonization of the Bard much appreciated by David Garrick, devotes a chapter to historical drama in which the author compares the naturalness of Shakespeare's historical personages and events to the 'Sister art' of Renaissance painting, which in turn inspired Kauffman's own Shakespearian work.[4]

Kauffman's popularity in England endured long after her departure for Italy in 1781. From Rome she produced history paintings, including Shakespearian subjects, for British engravers and printers. It is difficult to determine the exact extent of her Shakespearian repertory, partly because history painting – the genre of which she had been, together with Benjamin West, the most prominent exponent in England – is a narrative pictorial mode that comprehends subjects from historiographical, mythical, biblical, and literary sources, sometimes blurring the differences between them.[5] Kauffman drew frequently on classical history, and in some cases these coincide with characters and episodes dramatized in Shakespeare's Roman plays, without necessarily deriving from them. For example, her early 1764 painting *Coriolanus entreated by Vetturia and Volumnia*, commissioned by John Byng, is taken directly from Plutarch rather than from Shakespeare (*Coriolanus* 5.3), although presumably British interest in the subject was in part due to the play; her later print of Coriolanus and Volumnia (1785), instead, is certainly based on Shakespeare's Roman play. Another case in point is the series of oils on canvas dedicated to Cleopatra – who, together with Penelope, is the most recurrent and paradigmatic female figure in Kauffman's repertoire – which were frequently reproduced in print and even in furniture. These include *Cleopatra decorating the tomb of Mark Antony*, painted in England (1770), and *The death of Marc Antony* (1783) and *Cleopatra throwing herself at the feet of Augustus after the death of Marc Antony* (1783), both painted in Rome. The English painting – a pictorial paraphrase of Poussin's *Et in Arcadia Ego*[6] that also recalls Kauffman's own earlier *Fame decorating Shakespeare's tomb* (c. 1770), showing an allegorical lady sprinkling flowers on the Bard's memorial – has no direct counterpart in *Antony and Cleopatra*. The later Italian works, meanwhile, have been described by Kauffman scholars as 'two episodes from Shakespeare',[7] but in reality the scene of Cleopatra with Augustus is conspicuously and strategically omitted in Shakespeare's play.

Whatever the direct Shakespearian affinities or otherwise of the Cleopatra paintings, however, they share a central characteristic with the artist's more certain works from Shakespeare, namely female historical and personal agency, often disguised as submissiveness: as Sarah Hyde notes, Cleopatra appears to be passive, but Kauffman relied, for the pathos of the painted scenes, on her audience's knowledge that the Egyptian queen went on to take her own life rather than submit to Octavius.[8] The paintings privilege, in particular, female agency through posture and gesture, the most significant of which is that of imploration, a kinesic act that denotes subordination but in reality expresses a mode of power: 'Cleopatra' – reads the artist's description of her *throwing herself* painting – 'humble and prostrate at the feet of Augustus, imploring mercy'.[9]

Kauffman's more certain Shakespearian paintings likewise have primarily female protagonists. While her predecessors and contemporaries, from Hogarth on, privilege male characters (Macbeth, Lear, Falstaff, Orlando) seen in vigorous action, or male actors (notably Garrick) performing celebrated stage roles, Kauffman's heroines frequently appear engaged in more intimate and 'private' acts, and not via specific stage performances. What characterizes much of this work is again a particular attention to gesture, especially the position and movement of the hands. To some extent this reflects contemporary acting style, with its emphasis on gesture in the representation of the passions, but it also constitutes a precise pictorial and corporeal code in Kauffman's oeuvre. A good example of the use of such 'manual' signifiers is the 1782 painting for the carver and gilder James Birchall, which is described by Kauffman as '[an oval painting] that represents Cordelia invoking the help of Jove for her father King Lear who is in imminent danger of being betrayed – subject taken from Sakspire [*sic*].'[10] The description alludes to the apostrophe at 4.7.14–15:

O you kind gods,
Cure this great breach in his abused nature!

Kauffman shows the child-like Cordelia in a gesture of imploration, her left hand reaching up to the sky against the background of a picturesque landscape. Her supplication indicates a position of vulnerability, but at the same time suggests the determined and tragic agency of Cordelia in the last two acts of the play. Such direct 'quotation' of a precise moment in the text of the play, and especially its engagement with the gestural as well as discursive texture of the scene, distinguishes this and other Kauffman Shakespearian paintings from those of her male colleagues, as does an accentuated pathos in the representation of the female protagonist-victim. These works become what W. J. T. Mitchell in his seminal volume *Picture Theory* terms image-texts,[11] or what we might more properly term text-images, namely images whose reception and interpretation depends on an intimate dialectic with the texts in question, rather than a generic relationship with a given play or character, translating the speech-act dynamic of the drama into a mode of visual and especially corporeal performativity.

A further female gesture of imploration appears in the oil on canvas representing *The Tempest*, 3.1 (1782, for Birchall),[12] marked again by attention to the language and semiotics of the text, and in particular to the interplay of hands among the three characters present: Ferdinand is at his manual labour on the logs, as Miranda, placing her left hand on his right 'working' arm, makes a pleading gesture with her own right hand, while Prospero looks on from a cavernous space in the background ('a grotto in an uninhabited island'),[13] his right hand grasping a pen and his left a book of magic. Miranda's open mouth, meanwhile, suggests that she is speaking, and indeed her speech is readily identifiable:

Alas, now, pray you,
Work not so hard
[...] pray now, rest yourself;
He's safe for these three hours.

(3.1.15–21)

It is thus a speaking and gesticulating picture, halfway between a pictorial reading of Shakespeare's text in a precise dialogical moment, and the representation of an idealized stage production involving a careful gestural choreography against a colourful painted backcloth: the setting is a picturesque land- and seascape in the style of Salvator Rosa, whose flatness, however, betrays a certain staginess.[14] This is a further distinctive feature of Kauffman's Shakespeare paintings: they often erase the boundaries between the naturalistic and the theatrical. Stuart Sillars notes what he terms 'the move out of the theatre [through] the use of landscape' in late eighteenth-century Shakespeare paintings;[15] Kauffman modifies this move by bringing landscape back, as it were, into the theatrical arena.

The scene in Kauffman's representation of *Othello* 5.2 (for Joseph Collyer, printed 1783) is a dark and circumscribed domestic space that again could well be a stage set, especially given the presence of a raised bed (or perhaps stage) curtain and the bedroom (or possibly stage) door in the background.

Here is an extreme version of female agency in passive mode, figuring the sleeping Desdemona about to be murdered by Othello (the print identifies the discursive moment: the Moor's 'Yet I'll not shed her blood', 5.2.3).[16] Again the dramatic dynamics are entrusted to the interplay of hands: a distinctly oriental and turbaned Othello bears an exotic candle-holder in his left hand to illuminate his victim, while his right hand rests on the dagger he is simultaneously declaring he will not use. Desdemona's left hand, meanwhile, props up her sleeping head on the bed, while her right clasps a sheet in childlike fashion.

In 1787, by way of recognition of her double status as 'British' artist and painter of Shakespeare, Kauffman received two commissions from John Boydell – who had already printed several of her paintings – for his celebrated if doomed Shakespeare Gallery. Kauffman, the only woman painter included in the Gallery,[17] chose to illustrate episodes respectively from *Troilus and Cressida* 5.2 and *The Two Gentlemen of Verona* 5.4, both of which are choral scenes dramatizing the theme of infidelity. The paintings were displayed in Boydell's Gallery in Pall Mall, and then engraved for his illustrated edition of the plays.

The *Troilus* painting (Figure 2) presents what Kauffman describes as 'a night scene, by torchlight',[18] that again could well be theatrical (or operatic: Kauffman shows us a polyphonic quartet analogous, for example, to Mozart's 'Non ti fidar, oh misera' (*Don Giovanni*, 1787)). It pictures Diomedes's seduction of Cressida (and vice versa) before the eavesdropping and suffering Troilus, who is restrained from intervening by Ulysses. Frederick Burwick identifies Cressida's posture in the picture as one of imploration: 'Cressida plea[d]s with Diomed to release her from her oath',[19] (see line 28: 'I prithee, do not hold me to mine oath'). The inscription to the print, however, indicates a later moment in the scene, in which Cressida, having so far offered token resistance to Diomedes's advances, proffers a blatantly seductive gesture towards her suitor, made explicit by Troilus (this is the line he is shown uttering in the painting):

FIGURE 2 *Calchas' Tent. Diomed and Cressida, Troilus, Ulysses, and Thersites (1788/89), engraved by Luigi Schiavonetti*

Troilus: She strokes his cheek! (52)

It is true, however, that Kauffman renders the gesture ambiguous by figuring Cressida's body and face in an attitude of tension, as if divided between resistance and surrender, thereby creating a spatial synthesis between the earlier imploration and the later caress. Such ambiguity has considerable implications for the reading of the scene, since it partially redeems Cressida from the stereotyped icon – present in other illustrations for Boydell by Thomas Kirk[20] – as the proverbial embodiment of female treachery (a stereotype endorsed by Troilus himself: 'Let all untruths stand by thy stained name', 178). This redemptive reading accords with Elizabeth Griffith's benevolent view of Cressida in *The Morality of Shakespeare*.[21] Cressida's new-found moral dignity, moreover, is accentuated by the

FIGURE 3 *Valentine, Proteus, Sylvia and Giulia in the Forest (1788/89), oil on canvas.*

'grand style' adopted by Kauffman, which implicitly places the protagonist in the role of classical heroine.

The second painting for Boydell depicts the final scene of *Two Gentlemen*: another quartet in which Valentine intervenes to rescue Silvia from attempted rape by Proteus, while the cross-dressed Julia looks on 'observing with sadness the infidelity of her beloved'.[22] The forest setting is depicted as a landscape in the guise of bucolic backdrop, and the overall composition 'shows Angelica's best and most enticing way with colour – rococo pastel colours muted slightly, but not diluted to the point of boudoir prettiness'.[23] The painting is constructed on a horizontal line up of gestures, readable from left to right, in the form of an almost unbroken continuum of 'talking' arms that takes us from Proteus's thrusting aggressiveness to Valentine's civilized protectiveness to Silvia's alarmed self-defence to, finally, Julia's shocked impotence. This movement across expressive limbs corresponds precisely to the narrative and dialogic sequentiality of the episode, beginning with Proteus's 'I'll force thee yield to my desire.' (59) and ending with Julia's 'O me unhappy!' (84) prior to her fainting.

Angela Rosenthal justly notes the 'subtle gradations of gendered corporeal differences' at work in the picture, although she mistakenly identifies the character on the left as Valentine, observing that 'the figures of Valentine and Julia resemble each other';[24] in reality the figure in question represents Proteus, impeded in his intents by the intervening Valentine sporting his Robin Hood-like outlaw costume. Thus the gender gradations are centred on the couple Proteus-Julia, both seen in clinging tights that suggest a specular *Doppelgänger* affinity while simultaneously accentuating their differences in musculature and attitude. Silvia's discreet silken décolleté, meanwhile, reveals her soft and unambiguously feminine forms. Julia, physically marginal but dramatically central to the scene, embodies the androgyny of her cross-dressed role by mirroring Proteus corporeally and Silvia facially. Valentine himself betrays a certain softness of contour that associates him with Silvia, his face likewise resembling hers.

Much has been written about the androgyny or 'effeminacy' of Kauffman's male figures, beginning with the barbed comment of the great German critic and translator of Shakespeare, August Wilhelm Schlegel:

the soft femininity in thoughts and words, which draws one to the paintings of Angelica Kauffman, now and then sneaks into the figures in an unpermitted manner: one can see in the eyes of her young boys that they would like far too much to have a girl's breast, and if possible also such hips.[25]

Such dubious masculinity may be in part due to Kauffman's lack of experience in the study of male anatomy, but it also reflects the neoclassical aesthetic ideals of her friend and mentor Winckelmann, for whom androgyny 'represented the greatest perfection of Roman art'.[26] At the same time, there is in much of Kauffman's work a strategic eroding of gender confines, as if to underline a feminine and feminized reading of history and, more specifically, of Shakespeare himself.

Angelica Kauffman's reputation, especially in Britain and the United States, rests primarily on her supposed ability as decorative artist, even if in reality there are only two examples of decorative art directly attributable to her, the rest being the work of copyists and engravers. With regard to her Shakespearian subjects, there is little doubt that the abundant prints, furniture, porcelain, snuff-boxes, cameos and needlework reproducing her portraits of the Bard and her scenes and characters from the plays contributed quite considerably to the 'making' of Shakespeare as, literally, a household name, in the precise period in which he was being set up as national icon in chief.[27] Kauffman was not directly responsible for the domesticating effects of such reproductions, but they are not incompatible with the 'feminizing' character of her paintings, and she certainly encouraged the popularizing of her work through engraving and printing. Her popularity should not detract, however, from the seriousness and intelligence of her engagement with Shakespeare's texts in some of the most illuminating pictorial representations of her age.

Notes

1   See, for example, Stuart Sillars's excellent *Painting Shakespeare: The Artist as Critic, 1720–1820* (Cambridge, 2006).

2   Charlotte Yeldham's inventory of the paintings exhibited by women during the nineteenth century, for example, includes around 170 works dedicated to Shakespearian subjects (*Women Artists in Nineteenth-century France and England* (New York, 1984).

3   Respectively, *Shakespear Illustrated* (1753), *An Essay on the Writings and Genius of Shakespear* (1769) and *The Morality of Shakespeare's Drama Illustrated* (1775). See Ann Thompson and Sasha Roberts, *Women Reading Shakespeare, 1660–1900. An Anthology of Criticism* (Manchester, 1997), pp. 15–39.

4   Elizabeth Montagu, *An Essay on the Writings and Genius of Shakespear* (London, 1769), p. 64.

5   On Kauffman as historical painter, see Wendy W. Roworth ed., *Angelica Kauffman: A Continental Artist in Georgian England* (London, 1992), pp. 21–37. I am grateful to Wendy Wassyng Roworth for her generous advice regarding, among other matters, the Shakespearian provenance or otherwise of the paintings.

6   Ronald Paulson 'The Aesthetics of Mourning', in Ralph Cohen ed., *Studies in Eighteenth-Century British Art and Aesthetics* (Berkeley, CA, 1985), pp. 148–81, p. 165.

7   See Malise Forbes Adam and Mary Mauchline, 'Kauffman's Decorative Work', in Wendy Wassyng Roworth, 1992, pp. 111–40, p. 132. Copies of the two paintings appear together in a 1786 secretaire-bookcase: see Roworth 1992, p. 126.

8   Sarah Hyde, *Exhibiting Gender* (Manchester, 1997), p. 109.

9   Angelica Kauffman, in Carlo Knight ed., *La memoria delle piture* (Rome, 1998), p. 17.

10 Kauffman, p. 17. The painting was engraved by Francesco Bartolozzi and printed in 1784; see Roworth p. 185.

11 W. J. T Mitchell, *Picture Theory* (Chicago, 1994), p. 9

12 See Kauffman, pp. 26–7.

13 Kauffman, p. 17.

14 The only actual performance of the play she was likely to have seen was Thomas Sheridan's adaptation, performed regularly at Drury Lane from 1777 to 1786.

15 Sillars (2006), p. 16.

16 The print is reproduced in Thompson and Roberts 1997, p, 34.

17 Boydell also commissioned two reliefs from the sculptor Anne Seymour Damer.

18 Kauffman, p. 47.

19 Frederick Burwick, in Walter Pape and Frederick Burwick eds, *The Boydell Shakespeare Gallery* (Bottrop, 1996), p. 155.

20 Burwick (1996), p. 155.

21 Elizabeth Griffith, *The Morality of Shakespeare's Drama Illustrated* (London, 1775), p. 487; see Georgianna Ziegler, 'Suppliant Women and Monumental Maidens: Shakespeare's Heroines in the Boydell Gallery.' In Burwick and Pape, 1996, pp. 89–102, p. 94.

22 Kauffman, p. 47.

23 Winifred H. Friedman, *Boydell's Shakespeare Gallery* (New York, 1976), p. 156.

24 Angela Rosenthal, *Angelica Kauffman: Art and Sensibility* (New Haven, CT and London, 2007), p. 199.

25 Quoted in Rosenthal (2007), p. 191.

26 Roworth (1992), p. 83.

27 See Michael Dobson, *The Making of the National Poet: Shakespeare, Adaptation and Authorship, 1660–1769* (Oxford, 1992).

13

Women Reading Witches, 1800–1850

Lucy Munro
King's College London

I begin this essay with a woman reading *Macbeth* to a rapt audience in the early nineteenth century:

> there was no got-up illusion here: no scenes – no trickery of the stage; there needed no sceptred pall – no sweeping train, nor any of the gorgeous accompaniments of tragedy: – SHE was tragedy! When in reading Macbeth she said, 'give me the daggers!' they gleamed before our eyes. The witch scenes in the same play she rendered awfully terrific by the magic of looks and tones; she invested the weird sisters with all their own infernal fascinations; they were the serious, poetical, tragical personages which the poet intended them to be, and the wild grotesque horror of their enchantments made the blood curdle.[1]

The description is of the great actress Sarah Siddons, mainly retired from the public stage but continuing to perform in readings in which she read all parts – male and female, old and young. The author is Anna Jameson, who hoped at one stage to write the actor's biography, and whose own scholarly reading of *Macbeth* responded to Siddons' performances in the play.[2] In Jameson's analysis, Siddons' reading encapsulates the power of tragedy without any of the usual recourse to stage tricks. What interests me here in particular, however, is the attention that she pays to the ways in which the witches' lines are read, which restore, in Jameson's opinion, the powerfully tragic horror that Shakespeare intended for them.

Taking Jameson's account of Siddons reading as its starting point, this essay argues that women's activities as Shakespearean critics and performers helped to propel a nineteenth-century reappraisal of the role of the witches in *Macbeth*. Eighteenth- and early nineteenth- century performance traditions had ossified as far as the Weird Sisters were concerned. Following a tradition that stretched back to the Restoration, they were conventionally played by male comedians, and they were almost invariably accompanied by a full-blown chorus.[3] *The Daily News* remarked of a production at Drury Lane in 1864, '[t]he wild poetic grandeur of the drama is certainly diminished by the introduction of a hundred or more pretty singing witches, but trading managers are bound to be practical'.[4] In contrast, the activities of Shakespearean performers, critics and authors such as Siddons, Jameson, Fanny Kemble and Mary Cowden Clarke demonstrate that alternatives were available and that they were being actively explored. Focusing on the precise issue of how the witches were presented in *Macbeth* thus demonstrates once again the characteristics identified in women's Shakespeare criticism by Ann Thompson and Sasha Roberts: the depth of women's engagement with Shakespeare in the nineteenth century; the range of forms that this engagement took; and the impact that it might have on audiences and readers.[5]

The detailed attention that many commentators paid to Siddons' performance of Macbeth and the witches may perhaps seem surprising, given her fame in the role of

Lady Macbeth.[6] However, the very novelty of hearing the great actress read these roles appears to have been part of their appeal. Frances Williams-Wynn, for example, comments that '[p]robably Lady Macbeth, however excellent, had by frequent repetition lost some of her power', but she found Siddons' Macbeth and witches horribly convincing: 'I never saw Mrs Siddons with a good Macbeth; for Kemble I never reckoned tolerable; nor did I feel I knew what the character was till I heard Mrs Siddons read the play. Certainly, in that reading, some speeches of Macbeth's, and almost of the whole of the witches', were the parts that struck me most'. She singles out one moment from the witches' parts: 'I can hardly conceive anything finer than the expression which Mrs Siddons gave to the simple reply, '*A deed without a name.*' It seemed full of all the guilty dread belonging to witch-craft'.[7] For Williams-Wynn, Siddons' power is to reveal the hidden authenticity beneath layers of theatrical accretion; she uncovers both 'what [Macbeth] was' and the realistic emotion lying behind the witch's simple words.

A similar quality was noted in Kemble's readings of the witches' scenes some years later, of which a reviewer in *The Monthly Post* wrote:

All thought of the monotonous or unmeaning jingle of the mere words of the witches' chaunt, and all impression of anything approaching to the ludicrous, vanished utterly before the mystical and yet ferocious expression which Mrs Kemble threw into every line of these strange and unearthly scenes; while the exquisite skill evinced in modulating the voice to give a separate identity to the bold but stern tones of *Macbeth*, the discordant yet monotonous utterance of the Weird Sisters, and the shrill yet solemn tones of the child-like apparitions, was, indeed, above all praise.[8]

The reviewer describes the virtuosity with which Kemble was able to differentiate one character from another, noting the combination of vocal and facial expression; yet his or her attention seems to have been captured in particular by the way in which the reading facilitated a reassessment of the witches' lines and their potential dramatic impact. In accounts of both Siddons' and Kemble's readings, the actress's performance is able to render even potentially ludicrous material horribly plausible, lending supernatural fantasy a kind of queasy, fantastic realism.

The delighted surprise with which audience members received Siddons' and Kemble's representation of the witches is explained by two factors: first, these were roles that were not open to actresses on the public stage; second, they were treating seriously roles that were conventionally played for laughs. In George Daniel's *Love's Last Labour Not Lost*, 'Uncle Timothy' comments, 'I had been accustomed to hear these incantations greeted with rude laughter by the "groundlings" because they had been buffooned by drolls'.[9] Reviewers during this period frequently praise individual productions for their willingness to take the witches more seriously, but the fact that each hails this strategy as an innovation suggests the stubborn survival of the comic tradition.[10] Kemble herself complained in 1833:

> It has been always customary, – heavens only knows why, – to make low comedians act the witches, and to dress them like old fish-women. Instead of the wild unearthly appearance which Banquo describes, and which belongs to their most terrible and grotesquely poetical existence and surroundings, we have three jolly-faced fellows, – whom we are accustomed to laugh at, night after night, in every farce upon the stage, – with as due a proportion of petticoats as any woman, letting alone witch, might desire, jocose red faces, peaked hats, and broomsticks, which last addition alone makes their costume different from that of Moll Flagon.[11]

Kemble's final allusion compares the contemporary stage representation of *Macbeth*'s witches to that of the Amazonian character in John Burgoyne's comic opera *The Lord of the Manor* (1789), who enters in Act 3 with 'A Soldier's Coat over her Petticoat, a Gin-bottle by her Side, and a short Pipe in her Mouth', and was created by a male performer, Richard Suett.[12] Kemble's own solution is not, however, that women should play the witches; she writes:

> If I had the casting of Macbeth, I would give the witches to the first melo-dramatic actors on the stage, – such men as T.P. Cooke, and O. Smith, who understand all that belongs to picturesque devilry to perfection, – and give them such dresses, as, without ceasing to be grotesque, should be a little more fanciful, and less ridiculous than the established livery; something that would accord a little better with the blasted heath, the dark, fungus-grown wood, the desolate, misty hill-side, and the flickering light of the caldron [*sic*] cave.[13]

The comment 'If I had the casting of Macbeth' reminds us of the lack of creative input that women often had in theatrical productions outside their own performances; Kemble is able to sketch out in her diary an imaginary production that she could not effect on a real stage. Her willingness to consider the witches as serious figures rather than comic grotesques may have been influenced by her early exposure to Siddons' readings.[14] Moreover, her own comments had an afterlife and sustained impact: the diaries were widely published, and she is credited with the idea that the witches should be played by 'melodramatic actors' in an essay published by Wilfred Wisgast in 1860.[15]

In their responses to Siddons' or Kemble's performance as the witches, commentators registered their implicit critique of the assumptions regarding gender, casting and theatrical convention on which contemporary stage tradition was based.[16] The 'serious, poetical [and] tragical' potential of the witches was underlined by Jameson in an illustration published at the head of her essay on Lady Macbeth in *Characteristics of*

Women (1833). This drawing presents a revisionary image of the witches as heavily cloaked women, positioned above and behind an uneasily sleeping Lady Macbeth.[17] Within the essay, Jameson does not speculate on a specific thematic connection between the witches and Lady Macbeth, beyond saying that Macbeth's letter 'acts upon her mind as the prophecy of the Wierd [*sic*] Sisters on the mind of her husband' (315). However, the illustration points to interpretations developed by later scholars, keen to drawn links between the few female characters that appear in this male dominated narrative. While neither Kemble nor Jameson appears to have countenanced the idea that the witches might be played by women on the stage, each is alert in her different way – through performance and through illustration – to the possibilities offered by placing female bodies in those roles.

The extent to which conceptions of the witches were in flux is also suggested in Mary Cowden Clarke's 'The Thane's Daughter', published in *The Girlhood of Shakespeare's Heroines* in 1850.[18] Clarke gives Gruoch, the future Lady Macbeth, a supernatural prophecy to match Macbeth's, but it is delivered not by women but by a man. When Gruoch is a young girl, a strange Highland warrior predicts death in her father's castle and then turns his attention to Gruoch herself: 'steadily regarding the lady Gruoch for a few seconds, he added: – "What is it I trace on that fair young brow! But such weird shall not be read by me for one that has just proffered rest and refreshment".' [19] Because Gruoch has offered him hospitality, he refuses to describe his prophetic vision. Clarke thus teases her readers with the possibilities that the prophecy offers, and matches Shakespeare's deceptive prophets with a male equivalent. The use of the word 'weird' for 'fate' – repeated later in the story – also underlines the connections between Clarke's prophet and the witches that are simultaneously his predecessors and his successors. However, the Highlander at this stage in Clarke's narrative is a much less marginal figure than *Macbeth*'s witches, firmly embedded in the homosocial structures of the warrior class that Clarke depicts, and the father of a daughter of around Gruoch's age.

Later in the story, however, Gruoch causes the death of the Highlander's daughter by expelling her from the castle in foul weather because she is jealous of her effect on her suitor, Macbeth. The Highlander then appears before her:

> 'I am come to read thee thy weird at last!' said the Highlander. 'When first I looked upon thee, I beheld a crown spanning the fair young brow – but I beheld it through a red mist, and would not reveal the fearful secret to one who proffered aid.'
>
> 'A crown? – a crown said'st thou?' exclaimed the lady.
>
> 'Ay, a crown, a royal crown – the golden badge of sovereignty! I would not then foretel [*sic*] so dread, so fatal a vision. But thou hast sent me my child through the snow-storm, and I read thee thy weird through the red mist. A crown is thy weird; the red mist is blood!'
>
> 'What matters, so that the weird be a crown!' cried the lady Gruoch. 'Methinks to gain that, I could stem torrents of blood; scarcely heeding though some of my own were shed to mingle with the stream.'
>
> 'Thine own?' echoed the Highlander, with a scoffing laugh; 'That were too gentle a sentence.'

(152–3)

When Gruoch attempts to gain more information from the Highlander, and tries to lay her hand on his folded arms, he melts away: 'No tangible matter met her grasp, and with horror and awe unspeakable she recoiled; – then plunging desperately forward, she passed through the vivid shadow as if it had been a rainbow!' (153). Deprived of his daughter by Gruoch's thoughtless and callous actions, the Highlander becomes increasingly insubstantial and supernatural, and he disappears in a fashion similar to that of the witches in Act 1 of *Macbeth*. Clarke deliberately leaves it unclear, however, whether he has 'really' appeared or is the product of Gruoch's guilty conscience; foreshadowing Lady Macbeth's anguished progress around the castle at night, she has already begun to walk in her sleep. Like the witches, the Highlander provides his susceptible auditor with a prophecy of something that she may already secretly desire, yet the reversal of genders is unsettling, as is Gruoch's willingness to 'stem torrents of blood' in order to further her ambition.

The work of Siddons, Kemble, Jameson, and Clarke argues that women in the mid-nineteenth century began to develop their own 'readings' of Shakespeare's witches in a range of different media – performance, criticism, illustration and fiction. In Jameson's words, these women 'invested the weird sisters with all their own infernal fascinations', resisting and critiquing a theatrical tradition that excluded them from those roles. They were not, of course, the only commentators to raise objections to the performance of the witches by comedians, and none of them seems to have gone so far as to argue that these roles should be taken by women.[20] Nonetheless, their performances and writings made an implicit case for a renewed examination of the witches and their critical and theatrical potential.

Notes

1   'Mrs Siddons', *The New Monthly Magazine and Literary Journal* 32.2 (1831), 27–32 (31).

2   See Cheri Lin Larsen Hoeckley, 'Anna Jameson', in Gail Marshall ed., *Great Shakespeareans: Jameson, Cowden Clarke, Kemble, Cushman* (London, 2011), pp. 11–57; Georgiana Ziegler, 'Accommodating the Virago: Nineteenth-Century Representations of Lady Macbeth', in Christy Desmet and Robert Sawyer eds, *Shakespeare and Appropriation* (London, 1999), pp. 119–41.

3   See Dennis Bartholomeusz, *Macbeth and the Players* (Cambridge, 1969). Henry Irving's 1888 Lyceum production was widely praised for casting women in these roles, a move

that was seen as an important innovation. See Clement Scott, *Daily Telegraph*, 31 December 1888; *Morning Advertiser*, 31 December 1888.

4   'Drama: Drury-Lane', *The Daily News*, 4 November 1864. On choruses of witches in *Macbeth* see Bernice Kliman, *Shakespeare in Performance: Macbeth*, 2nd edn (Manchester, 2004), pp. 46–8.

5   See *Women Reading Shakespeare, 1660–1900* (Manchester, 1997). The title of the current essay signals its debt to this exemplary collection; its subject matter is also intended to pay tribute to Sasha Roberts, whose own research on theatrical witches was sadly cut short. For useful commentary see also Christy Desmet, '"Intercepting the Dew-Drop": Female Readers and Readings in Anna Jameson's Shakespearean Criticism', in Marianne Novy ed., *Women's Re-Visions of Shakespeare* (Urbana, IL, 1990), 41–57; Tricia A. Lootens, *Lost Saints: Silence, Gender, and Victorian Literary Canonization* (Charlottesville, VA, 1996), 77–115; Marshall ed., *Great Shakespeareans*; Ziegler, 'Women and Shakespeare', in Gail Marshall ed., *Shakespeare in the Nineteenth Century* (Cambridge, 2012), 205–28.

6   See Thompson and Roberts, 54–7; Bartholomeusz, *Macbeth and the Players*, 98–123; Ziegler, 'Accommodating'.

7   *Diaries of a Lady of Quality from 1797 to 1844*, ed. A. Hayward (London, 1864), 102, 104.

8   'Mrs Fanny Kemble's Shaksperian Readings', *Morning Post*, 5 April 1851. See also Fanny Appleton Longfellow's praise for Kemble's reading of the witches in a letter of 14 February 1849 (Edward Wagenknecht ed., *Mrs Longfellow: Selected Letters and Journals of Fanny Appleton Longfellow* (New York, 1956), 148–9). On Kemble's readings see Deirdre David, *Fanny Kemble: A Performed Life* (Philadelphia, 2007), 222–51; Jacky Bratton, 'Frances Anne Kemble', in Marshall ed., *Great Shakespeareans*, pp. 92–132 (117–31).

9   *Love's Last Labour Not Lost* (London, 1863), p. 121.

10 See, for instance, W. C. Oulton, *History of the Theatres of London*, 2 vols (London, 1796), vol. 2, p. 139–40 (on Garrick, Colman and Kemble); *St. James's Chronicle*, 19–21 January

1768 (on Powell's revival); *St. James's Chronicle*, 28–30 October 1773 (on Macklin's revival); 'The Termination of Mr Macready's Management of Covent-Garden', *The Odd Fellow*, 27 July 1839; 'The Stage', *The Southern Star and London and Brighton Patriot*, 12 July 1840 (on Charles Kean's revival); 'Music and the Drama', *The Era*, 3 April 1842 (on Macready's revival).

11 *Journal by Frances Anne Butler*, 2 vols. (London, 1835), 2, p. 157.

12 *The Dramatic and Poetical Works of the Late Lieut. Gen. J. Burgoyne* (London, 1808), vol. 1, p. 219. See Philip H. Highfill Jr., Kalman A. Burnim and Edward A. Langhans, *A Biographical Dictionary of Actors, Actresses, Musicians, Dancers, Managers and Other Stage Personnel in London, 1660–1800*, 16 vols. (Carbondale, IL, 1973–93), vol. 14, p. 331.

13 *Journal*, 2, pp. 157–8.

14 Anne Thackray Ritchie describes Kemble listening to Siddons read: see *Chapters from Some Memoirs* (New York, 1894), p. 207.

15 '*Macbeth*'s Witches', *The Players: A Dramatic and Literary Journal* 2, 30, Saturday 28 July 1860, 29–30 (29).

16 I am indebted here to the discussions of Siddons in Russ McDonald, *Look to the Lady: Sarah Siddons, Ellen Terry, and Judi Dench on the Shakespearean Stage* (Athens, GA, 2005), pp. 1–50; Celestine Woo, *Romantic Actors and Bardolotry: Performing Shakespeare from Garrick to Kean* (New York, 2008), pp. 87–132.

17 *Characteristics of Women, Moral, Poetical, and Historical*, 2 vols. (London, 1833), vol. 2, p. 304.

18 On Clarke's revision of *Macbeth* in 'The Thane's Daughter' see Erica Hateley, *Shakespeare in Children's Literature: Gender and Cultural Capital* (New York, 2009), pp. 40–3.

19 *The Girlhood of Shakespeare's Heroines*, vol. 1 (London, 1850), p. 116, pp. 152–3.

20 Wisgast does make this case in his 1860 essay, but he appears to have been heavily criticized for it (see 'Macbeth's Witches Again!', *The Players* 2, 35, 25 August 1860, pp. 61–2), and women do not appear to have played the roles for another thirty years.

14

Joanna Baillie: The Female Shakespeare

Fiona Ritchie
McGill University

Joanna Baillie, one of the most important dramatists of the Romantic period, was known to her contemporaries as 'the female Shakespeare'. Walter Scott, for example, identified her with the Bard in the introduction to canto three of *Marmion*:

> Or, if to touch such chord be thine,
> Restore the ancient tragic line,
> And emulate the notes that rung
> From the wild harp which silent hung,
> By silver Avon's holy shore,
> Till twice an hundred years rolled o'er;
> When she, the bold Enchantress, came,
> With fearless hand and heart on flame!
> From the pale willow snatched the treasure,
> And swept it with a kindred measure,
> Till Avon's swans, while rung the grove

With Monfort's hate and Basil's love,
Awakening at the inspired strain,
Deemed their own Shakespeare lived again.[1]

Baillie is here positioned as the inheritor of Shakespeare's natural genius, able to convince her contemporaries that his spirit lives again in her. This view was widely shared: the *Edinburgh Magazine and Literary Miscellany* for January 1818 ranked her only behind Shakespeare as a dramatist and *Fraser's Magazine* greeted the publication of her last volume of plays in 1836 by exclaiming 'Had we heard that a MS. play of Shakespeare's, or an early, but missing novel of Scott's had been discovered, and was already in the press, the information could not have been more welcome'.[2] In a poem published in 1827, William Sotheby also echoed Scott's assessment of Baillie, describing her as 'Sister of Shakespeare!' and 'artless Nature's simple child'.[3]

Author of seven volumes of plays, which contain lengthy prefatory material in which she theorizes about drama and the state of the contemporary theatre, Baillie was certainly prolific in print.[4] Her work was praised for its language but her plays were seen as less successful on the stage than on the page.[5] Recent critics have addressed Baillie's apparent lack of theatrical success and made a strong case for her significance to the Romantic stage. Catherine B. Burroughs explores Baillie's identification as a closet dramatist to argue that this should not preclude her from being considered as a writer for the theatre. Closet drama for Baillie, Burroughs contends, does not mean a play that is unperformed or unperformable but rather one that 'actually dramatizes scenes from a character's private closet', recognizing the theatrical potential of representing 'private emotions' or 'closeted moments' on stage.[6] Ellen Donkin counters the marginalization of Baillie's stage success by laying out the details of her achievements in the theatre. *De Monfort* was produced at Drury Lane in 1800 starring John Philip Kemble and Sarah Siddons and had a good run of eleven nights. It was revived in 1821 with Edmund Kean in the lead role. *The Family Legend* was successfully staged in Edinburgh in 1810.[7] Donkin ultimately ascribes Kemble's about-face over *Constantine Paleologus*, which he initially encouraged but later refused to stage, to the desire of the critical community to 'contain' Baillie, whose authoritative criticism of contemporary theatre practice posed a threat to the establishment.[8] This essay argues that one of the reasons for Baillie's success as a closet dramatist but apparent failure as a writer for the stage lies in the identification of her with Shakespeare, who was himself becoming increasingly divorced from the stage by critics at this time, despite his theatrical popularity.

There is ample evidence in Baillie's prefatory writing of her knowledge of current theatrical practice and much critical engagement with the state of the contemporary stage. In the address to the reader in the third volume of the *Plays on the Passions*, published in 1812, Baillie explores why her play *De Monfort* has not been revived in the theatre. She writes that while it may have had some 'merit in the writing', this could not be adequately transmitted 'in a theatre, so large and so ill calculated to convey sound as the one in which it was performed' so that 'it was impossible this [merit] could be felt or comprehended by even a third part of the audience'.[9] The patent theatres had become vast spaces – by the 1790s, both Covent Garden and Drury Lane accommodated over 3,000 people each – and this was a state of affairs much lamented by those who sought to promote the development of a canon of English dramatic literature. Indeed, the size of the patent theatre auditoria was cited as a reason for Edward Lytton Bulwer's call for a Parliamentary Inquiry into the State of the Drama in 1832 as he claimed that theatre had come to rely on 'noise, and glitter, and spectacle' rather than poetry because 'the enormous size of these houses rendered half the dialogue lost to half the audience'.[10]

Baillie notes particularly that soliloquy is 'the department of acting that will suffer most under these circumstances', a point which is crucial to her plays since she had earlier identified soliloquy as a key means for the dramatist 'to

open to us the mind he would display', making it central to
the unfolding of the passions which were at the heart of her
drama.[11] Shakespeare's works continue to succeed on the
Romantic stage because 'being familiar to the audience, they
can still understand and follow them pretty closely, though
but imperfectly heard'.[12] However, as long as the theatres
remain at their current size, 'it is a vain thing to complain
either of want of taste in the Public, or want of inclination
in the Managers to bring forward new pieces of merit'.[13]
Not only does Baillie effectively contextualize the fate of her
drama by elucidating the state of the contemporary stage,
she also offers suggestions for reform, for example in her
detailed footnote on lighting effects. Here Baillie criticizes the
use of footlights for distorting the actor's face and making it
unable to achieve subtlety of expression and advocates instead
'bringing forward the roof of the stage as far as its boards or
floor, and placing a row of lamps with reflectors along the
inside of the wooden front-piece' in order to provide a more
subtle light.[14]

Baillie also suggests that actresses suffer more 'from the
defects of a large theatre' and her playwriting and advocacy
for more intimate performance spaces might also be seen
as a way to rethink women's involvement in contemporary
performance.[15] Female readers and spectators such as Hester
Piozzi and Mary Berry noted that there was something
different and indeed innovative about Baillie's portrayal of
women characters: Piozzi commented of Baillie's work, 'I felt
it was a woman's writing; no man makes female characters
respectable – no man of the present day I mean, they only
make them lovely'.[16] And Siddons reportedly visited Baillie to
request that she 'Make me some more Jane De Monforts!'[17]
Siddons's appreciation of Baillie's dramaturgy may also have
sprung from her own awareness of the limitations imposed by
the size of the contemporary stage: she referred to the Drury
Lane theatre as 'this vast wilderness'.[18]

It is clear from the detailed discussion of the Romantic
stage in her prefaces that it was not a lack of knowledge about

the practicalities of the theatre that prevented Baillie being taken seriously as a dramatist for the stage as well as the page. Baillie's identification with the literary rather than the theatrical forms part of her connection with Shakespeare, who was at this time increasingly being moved from the stage to the closet. As Baillie noted, Shakespeare's plays remained popular in the theatre but influential critics such as William Hazlitt, Leigh Hunt and Charles Lamb argued that his works were better read than performed. Perhaps the most famous expression of this view comes from Lamb, who polemically claimed that 'the plays of Shakspeare are less calculated for performance on a stage, than those of almost any other dramatist whatever'.[19] Instead, Lamb believed that Shakespeare should be read in the study, suggesting that acting the plays in some way debased them and was merely a novelty which 'instead of realizing an idea, [...] materialized and brought down a fine vision to the standard of flesh and blood'.[20] Seeing the plays staged was limiting since it provided the audience with a physical embodiment of a character in a situation, rather than allowing the imagination mentally to construct that character and situation for oneself in order to achieve empathy. The imagination was considered by the Romantics to be the highest creative faculty and Shakespeare was of course the supreme embodiment of the imaginative writer.

Julie A. Carlson contends that Romantic antitheatricalism is 'a misogynist reaction against the visibility of "public women" in theatre', an argument which is pertinent to Baillie's position as a female dramatist.[21] Lamb objected to the performance of Shakespeare because 'the stage inverts all natural hierarchies by subordinating poet to player, forfeiting dreams to realities, privileging sense over imagination and action over intellect'.[22] But more than this, gender hierarchies were inverted on the stage since the most influential performer of the age was female, not male: it was Siddons who embodied Shakespeare in the Romantic period, elevating his female characters over the male ones. Furthermore, watching Siddons perform Shakespeare feminized the audience since she invariably provoked an intense and publicly demonstrated emotional reaction amongst her spectators.[23] The move to restrict Shakespeare to the page was therefore in part an attempt to keep his works free from this feminine influence. By advocating that her plays be performed, Baillie sought to make herself the kind of public and influential woman of the theatre that troubled the antitheatrical critics.

Baillie herself acknowledges in her writing the deep divide emerging between drama deemed fit for performance and that regarded as better suited for reading. In her 1812 preface, published the year after Lamb's essay, she explains why she intends this to be the last volume of her plays to appear in print:

> The Series of Plays was originally published in the hope that some of the pieces it contains, although first given to the Public from the press, might in time make their way to the stage, and there be received and supported with some degree of public favour. But the present situation of dramatic affairs is greatly against every hope of this kind; and should they ever become more favourable, I have now good reason to believe, that the circumstances of these plays having been already published, would operate strongly against their being received upon the stage. I am therefore strongly of opinion that I ought to reserve the remainder of the work in manuscript, if I would not run the risk of entirely frustrating my original design. Did I not believe that their having been already published would not afterwards obstruct their way to the stage, the untowardness of present circumstances should not prevent me from continuing to publish.[24]

Baillie reaffirms her commitment to writing for performance, rather than print, and asserts that play publication hinders the staging of her works. This seems to be a clear response to the attempts of critics such as Lamb to render great drama, epitomized by Shakespeare himself, antithetical to performance.

Baillie's writing recognizes the link with Shakespeare posited by Scott but fights against the closeting of the Bard. In the preface to her 1804 volume of *Miscellaneous Plays* she notes that she has a strong attachment to the drama of her native country, of which Shakespeare, 'one whom every British heart thinks of with pride', is the chief exemplar.[25] In her first preface, she extends the maxim of 'a sagacious Scotsman' – 'let who will make the laws of a nation, if I have the writing of its ballads' – to the drama, arguing that plays have an important ability to affect all classes of society.[26] She thus positions herself as part of a strong tradition of native British drama with Shakespeare at its head. In this way, Baillie anticipates the Parliamentary Inquiry into the State of the Drama of 1832, which aimed above all to reverse the deterioration of the national drama that was perceived in the contemporary patent theatres, largely as a result of their size. Baillie's advocacy for smaller auditoria and her attempts to produce plays suitable for performance in such spaces are her way of continuing the nation's dramatic tradition. Indeed, Lytton specifically requested that the drama return to the standards of 'the days of Massinger, and Beaumont and Fletcher, and Jonson and Shakespeare'.[27] Baillie's work attempts to revive British playwriting by returning to this heyday of the theatre. The fact that she insists so strongly on the suitability of her plays for performance throughout her writing whilst simultaneously linking herself with Shakespeare is a reaction to Romantic antitheatricality which sought to remove Shakespeare, and any form of high drama, from the stage.

In fact, Baillie responds to calls to reinvigorate British drama more successfully than her male peers. Wordsworth, Shelley, Byron, Coleridge, and Keats all experimented with writing for the theatre but, as Jeffrey N. Cox notes,

Of the major male writers of the period, only Coleridge had a clear success with *Remorse* (1813); even the wildly popular Byron, who had direct ties to the management of

Drury Lane, saw only one of his plays, *Marino Faliero*, produced during his lifetime, and it was a failure on stage.[28]

Baillie's work had more theatrical success and so it was she, rather than any of her male peers, whom Scott likened to Shakespeare and positioned as the true successor to the Bard. While critics such as Burroughs and Donkin have elucidated other forces that worked to constrain Baillie and that have negatively influenced her reputation, the role of her identification with Shakespeare in this process has not previously been explored. I contend that labelling Baillie 'the female Shakespeare' simultaneously elevated her to a position at the head of contemporary playwriting and precluded her success in the theatre by further associating her with closet drama rather than theatrical practice. However, Baillie's prefatory writing reveals a rich engagement with the stage that suggests that she wished to argue against this closeting and make a strong case for the place of her plays in the theatre. She hoped that her works would be appreciated, as Shakespeare's had historically been, as both literary texts and performance pieces.

Notes

1   Walter Scott, *Marmion; A Tale of Flodden Field*, 2nd edn (Edinburgh, 1808), p. 122. Monfort and Basil are characters in two of Baillie's plays. Catherine B. Burroughs notes that in some editions of the poem a footnote identifies the 'bold enchantress' as Baillie. Catherine B. Burroughs, *Closet Stages: Joanna Baillie and the Theater Theory of British Romantic Women Writers* (Philadelphia, 1997), p. 200.

2   Quoted in Jeffrey N. Cox, 'Baillie, Siddons, Larpent: Gender, Power, and Politics in the Theatre of Romanticism', in *Women in British Romantic Theatre: Drama, Performance, and Society, 1790–1840*, ed. Catherine Burroughs (Cambridge, 2000), pp. 23–47 (pp. 27–8).

3   Quoted in Burroughs, *Closet Stages*, p. 200.

4   Joanna Baillie, *A Series of Plays: In Which it Is Attempted to Delineate the Stronger Passions of the Mind. Each Passion Being the Subject of a Tragedy and a Comedy* (London, 1798); *A Series of Plays*, vol. 2 (London, 1802); *A Series of Plays*, vol. 3 (London, 1812); *Miscellaneous Plays* (London, 1804); *Dramas*, 3 vols. (London, 1832). In total, Baillie wrote twenty-six plays. Her most substantial theoretical writing is to be found in the prefaces to the 1798, 1804, and 1812 volumes.

5   Ellen Donkin, *Getting Into the Act: Women Playwrights in London 1776–1829* (London, 1995), p. 170.

6   Burroughs, p. 91.

7   Donkin, pp. 163–4, p. 174, p. 171.

8   Donkin, p. 172, pp. 176–7.

9   Joanna Baillie, 'To the Reader', in Jeffrey N. Cox and Michael Gamer *The Broadview Anthology of Romantic Drama* (Peterborough, Ontario, 2003), pp. 370–8 (p. 374). Subsequent references to the 1812 volume are to this edition.

10 'State of the Drama', *Hansard's Parliamentary Debates*, 3rd ser., vol. 13 (London, 1833), pp. 239–59 (p. 243).

11 Baillie (1812), p. 375; Joanna Baillie, 'Introductory Discourse', in Peter Duthie ed., *Plays on the Passions* (Peterborough, Ontario, 2001), pp. 67–113 (p. 105). Subsequent references to the 1798 volume are to this edition.

12 Baillie (1812), p. 374.

13 Baillie (1812), p. 374. It is exactly the problem that Baillie pinpoints in 1812 that the 1832 inquiry was set up to address.

14 Baillie (1812), p. 377.

15 Baillie (1812), p. 375.

16 Quoted in Donkin, p. 166.

17 Quoted in Donkin, p. 166.

18 Quoted in Iain Mackintosh and Geoffrey Ashton, *The Georgian Playhouse: Actors, Artists, Audiences and Architecture 1730–1830*, (London, 1975), exhibition catalogue, entry for items 227–31.

19 Lamb, Charles, 'From "On the Tragedies of Shakespeare,

Considered with Reference to their Fitness for Stage Representation" (1811)', in *The Romantics on Shakespeare*, ed. Jonathan Bate (London, 1992), pp. 111–27 (p. 113).

20 Lamb, p. 113.

21 Julie A. Carlson, *In the Theatre of Romanticism: Coleridge, Nationalism, Women* (Cambridge, 1994), p. 20.

22 Lamb, p. 113.

23 Carlson, pp. 168–72.

24 Baillie (1812), p. 373.

25 Joanna Baillie, 'To the Reader', *Miscellaneous Plays* (London, 1804), pp. [iii]–xix (p. ix).

26 Baillie (1798), p. 103.

27 'State of the Drama', p. 246.

28 Cox, 'Baillie, Siddons, Larpent', p. 26.

15

The Girlhood of Mary Cowden Clarke

Kate Chedgzoy
Newcastle University

Highly respected as a scholar and popular as a writer in her own time, later mocked by an academy unsympathetic to amateur female scholarship, Mary Cowden Clarke is once more being taken seriously as a formative influence on Victorian perceptions of and responses to Shakespeare. The inclusion of her work in the volume of women's critical responses to Shakespeare edited by Ann Thompson and Sasha Roberts, *Women Reading Shakespeare 1660–1900*, made a significant contribution to this revaluation, and it has more recently been consolidated by her inclusion in the pantheon of Great Shakespeareans in an essay by Ann Thompson and Gail Marshall.[1] This essay takes as its point of departure Cowden Clarke's recollections of her childhood in her memoir *My Long Life*. I argue that her early education, conducted within her family and by Mary Lamb, exemplifies the incorporation of Shakespeare into liberal pedagogic practice and the culture of childhood in the Romantic period, and prepared her for a remarkable Victorian career in which she engaged with Shakespeare as a scholar, actor, and creative writer.

My title alludes to *The Girlhood of Shakespeare's Heroines*, probably the work for which Cowden Clarke is now best known.[2] In 15 substantial narratives, it imagines the pre-history of Portia, Lady Macbeth, Helena, Desdemona, 'Meg and Alice the merry maids of Windsor' (contents page), Isabella, Katharina and Bianca, Ophelia, Rosalind and Celia, and Juliet, up to the point when they enter the scene of Shakespeare's play. Introducing the volume, Cowden Clarke explains that her goal was 'to imagine the possible circumstances and influences of scene, event, and associate, surrounding the infant life of his heroines, which might have conduced to originate and foster those germs of character recognized in their maturity, as by him developed' (Preface, p. 1). The idea that early experiences shape the adult self has become naturalized in modern Western conceptualizations of subjectivity, but for Cowden Clarke and her readers this was still a relatively new insight, and one which would be crucial to the development of the Victorian novel as a study of character. Cowden Clarke explained that her interest was in 'the development of character' (Ibid.) which she considered to be formed by the setting in which the child is brought up ('scene'), by childhood experiences ('event'), and by the influence of the people around the child ('associate'). How, then, did the setting, experiences, and influences of her own childhood prepare her to become the author of *The Girlhood of Shakespeare's Heroines*?

Mary Victoria Novello (known in childhood as Victoria) was the eldest of eleven children in a happy and affectionate family. She recalled her early years warmly in *My Long Life*, mapping for her readers a social and spatial world characterized by pleasure and sustenance, bodily and mental. Describing her childhood home near Hyde Park, she recalls how outings there with her brothers and her sisters combined 'enjoyment of those fine old elm trees, those stretches of grass' with the purchase of little mugs of curds and whey, a 'dainty refection [which] seemed properly rustic' (p. 2). These healthily pastoral physical pleasures are matched with the pleasures of textual culture which were also available in the park from the sellers of cheap printed materials: 'The railing adjacent to the gate was ... strung with rows of printed old-fashioned ballads, such as "Cruel Barbara Allen"' (pp. 2–3). In many ways, this is a verbal culture that could have been available to Shakespeare and his contemporaries, and stories from the oral tradition, too, shape her early encounters with her environment. The memory of escorting her brothers to their preparatory school is associated with a neighbourhood anecdote of a little boy who was lost, brought up under a false identity associated with a much more humble rank in life, and eventually found his way back to his home and mother (p. 8). Reminiscent of one of Shakespeare's late romances, this tale of loss and restitution comes immediately before Mary's account of the books her parents provided for their children: to be safely part of the family is to be nourished with reading material, as well as to be loved and sheltered.

Mary is at pains to explain that though her parents 'were bountiful in providing us with books' (p. 8), that bounty is moral and intellectual, rather than material. She contrasts the carefully-selected but 'plain, unornate' volumes of her childhood with the excessive abundance of gaudily-illustrated but unappreciated products of late-Victorian commercial publishing for children, highlighting the pleasurable intimacy that came from close, repeated study of a small, select library. Among the books 're-read and treasured by us young Novellos' (p. 8) were 'Miss Edgeworth's "Frank", "Rosamond" and "Parents' Assistant"; Day's "Sandford and Merton"... "The Book of Trades" and Aesop's Fables' (p. 9). Maria Edgeworth's didactic fictions for children and Thomas Day's *The History of Sandford and Merton* (1783) were hugely popular and combined instruction with delight for their enthusiastic early readers in a way that typified the impulses driving the growth of children's literature at the turn of the century. In contrast 'The Book of Trades' (a volume which illustrated workers displaying their skills) and Aesop's Fables are instances of genres that had enjoyed sustained popularity with youthful readers since at least the mid-sixteenth century. Thus both the distinctively innovative literary culture of Romantic-period English childhood, and a transnational popular textual culture with deep historical roots, played a formative role in Mary Cowden Clarke's early reading.

Pride of place in the Novello children's reading matter is accorded, however, to Shakespeare, who is introduced in a resonant passage in which father and children gather in the intimate space of the parental bedroom to enjoy a moment of easy community and shared study:

> Often, after a hard day's teaching, my father used to have his breakfast in bed next morning, when we children were allowed to scramble up to the counterpane and lie around him to see what new book he had bought for us, and listen to his description and explanation of it. Never can I forget the boundless joy and interest with which I heard him tell about the contents of two volumes he had just brought home, and showed me the printed pictures it had. It was an early edition of 'Lamb's Tales from Shakespeare.' And what a vast world of new ideas and new delights that opened to me – a world in which I have ever since much dwelt, and always with supreme pleasure and admiration.
>
> (p. 9)

This account of the youthful Mary's first encounter with Shakespeare recapitulates and develops the clustering of associations – pleasure in familial proximity, wholesome food, and the sharing of printed matter – repeatedly invoked in her recollections of her early years. In *My Long Life*, Mary Cowden Clarke attributes the integration in her life of professional success and a happy family existence to this early domestic introduction to Shakespeare.[3] It was in his works, she says, that she found 'the emotional warmth and loyalties of that family life best reflected' (p. 59), and in the prefaces to her scholarly works on Shakespeare she repeatedly attributes her devotion to Shakespeare to the early influence of her parents. When in 1845 she published in book form the first-ever concordance to Shakespeare's plays – widely acclaimed as a landmark achievement and reprinted in ten editions over the subsequent three decades – she remarked in the preface on her intellectual debt to her mother, 'who first inspired me with a love of all that is good and beautiful, and who therefore may well be said to have originated my love of Shakespeare'. [4] In the preface to her 1860 edition of *Shakespeare's Works* – the first edition produced by a sole female editor, Henrietta Bowdler having collaborated with her brother on the *Family Shakespeare* in 1807 – she echoes the cited passage from *My Long Life* in ascribing the origins of her interest in Shakespeare to her father's gift of the Lambs' *Tales* (Ibid.).

Communal reading aloud was a highly valued part of the culture of the educated middle-class family in this period: Henrietta Bowdler was inspired to produce her *Family Shakespeare* by her own memories of their father's domestic performances of carefully edited versions of the plays, while Charlotte Yonge staged a scene of domestic Shakespeare reading in which a brother and sister pore over *Henry V* together in her immensely popular novel *The Daisy Chain* (1856). [5] Later Yonge would concur with Cowden Clarke in citing both Bowdler's edition and the Lambs' *Tales* as 'the best stepping-stones to Shakespeare himself'. [6] Shakespeare is twice-mediated in Cowden Clarke's recollections: through Victor Novello's 'description and explanation' of the volume he presents to his children, and within that volume through Charles and Mary Lamb's retelling of the plays as stories for young readers. Gendered mediations within the family context are envisaged in the Preface to the Lambs' *Tales* as a vital part of the process whereby young girls may gain access to Shakespeare, and such practices have been construed by critics as underlining girls' marginalization from the world of print culture and the masculine control of their engagement with literature.[7] Yet Mary Lamb – like her contemporary Henrietta Bowdler – had to read Shakespeare's plays herself in order to mediate them, and for Mary Cowden Clarke too this first mediated encounter was to facilitate a life of extraordinarily extensive direct engagement with Shakespeare.

The Lambs' *Tales* constituted a site of first encounter with Shakespeare for many children in the nineteenth and twentieth centuries.[8] Mary Cowden Clarke celebrates their continuing presence in the reading lives of girls in particular in her 1887 article, 'Shakespeare as the Girl's Friend':

> Happy she who at eight or nine years old has a copy of 'Lamb's Tales from Shakespeare' given to her, opening a vista of even then understandable interest and enjoyment!

That they played an exceptionally significant role in her own early introduction to Shakespeare is not surprising, given that Charles and Mary Lamb were close friends of the Novellos and frequent visitors to the family home, alongside other figures from the London literary world such as Leigh Hunt, John Keats, and 'ever-welcome, ever young-hearted Charles Cowden Clarke' (p. 12), the man Victoria would eventually marry. This friendship network was to prove of particular value to the young Victoria when 'dear, kind Mary Lamb offered to give [her] lessons in Latin and to teach [her] to read verse properly' (p. 17). Cowden Clarke records three formative experiences associated with her education by Mary Lamb: meeting the distinguished actress Fanny Kelly, who was a close friend of the Lambs, when she arrived for her lessons one day ('Look at her well, Victoria', said Mary Lamb, 'for she is a woman to remember having seen', p. 18); attempting to imitate Hazlitt's son in 'scamper[ing]' through her Latin lesson at speed and being advised to work in a way more suited to her 'sober, steady' personality ('Best be natural in all you do', p. 19); and listening to Mary Lamb's 'beautifully natural and unaffected' way of reading poetry, especially *Paradise Lost*, which still 'remain[ed] on my mind's ear' (p. 19) at the time of writing.

Despite her beneficial pedagogic influence on Mary Victoria Novello, Mary Lamb had had relatively little formal education herself (family financial difficulties limited this to six months of part-time attendance at a day school), and was uncomfortably aware of the way this affected her as an adult. It was as a contribution to redressing the limitations of the education on offer to girls, Jean I. Marsden contends, that Mary Lamb would compose her *Tales from Shakespeare*.[9] But while Lamb was eager to offer girls wider educational opportunities and access to great literature, nonetheless, Marsden argues, the kind of education on offer remains limited in that it is primarily moral and social: its purpose is to form girls as virtuous members of society conforming to normatively gendered social expectations (p. 51). Demonstrating the remarkable durability of this gendered pedagogy (and the ideology of gender that informed it), Mary Cowden Clarke articulates her own understanding of the role Shakespeare could play in it as late as 1887, in 'Shakespeare as the Girl's Friend'.[10] By studying Shakespeare's 'feminine portraits' she argues, the girl reader can come to recognize what she must imitate or avoid 'in order to become a worthy and admirable woman':

> She can take her own disposition in hand, as it were, and endeavour to mould and form it into the best perfection of which it is capable, by carefully observing the women drawn by Shakespeare.

While the reading girl is positioned as an active subject here, she is required to deploy her agency to conform to gendered norms of behaviour. In other works, however, notably the tales which recount the *Girlhood of Shakespeare's Heroines*, Cowden Clarke undertakes more questioning negotiations with Victorian ideologies of gender.

As Kathryn Prince argues, 'Shakespeare as the Girl's Friend' is typical of much of the material published in the periodical where it first appeared, the *Girl's Own Paper*, in its 'blend of instruction and delight' and its focus on 'teach[ing] Victorian girls how to become exemplary women'.[10] What in practice this meant, for a girl of Mary Victoria Novello's background, was an education that prepared her for a transitional period spent educating other people's children before settling into marriage, a process described in her autobiography. This life course is prefigured in the way that the romances and comedies in Lambs' *Tales* all become, in the absence of subplots and lower-class characters, narratives centred on the elite young woman's journey towards heterosexual courtship and marriage. The Lambs' *Tales* clearly provided Mary Cowden Clarke with a model for her own efforts to frame Shakespeare for girl readers, and such a narrative focus on the female journey through life-stages from girlhood to womanhood, accompanied by a powerfully gendered 'moral pedagogy',[12] is also pervasive in the book for which she remains best known, *The Girlhood of Shakespeare's Heroines*. These dramatically inspired novellas celebrate good and dutiful daughters, but they do not merely reproduce a gendering of culture through a pedagogic and affective emphasis on virtuous feminine behaviour. They also expose and critique the factors that constrain feminine education and the sphere of activity open to girls and women, and explore what other opportunities girls might be able to seek out to learn, develop as women, and exercise agency. As Seth Lerer puts it, Clarke's heroines 'constantly need to find a middle way between the demands of private life and the temptations of public life', negotiating the ideological complexities of 'mid-Victorian girlhood' in ways that are not wholly compliant.[13]

Indeed, Gail Marshall and Ann Thompson have argued that Cowden Clarke explicitly challenges some of the limitations on Victorian girls and women by framing several of the stories to illustrate the damaging effects of 'women's exclusion from education and consequently from the professions' (p. 64) – an exclusion visible in her renditions of *The Taming of the*

Shrew and *The Merchant of Venice* and still in force when she was writing these tales in mid-Victorian England. When Cowden Clarke was writing *The Girlhood of Shakespeare's Heroines* the admission of women to London University – the first university in Britain to accept them – was still two decades away, and entrance to the professions would take a good deal longer. Cowden Clarke's reminiscences of her early years in *My Long Life* make plain that she herself benefited immensely from home education, within a family circle in which she chose to remain for much of an adult life which saw her making a significant contribution to public literary culture. Her experience shows that familial education for girls was not necessarily inferior to schooling, and did not inevitably limit their ability to engage with a wider world. However, many of the stories in *Girlhood* produce a less positive sense of familial education: they suggest that a lack of adequate moral pedagogy within the home is often at fault in producing difficult daughters. These narratives reflect on the limitations and possibilities of the institutions and experiences that shape girls' education and form them as women. At a time of considerable social constraint on the possibilities for women's and girls' lives, by imagining pre-histories for a number of Shakespearean heroines Cowden Clarke opened up for herself and her readers a larger creative space in which to imagine the lives and choices of Shakespeare's female characters, and thereby provided a template – as, in many ways, she did in her own life – for thinking differently about female lives and choices.

Notes

1   Ann Thompson and Sasha Roberts, *Women Reading Shakespeare 1660–1900* (Manchester), 1997; Gail Marshall and Ann Thompson, 'Mary Cowden Clarke', in Gail Marshall ed., *Great Shakespeareans* Volume VII: *Jameson, Cowden Clarke, Kemble, Cushman* (London: 2011), pp. 58–91.

2   Mary Cowden Clarke, *The Girlhood of Shakespeare's Heroines in a Series of Tales* (London, 1851–52).

3   Mary Cowden Clarke, *My Long Life: An Autobiographic Sketch* (London, 1896).

4   Marshall and Thompson, pp. 61–2.

5   Georgianna Ziegler, 'Introducing Shakespeare: the Earliest Versions for Children', *Shakespeare* 2, 2(2006), 132–51 (133).

6   Charlotte Yonge, *What Books to Lend and What to Give* (London, 1887), p. 61.

7   Erica Hateley, *Shakespeare in Children's Literature: Gender and Cultural Capital* (London, 2009).

8   Naomi J. Miller, 'Play's the Thing: Agency in Children's Shakespeares', in Kate Chedgzoy, Susanne Greenhalgh, and Robert Shaughnessy (eds), *Shakespeare and Childhood* (Cambridge, 2007), pp. 137–52.

9   Jean I. Marsden 'Shakespeare for girls: Mary Lamb and Tales from Shakespeare', *Children's Literature* 17 (1989), 47–63 (48).

10 Reprinted in Thompson and Roberts, pp. 101–3 (p. 101).

11 Kathryn Prince, *Shakespeare in the Victorian Periodicals* (London, 2008), p. 7.

12 Marshall and Thompson, p. 63.

13 Seth Lerer, *Children's Literature: A Reader's History from Aesop to Harry Potter* (Chicago, 2008), p. 233.

16

'A Sacred Trust': Helen Faucit, Geraldine Jewsbury, and the Idealized Shakespeare

Lois Potter

University of Delaware

It was for Geraldine Jewsbury, dying of cancer, that Helen Faucit wrote the first of the letters that were collected and published in 1885 as *On Some of Shakespeare's Female Characters: By One Who Has Personated Them*. Her letters on Ophelia and Portia were sent to Jewsbury; one on Desdemona, put aside when she realized that her friend would never read it, was completed a year later. Two further letters on Juliet were written for another old friend, Anna Maria Hall, who also died before they were completed. Faucit addressed the final four letters to Anna Swanwick (novelist, scholar and feminist) and to three famous men: Browning, Ruskin, and Tennyson (this last one, on Hermione, was added only in 1891). While Mary Cowden Clarke had dedicated each chapter of

The Girlhood of Shakespeare's Heroines (1852–1852) to a
different recipient, in gratitude for particular accomplishments
or personal favours, the dedication of Faucit's book was to
Queen Victoria, who had let it be known that she would
accept it.

That this book began as a letter to a dying friend is
important. As Ann Thompson and Sasha Roberts point
out, women's criticism of Shakespeare often takes unusual
forms.[1] Faucit, according to her husband, had always been
'impatient of commentators and theorists where Shakespeare
was concerned. They had never helped her, she said, to a
clearer understanding of his works, and they had constantly
encumbered his texts with annotations where no explanation
was needed, and missed the indications which only a sympa-
thetic imagination could observe, and the action of the stage
could alone develope [*sic*].'[2] What overcame her hesitation
about attempting any kind of critical writing was the sense
that in this case it was a duty she could not refuse.

But her letters were also affected by her knowledge of their
recipient. In 1848, before she had ever met Faucit, Jewsbury
published *The Half Sisters* (1848). As its title indicates, the
novel tells of two young women who have the same father but
totally different upbringings. Alice grows up in comfort and
marries a rich northern industrialist, but, lacking occupation
or purpose, nearly elopes with a lover; her hysterical feelings
of guilt finally kill her. Her sister Bianca, wretchedly poor,
works hard (initially as a circus performer), becomes a famous
actress and marries a lord. The novel draws on Jewsbury's
friendship with the American actress Charlotte Cushman –
who in fact had a sister, also an actress, who left the stage
to marry a Liverpool industrialist. Moreover, as several
critics have pointed out, the plot of *The Half Sisters* derives
ultimately from Germaine de Staël's famous *Corinne*.[3] Yet,
because Jewsbury removed most of the identifying features of
her model (including Cushman's lesbianism), Bianca's story
might well have struck Faucit as a more sensational version
of her own life. Faucit, though not so beautiful as Bianca,

nevertheless gave an impression of beauty and grace on the stage, whereas Cushman was notoriously ugly and famous for playing Romeo, Lady Macbeth, and the old hag Meg Merrilies. Bianca at the start of her career is mentored by an older actor. She suffers a long and desperate love for a man who despises the acting profession, and finally marries a rich and distinguished man who has waited patiently for several years. The young Faucit had learnt much, as she often acknowledges, from the elderly Charles Kemble and from acting with William Charles Macready. But Macready, whose diary is full of diatribes against his own profession, was also the object of Faucit's unhappy love for many years (he was married and a model of moral rectitude). She married her longstanding admirer – and first biographer – Theodore Martin, in 1851; as her second biographer, Carol Carlisle, points out, this was only six months after Macready retired from acting.

The Half Sisters may help to explain one aspect of *On Some of Shakespeare's Heroines* that has seemed excessive to readers. Jewsbury treats her characters even more harshly than the typical Victorian novelist, constantly subjecting them to accidents and illness. Bianca, Alice, and the man who successively loves them both, all collapse, under emotional pressure, into serious – in Alice's case, fatal – hysterical illness. Both Faucit and Martin, in his biography, often refer to her 'delicate health' and emotional exhaustion; Macready's playing of Leontes' reunion with Hermione in the final scene of *The Winter's Tale* was so overwhelming 'that I suppose I cried out hysterically'.[4] In her analysis of Shakespeare's characters she often assumes a propensity to psychosomatic illness. Shylock, she thinks, 'will not live long' after the trial scene (42); Imogen will never recover from the emotional shock of her husband's accusation of her: 'The "piece of tender air" very gently, but very surely, will fade out like an exhalation of the dawn' (222). Such imagining of events before and after the play was not new: Mary Cowden Clarke writes, as Faucit would do, that Ophelia spent her childhood in the country where she learned the songs she sings in her madness, and in Elizabeth Macauley's retelling of *The Merchant of Venice* Shylock dies soon after leaving the Venetian court.[5] The stories Faucit tells are gentler.

At this distance, it's clear that her treatment of the play's authority figures draws on feelings she could not openly acknowledge. The only good father is Portia's, who is dead. Of living parents, she sympathizes only with Lady Montague, who dies of grief after Romeo's banishment. Perhaps, as Carol Carlisle suggests, the actress is reflecting the absence of parental affection in her own life.[6] Cymbeline is weak; the Banished Duke in *As You Like It* shows so little concern for the daughter he left behind at his brother's court that Rosalind 'has no temptation to make herself known to him' (253); Polonius is self-serving, telling Ophelia to deny access to Hamlet because he thinks 'that this will make the Prince openly avow his love' (10). Brabantio was tragic for many Victorian critics, but not for Faucit, who points out that for Desdemona he was only 'the lord of duty' (71).

The heroes compare poorly to the heroines. Surprisingly, even Lady Macbeth is superior to her husband. 'It was not Macbeth alone [...] whose sleep was haunted by the addiction of terrible dreams. She says nothing of them, for hers was the braver, more self-sustained nature of the two; but I always felt an involuntary shudder creep over me when, in the scene before the banquet scene, he mentions them as afflicting himself. He has no thought of what she, too, is suffering' (232–3). Of Hamlet, she writes, 'there is not much sign of his love being at any time worthy of the sweet life lost for it' (18). The one act usually held against Ophelia – that she lies when Hamlet asks, 'Where is your father?' – is to Faucit a courageous attempt to protect the old man, comparable to Desdemona's deathbed lie to protect Othello: 'she takes it upon her own soul' (14). The three plays that affect her most strongly – *Othello, Cymbeline,* and *The Winter's Tale* – are also those in which the hero most fully recognizes the wrong he has done the heroine. Othello's agonized vision of his soul being thrown from heaven by the sight of Desdemona's dead face clearly recurred to her when she wrote her essay on Ophelia: 'when they shall meet at compt', Hamlet will feel the remorse that he has failed to show in the play (17–18). In case Posthumus and Iachimo do not realize how much anguish they have caused Imogen, her death will give them a lifetime of well-deserved remorse. Her notorious post-play vision of Portia looking after the dying Shylock and helping to reconcile him to his daughter contains echoes of the other Venetian play that perhaps suggest a different fantasy: the rich Venetian lady, no longer in disguise, will listen to this foreigner's sad history and respond with 'a world of sighs' (41). Shylock, like Othello, was played by Macready.

To an unsympathetic reader, then, Faucit's book could be called, as it is by Jacky Bratton, 'a grotesque effort of self-justification and appropriation'.[7] Yet this identification of actor with role is hardly unusual even now. In 2010, Neil Taylor, who sent a questionnaire to women who had played Ophelia professionally, was surprised to find how many of them had imagined histories for her. All noted that Ophelia's mother was dead, and two of them agreed with Faucit that she had died in childbirth; one used the phrase 'a sensitive kindred spirit' to describe Ophelia's feelings about Hamlet,[8] just as Faucit had written that Ophelia is attracted to Hamlet because of 'a certain loneliness in his position not very unlike her own' (9). Faucit, when she comes to the scene in *Cymbeline* where Imogen discovers that Posthumus has ordered her murder, writes 'My pen stops here. I know not how to write. […] I used to feel tied to the earth' (190). Similarly, Alexandra Gilbreath, writing in *Players of Shakespeare* of the final scene of *The Winter's Tale*, where she played Hermione in 1998–9, also finds it impossible to go on: 'How can I describe this moment for you? Every attempt I make seems inadequate.'[9] One reason why actors' accounts of their performance experience interest us is that they can connect with aspects of the plays – including the emotional response – that seem inaccessible to much literary criticism.

As a Shakespeare interpreter, Faucit was both ahead of her time and part of it. Though she first read the plays in a heavily cut acting edition, she soon recognized the importance of studying the full text and often makes perceptive comments: for example, that although Ophelia in the theatre always exits after her speech at the end of the 'nunnery' scene, it would be more effective if, as in the text, she heard Polonius's unfeeling reaction (15). Yet she acted *Romeo and Juliet* in the Garrick text for years. As a touring star, she could not easily ask actors in another theatre company to learn new lines for her visit, but she cut even more of Juliet's wedding night soliloquy than was usually omitted.[10] She never restored the 'willow scene' of *Othello*, much as she would have liked to play it. No wonder her interpretations often seem incomplete. Though she realizes that Shylock's enforced conversion means that he becomes 'an outcast even from his tribe' (43), her *Merchant of Venice* otherwise is simply a good-natured comedy: Portia likes her amusing French suitor, Monsieur le Bon, and will invite him to Belmont someday (28); the episode with the rings is just a 'pleasant little embarrassment'; at the end there's 'no trace of sadness left in the merchant's heart' (39); Portia will be blissfully happy with Bassanio, who will appreciate how much he owes to her.

The idealization of the heroine, in other words, leads to a simplification of the plays. This had already happened to some extent through the cuts traditionally made in performance. But Faucit's performances could almost be called Bowdlerizations of Shakespeare. As a reviewer in the *Glasgow Herald* (1848) put it, 'her delicacy of taste and elevation of thought have succeeded in banishing from his characters, without the omission of any expression, all that, from the change of manners, sometimes in the hands of others, has become painful. Such is the atmosphere of purity with which she is surrounded, that nothing at variance with it can enter even her most playful conceptions' (Martin, 198). Her performances of 'the types of noble womanly nature' (Martin, 166) reinforced Coleridge and Ruskin's views on the high moral tone of the plays and of their female characters in particular. Ruskin, to whom Faucit dedicated her letter on Beatrice, declared in *Sesame and Lilies* (1865): 'The catastrophe of every play is caused always by the folly or fault of a man; the redemption, if there be any, is by the wisdom and virtue of a woman, and, failing that, there is none.'[11] In April of 1864, Shakespeare's tercentenary, the Archbishop of Canterbury, Richard Chenevix Trench, preached the Shakespeare sermon at Stratford, praising in particular the 'ideals of perfect womanhood' exemplified in Miranda, Imogen, and Cordelia.[12]

Not everyone liked seeing female characters portrayed as the embodiment of an ideal. In October of that year, Richard Hutton, reviewing Faucit's performance as Imogen, agreed that she spoke the poetic passages 'with perfect melody and taste' (61), but complained that 'There is too little of wounded self-love in her later anguish; too little of the rainbow tints of girlish feeling; too little of that variety of impulse which helps us to see how Imogen though a poetic ideal might really have existed' (65). But this 'realistic' approach, which anticipates Bernard Shaw by several decades, fails to recognize the political importance of depicting the drama as morally uplifting in order to reclaim Shakespeare not only for the reader but also for the spectator. It was a time when some clergymen still refused to enter the theatre at all and when, as Tracy C. Davis has shown, actresses were generally equated with prostitutes.[13] It is in this context that one has to understand the admirer whose lines to Faucit now sound so chilling (if prophetic, as regards Shakespeare): 'Prove the stage as it was meant, / Education's instrument!' (Martin, 234).

The moral effect of the stage receives extended discussion in *The Half Sisters*. The old actor urges Bianca, 'You must not only take the head of your profession, but you must make that profession what it has never been made yet. [...]The stage has had glorious actors, but the art has had no priests; all have wanted to be better than their profession, instead of reverencing it beyond all earthly things.' Bianca protests that she can 'conceive no higher motive, or more enobling, than the desire to become worthy of one we love.'[14] The man she loves is violently opposed to women acting, but the man she eventually marries defends their right to have a profession. Yet, disappointingly, he makes no protest when his more rigid sister urges Bianca to leave the stage, and Bianca apparently finds no difficulty in agreeing. If Faucit read this novel soon after its publication, it might well have contributed to her nervousness about marrying three years later. Her story however diverges from Bianca's at this point. She did not give up acting (admittedly, she was now able to pick and choose her roles). Martin understood her need to perform. A theatre enthusiast himself, he told audiences at the ground-breaking for the first Shakespeare Memorial Theatre in Stratford-upon-Avon that Shakespeare 'never would have been so great a dramatist, had he not begun by being an actor' (Martin, 343). Faucit did not speak, but she acted in the first performance at that theatre.

Henry Howard Furness thought that Faucit's book 'outweighs tons of commentaries'.[15] According to her husband, an anonymous reviewer said the same of her acting.[16] Her performances may have lacked the realistic characterization that Hutton wanted, but her focus on the language, accentuated when she performed readings from the plays, was a revelation to many. 'Scholarly men, who had thought they knew their Shakespeare well,' Martin declared, 'admitted that his creations had a light thrown by her upon them far beyond what they had dreamed' (Martin, 120). James Orchard Halliwell-Phillips said that 'what sent him first to the study of Shakespeare was her performance of Imogen at Drury Lane in Mr Macready's Company, and especially the sense, with which she inspired him by her delivery, of the rich and varied music of Shakespeare's versification' (Martin, 401–2). Jewsbury may have been confused about what Bianca should do with her life, but Faucit was not: 'Whatever gifts I had as an actress were ever regarded by me as a sacred trust to be used for widening and refining the sympathies of my audiences, by transporting them into a world larger, purer, brighter, grander than that of their everyday life' (Martin, 405).

Notes

1   Ann Thompson and Sasha Roberts (eds) *Women Reading Shakespeare 1660–1900: An Anthology of Criticism* (Manchester, 1997), p. 7.

2   Sir Theodore Martin, *Helena Faucit (Lady Martin)* (Edinburgh and London, 1890), p. 208. Hereafter cited parenthetically as Martin.

3   Introduction to Joanne Wilkes, ed., Geraldine Jewsbury, *The Half Sisters* (Oxford, 1994), pp. xviii–xx.

4   Helen Faucit, *On Some of Shakespeare's Female Characters* (Edinburgh, 1890), p. 390. Unless otherwise indicated, parenthetical page numbers refer to this book.

5   Mary Cowden Clarke, *The Girlhood of Shakespeare's Heroines,* 1850–2, in Thompson and Roberts, pp. 96–7; Elizabeth Macauley, *Tales of the Drama,* 1833, in Thompson and Roberts, p. 60. I should acknowledge here that much of my knowledge of women's criticism of this period, apart from Faucit's, derives from this excellent collection.

6   Carol Jones Carlisle, *Helen Faucit: Fire and Ice on the Victorian Stage* (London, 2000), p. 19.

7   Jacky Bratton, *New Readings in Theatre History* (Cambridge, 2003), p. 180.

8   Neil Taylor, 'An Actress Prepares: Seven Ophelias', in Kaara L. Petersen and Deanne Williams (eds), *The Afterlife of Ophelia* (New York, 2012), p. 50, p. 54.

9   Alexandra Gilbreath, 'Hermione in *The Winter's Tale*' in Robert Smallwood, ed., *Players of Shakespeare 5* (Cambridge, 2003), p. 90.

10   Carlisle, *Fire and Ice*, p. 281.

11   Quoted in Katherine Newey and Jeffrey Richards, *John Ruskin and the Victorian Theatre* (Houndmills, 2010), pp. 40–1. This last sentence, incidentally, is plagiarized by Laura Stubbs,

in an essay arguing 'That Shakespeare's Women Are Ideals', *Stratford-upon-Avon Herald,* July 1898, quoted in Thompson-Roberts, p. 247.

12 Quoted in Richard Foulkes, *Church and Stage in Victorian England* (Cambridge, 1997), p. 101.

13 Tracy C. Davis, *Actresses as Working Women: Their Social Identity in Victorian Culture* (London, 1991), p. 100.

14 Jewsbury, *The Half Sisters*, pp. 160, 161.

15 *The Letters of Henry Howard Furness,* ed. Horace Howard Furness Jayne, 2 vols (Boston, 1922), quoted in Thompson and Roberts, p. 185.

16 *The Caledonian Mercury,* 5 December, 1843, quoted by Carlisle (113), who suggests that the reviewer was Martin himself.

17

Invisible Women: Mary Dunbar and *The Shakespeare Birthday Book*

Anne Isherwood

King's College London

When she died I inherited my grandmother's library. It comprised a Bible, an Anglican prayer book and a tiny pocket-book inscribed 'Shakespeare' on the cover. This last item was a birthday book given to her by her parents on her twenty-fourth birthday in 1914. As with all such books the days of each month are listed on one page diary-fashion with, in this case, short quotations from Shakespeare allocated to each day. The facing pages are left blank for the owner to write the names of friends and family opposite their birthday dates. My grandmother's life was unremarkable. She was born in 1891, one of nine children, and spent her entire life in Watford and its environs. She had an elementary education to age thirteen, and until her marriage in 1922 worked as a machinist. I never knew her own any books other than those I inherited except for a children's picture history book given to her father in 1869 as a school prize and which was passed on to my brother and myself as children. Nor do I remember her reading anything other than women's magazines passed on by a neighbour, *The Daily Mirror* and *The News of the World*. Her cheap and badly printed Shakespeare birthday book is probably the closest she got to a Complete Works of Shakespeare.

My grandmother used her birthday book throughout her life to record the birthdays of family and friends and other significant events like deaths and marriages. She treated the endpapers rather like a family Bible to note the deaths of her son, husband, parents and a sweetheart killed in action in 1915. There is a poignant note of the death 'aged eighteen years three months' of one of her two sons; he died on 31 March and the quotation against that date in the birthday book is taken from Sonnet 104:

> To me, fair friend, you never can be old;
> For as you were when first your eye I eyed,
> Such seems your beauty still.

My grandmother crossed out 'fair friend' and wrote 'Dear Son'. Her lifelong use of her Shakespeare birthday book demonstrates an important but overlooked method by which Shakespeare was disseminated to a large readership in the late nineteenth and early twentieth centuries. Then, as now, many ordinary people did not think Shakespeare was for them; they did not read Shakespeare or see performances of his plays but, like my grandmother, became aware of Shakespeare's texts and engaged with them by means of secondary sources such as poetry anthologies and birthday books.

* * *

Few will have heard of Mary Frederica P. Dunbar, but in the last quarter of the nineteenth century her books sold in the tens of thousands.[1] She was the creator of *The Shakespeare*

Birthday Book, which was first published by Hatchards in the 1870s and proceeded to sell remarkable numbers over a decade or so. The British Library holds three copies: the earliest, dated 1875, describes itself as the 'third thousand'; the second, to which photographs were added, is dated 1876; and the third copy, dated 1879, is from the 'fifty-ninth thousand'. I own a copy dated 1877, one of the 'forty-fifth thousand'. An American edition of 1883 published in New York by Thomas Whittaker is the 'eighty-seventh thousand'. To put this into context, the nineteenth century's 'best-selling' anthology, Palgrave's *The Golden Treasury*, first published in 1861 had only reached 'the 67th thousand' in 1886.[2] Given these publication figures, it is perhaps not surprising that *The Shakespeare Birthday Book* was not Mary Dunbar's only compilation. The British Library catalogue also lists her *The Triplet of Life; or a Book of Records for Birth, Marriages and Death, with suitable passages for each. Selected and arranged by M.F.P.D.* published in 1883 and *The Queen's Birthday Book* published in 1887, presumably to celebrate and coincide with Queen Victoria's Golden Jubilee.

The publication of birthday books boomed in the last quarter of the nineteenth century. The British Library's catalogue for books published in the century with the words 'birthday book' in the title lists hundreds of titles; there were probably others without the words 'birthday book' in their title. Only two predate 1875: *The Birthday Motto Book and Calendar of Nature* (1871) and *The Birthday Book of Proverbs: consisting of a serious, satirical or humorous sentence, proverb and verse of poetry for everyday in the year* (1872). The themes chosen for these books are manifold: quotations from a variety of writers are used as well as extracts from the speeches of politicians such as Joseph Chamberlain, examples being the *Carlyle Birthday Book* (1879), *The Bronte Birthday Book* (1879) and *The Chamberlain Birthday Book* (1898). Others are concerned with the language of flowers or the birth dates of famous people in history. The largest single group uses biblical texts or devotional writings, with at least thirty devoted to such themes in the last quarter of the century. Next in number are those devoted to Shakespeare. In addition to Mary Dunbar's book, a further ten are listed as having been published between 1875 and 1894, and there were probably many others since such books fall into a grey area between diaries and calendars which are not subject to legal library deposit and collections of quotations or extracts which are. My grandmother's *Shakespeare Birthday Book* bears no indication of publisher, date of publication or compiler and is not listed by the British Library. The nineteenth-century Shakespearean birthday books which the British Library does record appear to be those produced by recognized book publishers; others, including my grandmother's, were probably produced by gift trade manufacturers who were either unaware of or ignored the legal deposit requirements or perhaps simply did not consider that they were publishing a book.

The wide range available is demonstrated in the advertisement printed at the back of the 1879 edition of Mary Dunbar's *The Shakespeare Birthday Book,* which advertises four of the publisher's birthday books and indicates that *The Shakespeare Birthday Book* was a best seller. It also reveals that *The Shakespeare Birthday Book* was available in a large variety of sizes and bindings to accommodate a range of incomes, from the calf bound 'Drawing Room' illustrated edition at twenty-four shillings to the 'Pocket' edition in a 'limp cloth' binding at two shillings. A passage from a review in *Queen* magazine is printed as part of the advertisement, indicating that Hatchards was aiming at the female and gift markets. The book is 'prettily illustrated with photographs', the 'selections are judiciously made' and the potential purchaser is told that '[m]any ladies would be glad of so pretty a depository for the memoranda of birthdays.' For the reasons outlined it is impossible to know exactly how many Shakespeare birthday books circulated in the nineteenth century but it is clear that there were enough for them to be a significant means of disseminating Shakespeare's texts, in particular to women and girls. It is clear that Mary Dunbar's Shakespearean birthday book was especially popular, selling tens of thousands of copies in a period of less than ten years.

* * *

Women anthologists, like female Shakespeare scholars, were rare in the nineteenth century. Most nineteenth-century printed anthologies drawing from Shakespeare's texts and more general anthologies of poetry were either attributed to male editors or anonymously compiled. One notable exception was the Shakespeare scholar Mary Cowden Clarke, whose work Ann Thompson has helped bring to wider attention. Clarke's collection of Shakespearean extracts, *Shakspeare's Proverbs* was published in 1848. She may have had a hand also in another tiny, anonymous anthology published in 1864, the *Shakespeare Tercentary Pocket Keepsake,* since this promoted Cassell's *Illustrated Shakespeare* that used the edition of the plays prepared by Mary Cowden Clarke and her husband Charles. Mary Dunbar was clearly another successful Shakespearean anthologist, although almost invisible because she worked outside the scholarly mainstream.

Mary Dunbar may have been the first to create a birthday book using Shakespeare's texts; if not, she was certainly among the first. Her paratextual note informing readers that her source text was the Globe Edition of Shakespeare is dated 1874, and her book was first published in 1874 or 1875. So far as I am aware, no other Shakespearean birthday books were published before 1875 and the only other contemporary examples that I have found are G[eorge]. Johnston's *Cupid's Birthday Book: one thousand love darts from Shakespeare gathered and arranged for every day in the year,* published in 1875 and *The Birthday Register with Sentiments from Shakspere,* compiled by J. A. K., which appeared in 1876. Others followed in the 1880s and 1890s.

As in all birthday books, the arrangement of Mary Dunbar's collection of extracts from Shakespeare's texts is dictated by the book's calendar format, but the work of selection and placement and the use of paratextual material is not insignificant. The title page declares the book to have been 'edited' by Mary F. P. Dunbar and prints the short epithet 'My blessing with thee, And these few precepts in thy memory'.[3] The title page conventionally identifies place of publication and the publisher Hatchards, but it adds a detail of the publisher's exclusive address: 'Piccadilly'. The following recto page contains a simple dedication 'By Permission' to HRH The Princess Mary Adelaide, The Duchess of Teck.[4] These links with Hatchards, one of London's premier booksellers with a history of supplying books to members of the Royal Family, and the dedication to a member of that Royal Family lent a touch of class to the product.

As in many other birthday books each double page opening covers three days, with the right hand page divided horizontally into three and, apart from the number of the day and the month, left blank for the owner to write on. On the left hand page, also divided into three horizontally, two or three extracts from Shakespeare's texts are printed in each day's section. Occasionally special days that occur on the same day each year are indicated: St Valentine's Day, St George's, St David's, St Patrick's and St Andrew's Days, Hallowe'en and Christmas Day. The extracts selected for the calendar pages are all short, a maximum of six lines and often only one or fewer. In addition each month has its own inner title-page headed with the month and with two or three quotations, often longer than those on the calendar pages and usually thematically linked to the month or time of year. There is also a 'New Year' page at the front of the book quoting lines deemed appropriate from *King John* and after the December 31 section a number of farewell themed extracts.

Around 900 extracts are used and these are taken from all of the plays in the established canon of that time, from the *Sonnets* and from two poems in *The Passionate Pilgrim*. The source text and act and scene details in the case of plays are given for each extract but since there are no line numbers this provides authenticity for the extract rather than a means for readers readily to locate the extract and read more. The organization of the extracts is not generally thematic and only occasionally does an extract seem directly to relate to the day in question. For example, one of the three passages for 1 April refers to a fool with lines from *As You Like It* and one of the three passages for 30 November (St Andrew's Day) refers to Scotland.[5]

Polonius' lines on the title page indicate the nature of most of the extracts. Extracts are edited and part-lines used to create universal precepts; interjections and references to the play are omitted. For example, Pistol's lines from *Henry V*, 'Bardolph, a soldier firm and sound of heart ...' are edited for 26 March to 'a soldier firm and sound of heart'.[6] The extracts are not, as is the case in many nineteenth-century anthologies, primarily short poems or snippets of poetry, nor due to its calendar structure can the book readily be used as a dictionary of quotations. In Dunbar's collection the extracts become proverbs or, as the title page epithet suggests, precepts. All the Victorian Shakespeare birthday books I have examined adopt a similar methodology. Some passages tend to self-select: 'The uncertain glory of an April day' from *The Two Gentlemen of Verona,* say, or Horatio's lines from *Hamlet*: 'Some say that ever 'gainst that season comes / Wherein our Saviour's Birth is celebrated'.[7]

As one of the innovators of the genre, Dunbar seems to have selected material directly from an edition of the works, as her paratextual note indicates. She was a careful and sensitive reader of Shakespeare but she read looking first for 'commonplaces' and second for extracts which delight with their poetic expression. In selecting in this way, Dunbar reinforces the image of a Shakespeare, one created by eighteenth- and nineteenth-century anthologies, who provides a secular scripture, a universal philosopher and moralist with an appropriate thought or 'text' for every situation. Just as the Anglican Book of Common Prayer prescribes daily Bible readings or 'texts', so *The Shakespeare Birthday Book* provides Shakespearean 'texts' for every day of the year, an overlap that is apparent in the titles of some later birthday books, e.g. *The Bard of Avon Birthday Text Book* (1880) and *Birthday Chimes from Shakespeare: A Text-Book of Choice Extracts from the Works of William Shakespeare for every day of the year* (1886).

The pictures selected for the 'Drawing Room' illustrated version of Dunbar's Birthday Book have a narrative of their own. They include photographic reproductions of the Chandos portrait, Shakespeare's Birthplace, John Brooks's paintings 'Shakespeare's Courtship' and 'Shakespeare before Sir Thomas Lucy', John Fead's painting 'Shakespeare and his Contemporaries' and paintings by a variety of artists inspired by the plays, but these are not pictures of the plays in performance.[8] These illustrations present the man created by 'traditional' and imagined biographies of Shakespeare and also a Shakespeare who is the inventor of fictional situations rather than a dramatist, but the primary Shakespeare that the birthday book reinforces is that of the provider of moral guidance.

It would be easy to denigrate Dunbar's presentation of Shakespeare's texts in cosy, readily digestible fragments for a predominantly female readership, but I would argue that the cultural importance of anthologies such as *The Shakespeare Birthday Book* should be recognized. Books of this kind disseminated the Shakespearean text to readers who might not have had the education, inclination, or opportunity to read the plays and poems in their entirety; even in households with a *Complete Works of Shakespeare,* it often sits unread on the shelf. Like my grandmother, Dunbar's readers may only have engaged with Shakespeare's texts through the medium of their birthday books. The invisible Mary Dunbar should be recognized, then, for facilitating an engagement with Shakespeare by other invisible women.

Notes

1   There is scarcely a trace of Mary Dunbar outside the title pages
     of her birthday books, where she is usually identified as Mary
     F. P. Dunbar. I believe that she is the Mary Frederica Pir[r]ie
     Dunbar, born in Aberdeen in 1844, who was the daughter of
     the Reverend William Dunbar, rector of Dummer in Hampshire
     until his death in 1881. Following his death, Mary, who never
     married, and her widowed mother moved to Hampstead where
     Mary died in 1891 aged 47. She is buried in the churchyard of
     All Saints', Dummer. I am grateful to the Assistant Rector Steve
     Mourant and members of All Saints' for their assistance, in
     particular Sheila Harden, Stafford Napier, and Alastair Stobart.

2   Megan Jane Nelson, 'Francis Turner Palgrave and *The Golden
     Treasury*,' PhD Thesis, University of British Columbia, Canada,
     1985. Available at http://circle.ubc.ca/handle/2429/25947

3   *Ham* 1.3.57/58.

4   A granddaughter of George III, cousin to Queen Victoria and
     mother of Queen Mary, grandmother of Queen Elizabeth II.

5

     Jaq. By my troth, I was seeking for a fool when I found you.
     Orl. He is drowned in the brook, look but in and you shall
        see him.

                                              (*AYL* 3.2.279–80)

     A heart can think: there is not such a word
     Spoke of in Scotland as this term fear.

                                              (*1H4* 4.1.83–4)

6   *H5* 3.6.24.

7   *TGV* 1.3.84ff; *Ham* 1.1.163ff.

8   G. S. Newton's 'Shylock and Jessica', 'King Lear' and 'Bassanio
     reading the Scroll'; C. R. Leslie's 'Petruchio and Katherina';
     Daniel Maclise's 'Play Scene' (*Hamlet*); W. Cowpers's 'Othello
     relating his Adventures'; B. West's 'A Storm on the Heath';
     Joshua Reynold's 'Puck' and G. H. Harlowe's 'The Trial of
     Queen Katherine'.

18

'A marvelous convenient place': Women Reading Shakespeare in Montana, 1890–1918

Gretchen E. Minton

Montana State University

The Montana young woman is a splendid type of femininity. She is not only blessed with a fine physique, but is possessed of a moral and mental strength not to be surpassed by the young women of other states.

W. J. CHRISTIE, 'THE WOMEN'S CLUBS OF MONTANA'[1]

In 1890, a group of women from Dillon, Montana picnicked in Sheep Creek Canyon, where one read aloud a letter she had received from her sister. The subject was a Shakespeare club that a group of women had formed in Kentucky; this club was quite successful and clearly inspired the women and their community. The picnicking Dillon women discussed this idea and decided to form a club of their own. As a later club historian puts it, '[t]he letter, the suggestion, the picnic, too, perhaps, furnished inspiration, and the outcome was the Shakespeare Club.'[2] This club, which is still active today, continues to bear the Shakespearean label, although most of the reading list is now more contemporary. Nevertheless, like many of its kind, this club started with the intention of studying the works of Shakespeare.

Reading and discussing Shakespeare's works on the American frontier might seem unusual, but there is plenty of evidence that the early mountain men and pioneers did just that decades before these clubs were formed.[3] As Montana was settled, the women who joined their men on the frontier showed their own interest in Shakespeare, especially in the context of women's literary groups. The women's club movement began in the East in the late 1860s and gradually moved westward; recent studies by Ann Thompson and others have provided a thorough picture of these women's clubs, even the specifically Shakespearean clubs, but insufficient attention has been devoted to the club women of the inter-mountain West.[4]

By the early 1890s Montana boasted clubs in five locations across the state, several of which took names inspired by Shakespeare, such as the West Side Shakespeare Club of Butte, the Dillon Shakespeare Club, and the As You Like It Club of Missoula. The Montana Federation of Women's Clubs, a subset of the national federation, was founded in 1904; many of the clubs joined this central organization, anxious to become part of a national community of like-minded women. Jane Croly, the earliest historian of the women's club movement in America, wrote in 1898 that 'Montana is a State of magnificent distances. Its social life is of but recent date, and its club life among women, of still more recent origin. Its sparse and scattered populations are separated by mountains and mines, by rivers and ravines, by rock-bound territory and limitless extent of plain.'[5] Croly's poetic portrait, however, under-represents the complexity of life in turn-of-the-century Montana. While it is true that the distances were vast, the towns new, and nature more immediate, it is also the case that, by 1900, Butte had a booming economy and a population of 60,000. The women who formed these clubs weren't living in isolated frontier cabins, but instead were inhabitants of growing cities who sought to fashion themselves as well-educated, cultured women rivalling those in the eastern part of the country. Shakespeare, of course, was an important signifier of this project. These women used Shakespeare as cultural capital to foster a sense of community in the new state of Montana – a project that involved both embracing their environment and establishing their role as increasingly politically active women.

In the late nineteenth century, women accounted for a small percentage of Montana's population, even in growing urban centres. Whereas the mountain men had carried Shakespeare as they crisscrossed the state in exploration, the women appropriated him, not surprisingly, as a necessary tool in the domestification of their new home. Montana became a state on 8 November 1889, and eight months later the area's first women's club was formed – in Deer Lodge, which was also home to Montana's first college, established twelve years earlier. Despite these advances, the women were still operating in a decidedly new town; they walked to and from meetings on the street, carrying lanterns, and bought cords of wood so they could keep warm in the Masonic lodge where they met.[6]

The clubs were almost invariably formed by women who had moved to Montana from the East, such as Mary Hooker of Connecticut, founder of the Dillon Shakespeare Club and a relative of Harriet Beecher Stowe, or Mrs Wickes of New York, who 'founded the little society [Helena's Fortnightly Club] in the realization that social and literary activities for young girls were somewhat limited in those years.'[7] Yet the aim of these clubs was not primarily social in those early decades; the stated objective of the West Side Shakespeare Club – 'the mutual improvement of its members in literature, art, and science and the vital interests of the day' – was typical. In the words of Scheil, 'starting a Shakespeare reading club was a way of re-establishing a cultural life from a former place of residence and an important part of community building.'[8] These communities were often exclusionary, comprised of upper- and upper-middle class women who embraced an elite view of literary study. Club members demonstrated their engagement with the material by having Shakespearean quotations memorized for roll call.[9] This oral exercise highlights the clubs' interest in 'right speaking,' for the Club Critic often corrected the women who were not pronouncing words properly.[10] Shakespearean language seemed an ideal subject for elocution, thus his words became the standard by which frontier women measured their ability to *sound* as if they were still in the East.

The yearly programs of these clubs, sometimes relying upon correspondence courses such as Bay View or Chautauqua, and other times developed by the women themselves, covered a range of Shakespearean material, with a particular fondness for the history plays. Club members did their own extensive research and gave papers on topics such as Shakespeare's biography, knowledge of the law, contribution to the English language, and use of history. We might assume that these women had no direct experience with Shakespeare other than memories of eastern life and their own reading, but the boom of these frontier towns meant that Montana hosted itinerant actors and lavish theatrical productions. In Butte's Columbia Gardens, an outdoor amphitheatre, a production of *A Midsummer Night's Dream* in 1900 drew 5,000 spectators and featured 'an elaborate system of transparencies, electrical colour lights … and moving panoramas.'[11] Club members did present papers on such performances,[12] and they also took advantage of actors' expertise. Frederick Warde, for instance, spoke at a reception sponsored by the West Side Shakespeare Club, which the newspaper described as 'one of the most brilliant social functions ever witnessed in Butte.'[13]

The women regularly read parts aloud when studying Shakespeare – a practice that Gere sees as deviant because 'clubwomen could hide under the protective colouring of domestic practices that had emerged earlier in the nineteenth century in response to social concern about the dangerous delights of solitary reading for women.'[14] Such performative practices quickly expanded to semi-public entertainments and performances. In these events we can see the line these Montana women walked in order to embrace both their cultured communities and their 'wild' surroundings – in fact, their environment became a key component of their self-identities. In 1899, Mrs Christie of the Homer Club in Butte was invited to Dillon for a celebration featuring *A Midsummer Night's Dream*, which included instrumental and vocal solos, abridged scenes entitled 'The complaint of Egeus' and 'The Mechanics Planning their Play,' and a tableau representing Lysander and Hermia. Guests then enjoyed a meal where all of the courses were accompanied by an appropriate quotation from Shakespeare: 'The boar will use us kindly' (*Richard III*) for the ham, 'I have not slept one wink' (*Cymbeline*) for the coffee, 'such lack of kindly warmth?' (*Timon*) for the ice cream, and even 'Here's a dish I like not: / I cannot endure my lady Tongue' (*Much Ado*) for this unexpected appetizer.[15] Christie's narration of this creatively domestic approach to Shakespeare is juxtaposed with the physical conditions of life in Montana: 'Saturday morning the storm clouds hovered near and ... burst into a blinding snow storm; but a storm was a little thing to the visiting club women after the cordial welcome of the evening before.'[16] Scheil has noted that, in many frontier clubs, Shakespeare is seen 'as the apex of intellectual achievement even in adverse conditions'[17]; in this case, however, the Shakespearean event manages to thoroughly neutralize the discomforts of the physical environment.

An account of a performance of *A Midsummer Night's Dream* in Great Falls shows both the same interest in food inspired by Shakespeare – 'Now here is one fairy named Peaseblossom and another one Mustardseed. How about

[serving] split pea soup and sandwiches of meat and mustard?'
– and also the same focus upon the challenges of nature.
Participants rode upon a hay wagon to a large field, where
these 'housewives in lacy muslin' had prepared to play all of
the parts (except for Bottom, who was played by an actual
donkey). The wagon became mired in a slough and the
performance was eventually rained out, but not before one of
the actors confidently gestured toward the field and declared,
'Here's a marvelous convenient place for our rehearsal!' The
event was memorialized in a painting by Charlie Russell,
whose wife happened to be in attendance, with the caption:
'*A Midsummer Night's Dream* turns *Tempest*, but *All's Well
That Ends Well*.'[18]

Club programs, minute books, and histories provide a
wealth of information about the study topics that interested
these women most – topics that suggest an active attempt to
relate Shakespeare to their own situations. Although some
clubs did include single and even working women, more were
comprised of married women who were undoubtedly reading
Shakespearean texts through the lens of their experience
as wives and mothers. Not surprisingly, therefore, several
clubs examined characters such as *King John*'s Constance
'as woman and mother'.[19] Flora McNulty of Virginia City
extended this interest to Shakespeare's biography as well,
writing,

> Mary Arden, Shakespeare's mother, was of gentle birth
> and wealthy. Her ancestors are traced back not only to the
> Normans but to the Anglo-Saxons. She brought culture
> and refinement into her husband's family. She was an ideal
> Mother and became the Storehouse from which the great
> dramatist in after-years drew material for his matchless
> pictures of women.[20]

'Culture' and 'refinement' are indeed the operative words
here, for, as Scheil suggests, in such outposts Shakespeare
often became 'part of the civilizing process'.[21]

Club programs also show topics such as the women of *Hamlet*, the girlhood of Lady Macbeth, Shakespeare's ideal woman, laws affecting women, and the strength of Shakespeare's women.[22] The questions they posed tell us even more: 'Which is the truest wife? Catherine, Hermione, or Lady Macbeth?';[23] 'Is it Apparent in Act I, that the Love of Desdemona and Othello holds within itself the Promise of a Violent Future?'; and 'Is Hermione more highly developed than other of Shakespeare's suspected wives?'[24] The West Side Shakespeare Club discussed 'Beatrice's test of Benedick as it appeals to the modern woman',[25] which provocatively sets the stage for how these women related Shakespeare to their own concerns. We are unfortunately left with far more questions than answers, for the minute books almost never provide any details about *how* the club members responded to these prompts. Thus, when the minutes of this club record that 'The members discussed Claudio's treatment of Hero most seriously and earnestly',[26] we can only imagine what the women thought and said, but these self-described 'modern women' surely had some strenuous objections to Claudio's behaviour.

Shakespearean clubs also frequently engaged with contemporary literature – most interestingly, in the early years of the twentieth century, several clubs were discussing and even seeing productions of Ibsen's *A Doll's House*.[27] Undoubtedly characters such as Hero, Hermione, and Desdemona were measured against the example of Nora in these women's minds. Van Orman posits an even stronger connection between the way Western club women read Shakespeare and turn-of-the-century politics, suggesting that '[t]hose members involved with women's suffrage used certain lines from the Bard's plays and from his virtuous women like Portia and Cordelia to strengthen their appeal for the vote.'[28] Although the link between Shakespeare and suffrage is tantalizing, the exact relationship between them in the Montana archives remains opaque. A possible clue, however, lies in the comment by a Dillon Shakespeare club member:

> The wide range of subjects treated [in Shakespeare] has deepened our understanding of people in varied environments, living under varied circumstances with varied background and opportunities, or lack of opportunity, living in other countries and in other times. Our sympathies have been broadened and our tolerance increased.[29]

This broadening of horizons, as it were, paved the way for the women to consider their own positionality. Thus the Dillon club moved from their initial focus on Shakespeare to cover other topics, such as women's suffrage, prohibition, and civil service reform; similarly, the As You Like it Club took up the question 'Should marriage laws be revised?' and read an article entitled 'The Unquiet Sex', which argued that women's clubs are different from men's, because 'instead of being a place for recreation they are only another place for hard work.'[30] The *work* of the reading groups and the *work* of women on the frontier – whether it be ranching, teaching, home-making, or building a society that could counter-act the threatening forces of the wild west – was something that united these women in a shared sense of purpose. As a result, the women became increasingly confident of their own contributions to society.

Women's suffrage gained support much earlier in the inter-mountain West than it did in many other parts of the country; furthermore, Montana elected the first female to congress. This representative, Jeanette Rankin, was invited by the Dillon Shakespeare Club to speak about women's suffrage in 1912,[31] and she spoke in Livingston at the Montana State Federation of Women's Clubs convention in 1913. The event was hosted by the Yellowstone Club, which had been reading and discussing Shakespeare since its inception. The woman who recorded this event, however, makes brief mention of Rankin's talk, and then spends a longer time telling a story about the large group that travelled from the convention site to the local hot springs; participants rode in 'cabs, buggies, wagons and even hayracks', but 'it was up to the hostesses to walk. It had rained in the meantime, and picture ... this unusual sight – plodding through the mud.'[32] This return to Montana's physical environment, even in the midst of a momentous change in women's rights, indicates a complex negotiation between politics, literary study, and life on the quickly shrinking frontier.

The As You Like It Club printed an epigraph on many of its early programmes:

> And this our life, exempt from public haunt
> Finds tongues in trees, books in murm'ing brooks,
> Sermons in stones, and good in every thing.

This idyllic picture of woodland life from *As You Like It* 2.1 highlights the unique position that these Montana women took with respect to their environment. As frontier women, their awareness of nature's role was heightened, because it was integral to how they fashioned themselves. Like Duke Senior's exiled court in Shakespeare's play, these women felt that nature itself – including trees and brooks, but also motherhood, food, and communal activities outside – could teach them a great deal. And yet their narratives suggest a very 'civilized' approach to life in nature; trees were really metaphors for books that pointed the way towards cultured self-improvement. By forming these clubs, Montana's turn-of-the-century women negotiated between public and private space, but also between wilderness and civilization, to form a new identity. Shakespeare, speaking loudly in the American West since the time of the mountain men, helped these women to find their own lady tongues.

Notes

1   *Rocky Mountain Magazine* 2.1 (March 1901), p. 587.

2   Dillon Shakespeare Club history.

3   Mountain man Jim Bridger, illiterate himself, hired a boy to

read him the plays, and pioneer Granville Stuart travelled a long distance just to acquire Shakespearean material. See Richard A. van Orman, 'The Bard in the West,' *Western Historical Quarterly* 5, 1, pp. 34–5.

4   See Anne Ruggles Gere, *Intimate Practices: Literacy and Cultural Work in U.S. Women's Clubs, 1880–1920* (Urbana, IL, 1997); Ann Thompson, 'A Club of Our Own: Women's Play Readings in the Nineteenth Century', *Borrowers and Lenders* 2, 2, pp. 1–7; and Katherine West Scheil, *She Hath Been Reading: Women and Shakespeare Clubs in America* (Ithaca, NY, 2012).

5   Jane C. Croly, *The History of the Women's Club Movement in America* (New York, 1898), p. 767.

6   Deer Lodge Club history.

7   Fortnightly Club history.

8   Scheil, p. 80.

9   West Side Shakespeare Club, 1910–11; Deer Lodge Club, 1890.

10 West Side Shakespeare Club by-laws 4.7.

11 *Anaconda Standard*, 2 September 1900.

12 Fortnightly Club minutes, 16 and 30 November 1912.

13 *Butte Miner*, 4 February 1900.

14 Gere, p. 149.

15 Event programme, 21 April 1899.

16 Frank Eliel, *Southwestern Montana: Beaverhead Revisited* (Dillon, MT, 1966), pp. 74–5.

17 Scheil, p. 83.

18 Elizabeth Greenfield, 'Shakespearean "Culture" in Montana, 1902,' *Montana the Magazine of Western History* 22.2 (1972), p. 50, pp. 53–4

19 West Side Shakespeare Club 18 March 1899; As You Like It Club minutes, 19 March 1907.

20 Ladies' Reading Circle minutes, 2 March 1893.

21 Scheil, p. 82.

22 Fortnightly Club, 1892; West Side Shakespeare Club, 1900–2.

23 West Side Shakespeare Club programs, 1900–1, 1904–5.

24 Fortnightly Club minutes, 7 November and 5 December 1896.

25 West Side Shakespeare Club Yearbook, 1916–17.

26 West Side Shakespeare Club minutes, 16 January 1917.

27 West Side Shakespeare Club, 1909–10; see also Yellowstone Club history, p. 6. Interest in this play was common in women's clubs: 'Writing in 1907, Annette Meakin observed that Ibsen's *Doll's House* has "shown the world that motherhood, even though it be woman's most sacred duty, can never more be looked upon as her final destiny"' (Gere, p. 231).

28 Van Orman, p. 37–8.

29 Dillon Shakespeare Club history.

30 Stephanie Ambrose Tubbs, 'Turn-of-the-century Women's Clubs in America' (MA Thesis, University of Montana, 1986).

31 Ethel Picton, '110 Years of Shakespeare Club'.

32 Yellowstone Club history, p. 9.

19

Remembering Charlotte Stopes

Kathleen E. McLuskie

University of Birmingham

One of the major achievements of the late twentieth-century women's movement has been its capacity for memorialization. From Sheila Rowbotham's *Hidden from History*[1] onwards, feminist scholars have rediscovered forgotten women writers, created a field for future research and authorized the development of new academic disciplines. Never again would women scholars feel women were exceptional intruders in a public world that was, by precedent and practice, male. Among these pioneering canon formers, Ann Thompson, and the much-missed Sasha Roberts, broke new ground by mapping the continuity from 1799 of *Women Reading Shakespeare.*[2]

Two decades later, the new generation of feminist scholars has not only identified many more women in literary and public life: they have also raised new questions about the terms in which we might remember them. They have reminded us that women's roles were not always circumscribed by the 'separate-spheres gender economy' that depended upon 'women's culture of sisterly co-operation and emotional intimacy'. Women's and men's work, they suggest, also took place within existing institutions and social networks; and the achievements that made them memorable might as easily be identified with long and contentious political traditions as in their individual struggles to be heard.[3]

That tension between individual achievement and social context is particularly evident in the case of the late Victorian Shakespeare critic and feminist, Charlotte Carmichael Stopes. Her ten books and the magazine articles from which she constructed[4] them are still in major libraries: her papers are collected in the British Library, University College Library, the Women's Library at the London School of Economics, and recently identified in the collections of the Shakespeare Centre Library in Stratford-upon-Avon. She is hardly 'hidden from history'. Yet the conditions in which she worked and the characteristics of her publications offer an insight into the relationships between institutions and individuals that framed the achievement of this late Victorian feminist Shakespeare scholar.

Charlotte Stopes's work was driven by her engagement with history. She pursued it through archive records and though, like many of her contemporaries, she was seeking records for the world of Shakespeare, she also found a firm connection between the present and the past. Her book on 'British Freewomen: Their Historical Privilege,[5] presented a history of women's legal position that showed the late Victorian struggle for women's rights as a decline from an idealized, pre-modern past:

> There was no necessity for a Married Women's Property Act then, the common custom of the country recognised as justice that a woman should freely enjoy and control what she freely earned or inherited, and Common Law followed common custom.[6]

In later times, as men were increasingly enfranchised, women, in Charlotte's view, became disenfranchised only 'by the use of a single statutory word', 'men' from the new legislation.[7]

By the standards of modern historiography, Stopes's case is methodologically weak.[8] However, it provided both a scholarly justification for some sections of the feminist movement and the intellectual framework for Stopes's work on Shakespeare's women. She presents Shakespeare, quite simply, as the champion of strong women:

Though he paints the weak submissive women because such there were, his own ideal characters in women are always fearless, independent and self-determining'.[9]

Her account of women in the plays often resorts to a fanciful back story to explain their behaviour: Kate's 'unladylike violence of temper' (p. 144) is the effect of being a 'motherless girl'; Lady Macbeth is 'utterly unconscious that she is mentally so far (Macbeth's) superior' as she 'gazes longingly from the high window of the castle of Inverness, awaiting the return of her hero'. Yet Stopes writing on *Macbeth* is also informed by developments in Scottish archaeology communicated to her by 'Miss Christian Maclagan veteran antiquarian of Scotland'[10] (*Industry* p. 79); her account of the *Shrew* includes a discussion of the history of Warwickshire taverns, and she counters Kate's submissive case for men's right to rule with a brisk reminder of her financial contribution to their marriage: 'If this argument has any force, if the *bread-provider* was to rule, she was more entitled to pre-eminence than he!' (Industry p. 149).

These incursions from archival data into the conventional readings of the plays illustrate the tensions between different ideas of womanhood that were being argued out in the feminist politics of the early women campaigners. Unlike the later militant women whose violent protests have framed the memory of the suffrage movement, these earlier campaigners insisted on the long-standing rights of women as workers

and citizens in order to show that 'Political democracy would
not crumble if women were admitted as full citizens, ... since
reforming legislation would simply restore the status quo
ante'.[11] The organizations in which their ideas were discussed
provided Charlotte with a framework for debate, action, and
writing. She undertook a lecture tour of northern towns on
behalf of the Scottish Suffrage Society in 1896, read a version
of her paper on 'Errors in Women's Dress' at an International
Congress of Women in Paris in 1913 and in a 1904 letter to
Richard Savage, the archivist at the Shakespeare Birthplace
Trust Library,[12] she writes of returning from a lecture tour of
Cheshire. At the same time her work with suffrage campaigns
was not her only preoccupation. In the same letter to Savage,
she indicates she is 'writing about the Lighthouses of Japan
for their architect; and on flint implements in memory of my
husband'[13] while also thanking him for information about
'your Hathaways' that have helped her 'trace the fate of the
other "Annes"'.

The frantic dispersed energy of Charlotte's writing,
lecturing and publication connects her to the image of the
'battered hack, struggling to grasp her opportunities in the
expansive but damaging world of journalism'[14] but that unkind
caricature plays down both the important roles of social
institutions in sustaining women scholars and the economic
realities for women who supplemented a meagre income
with publication. Charlotte had established a Shakespeare
Reading group in north London soon after her marriage, and
provided meeting spaces for the existing groups of Women in
Local Government, Women's Suffrage and Rational Dress. In
doing so, she followed the trend, adding yet another social
organization for 'educated brain workers lacking independent
means' to 'the myriad, often overlapping, coteries and clubs
of the late Victorian metropolis'.[15] She had met her husband,
Henry Stopes, at a meeting of the British Association for
the Advancement of Science and she joined Furnivall's New
Shakespeare Society soon after its inauguration, entering
energetically into its debates about the identity of Shakespeare's

patron, the disputed provenance of the Revels Accounts, and the connection between the chronology of the plays and Shakespeare's life.

Though organizations provided an important framework for intellectual work, they offered influence rather than income. In his biography of Stopes, F.S. Boas indicates that the entire first edition of the pamphlet version of her history of women was, 'bought by Helen Blackburn and sent to members of the House of Commons'[16] but none of the money came to Charlotte. In December, 1899, Stopes tells Savage 'I have managed at last to finish my Hunnis Book and Mr Francis of the Athenaeum is going to look out for a publisher for me in the New Year'. Members of the associations might provide some endorsement of scholarly credibility but none of their publications paid for the work they distributed.[17] Indeed, the authors themselves had to sell them. On the 14 June 1911, Stopes thanks Richard Savage for selling 'my few remaining copies of "Bacon-Shakespeare"', a work that was first published in 1888 out of 'a series of articles on Stimulants in the Trade Journal WINE SPIRIT & BEER'.[18]

The social and financial pressures of these conditions are revealed in Charlotte's letters and prefaces where she often seems anxious and vain: quick to be flattered by attention when she could get it and thick-skinned in seeking it elsewhere. An account of the cold-shouldering that she received from the editors of Oscar Wilde's magazine *Woman's World*[19] reveals the over-supply of content in the literary industry of the 1890s: editors selected material that aligned writers to the niche markets in which writing by affluent, or well connected, bohemians could be differentiated from the labours of historical scholars. As Stephanie Green explains,

> Stopes ... was not a glamorous woman of fashion, nor a dazzling and mysterious figure of the European intelligentsia, nor a member of the British social and cultural elite whom Wilde aspired to publish.[20]

Within the world of Shakespeare scholarship competition was equally intense. The continuing Bacon/Shakespeare controversy kept interest high on the lecture circuit[21] but new insights based on archive work brought much higher status. At a time when collections of papers were not all calendered and access depended upon curators, Stopes's letters and prefaces reveal her enraged competition with Professor and Mrs Wallace from Nebraska (who made important discoveries in the PRO), her insistence that 'Mr E.K. Chambers and I seem to have been working independently at the same time on the same papers, as may be proved by our publications'[22] and her frequent complaints that other scholars had enjoyed preferential access to archives.

In spite of these difficulties, Charlotte persevered with her archive research, with publications on the revels accounts, on the first Blackfriars theatre and on Burbage. Her connection with Richard Savage proved invaluable: he identified records, helped distribute her books and may have secured the publication with the Stratford upon Avon Herald of twelve monthly articles that she collected as *Shakespeare's Warwickshire Contemporaries* (1907). In the new century, some recognition came. She wrote to Richard Savage on 24 December 1913:

> Instead of a Christmas Card, I send you a copy of my Burbage book. It has been splendidly reviewed in spite of Sidney Lee's deliberate attempt to crush it in the Times September 18th. The most enthusiastic come from abroad and Professor Feuillerat has an ideal review due to appear in the 'Revue Germanique'.

She was made a member of the Royal Society of Literature (the first woman) and in 1916 was the first recipient of the Rosemary Crawshay prize.[23] She was also pleased to be asked to speak at the annual Shakespeare's birthday commemoration dinner in London, even if it was as a last minute replacement for an absent speaker. She was, characteristically, fully prepared, gave an eloquent account of Shakespeare's 'fortune', and published it as the preface to her 1918 collection, '*Shakespeare's Environment*'. Those forms of recognition endorsed her foundation of the Shakespeare Association in 1914, honoured by an opening 'Lecture by Professor Gollancz'.[24] It may also have given her a minimal financial boost. As she told Savage on December 1914, 'I have no copies, (of *Shakespeare's Environment*) to give away this year, as I did not pay for publication.'

The combination of sometimes humiliating social endeavours, friendships with curators and archivists and tireless re-publication of lectures and papers given in the emerging literary organizations, all contributed to the complex work of establishing scholarly standing at the turn of the nineteenth century. Understanding Charlotte Stopes's case, however, has been made even more difficult because her afterlife is entangled with that of her more famous daughter, the birth-control champion, Marie Stopes.[25] In spite of their mutually unsympathetic relationship Marie asked F. S. Boas to prepare a biography of her mother. She

> put at (his) disposal the large mass of printed and manuscript materials left by Mrs Stopes. The somewhat laborious task of going through these was mainly undertaken by Miss Gwendolen Murphy.[26]

By 1931, Boas could write from the perspective of a more securely established scholarly consensus about Shakespeare, and from the position of a distinguished career in established universities. Though he provides useful information about her education at an external student at Edinburgh University, he also manages her story to make it fit the commonplaces of post-suffrage views of women. He imagines Charlotte's resentment at her brother's education and he presents her connection to the New Shakespeare Society with the arch observation that it was where she met 'kindred spirits, including her life-long friend Miss Grace Latham' (p. 85). A similar condescension is clear in a *Sunday Times* reporter's description of Charlotte as

> A little grey-haired old lady with an old-fashioned Bonnet
> ... she is constantly to be seen in the Public Record Office,
> or in the reading room of the British Museum, where she
> pursues her studies with unbated enthusiasm.[27]

In fact, she was supporting Marie in a court case following the publication of *Married Love*.

Those who knew of Charlotte only through Marie also placed her among the 'Victorians' as they had been characterized by the new progressives of the twentieth century. Marie Stopes's modern biographer, Ruth Hall, seems to have accepted Marie's view that she was brought up in a sexless environment dominated by her mother's restrictive, Scottish religiosity. Hall's evidence came from a touching letter from Henry to Charlotte, in which he laments their lack of closeness.[28] However, the case is clinched by Hall's observation that '[c]ontemporary photographs of Charlotte show an unsmiling, thin lipped rather hard eyed woman, secure in her own rectitude'.[29] The conventions and technical restrictions of early photography, together with the settling conformity of new forms of feminism, had begun to close the case on Charlotte Stopes.

It is unlikely that Charlotte Stopes will loom large in the bibliography or research projects of busy academic Shakespereans today. We would not turn now to Charlotte Stopes's writing for reliable information about Shakespeare. She often got things wrong and touchingly confessed, 'I know that I am a bad proof-reader, and I have no help; my mind is so filled with things in themselves.'[30] She recognized that 'The time for romancing is gone by, and nothing more can be done concerning the poet's life except through careful study and through patient research'.[31] But she cannot resist the lure of the good old stories about Queen Elizabeth attending the first production of *A Midsummer's Night Dream*, about the tale of Katherine Hamlet, drowned in a brook outside

Stratford-upon-Avon or of 'Snug the *joiner...* who had nothing to do now but *to roar*', being modelled on the querulous James Burbage.[32]

Since Charlotte's time, the gap between romance and research had widened and opened into two distinct paths: the one towards academic protocols of editing and historical evidence; the other to the more playful biographical fantasies of 'Shakespeare in Love' or the creative adaptations of 'remotivated narrative'.[33] Charlotte's career nonetheless reminds us of the forces that govern their convergence and separation and may make us rather less certain which path will leave more lasting memorials.

Notes

1   Rowbotham, Sheila, *Hidden from History* (London, 1973).

2   *Women Reading Shakespeare 1660–1900*, ed. Ann Thompson and Sasha Roberts (eds) (Manchester, 1997).

3   See Amanda Vickery, 'Golden Age to Separate Spheres? A Review of the Categories and Chronology of English Women's History', *The Historical Journal* 36 (1993), 383–414.

4   Published as a suffrage tract in 1873, with two expanded editions in 1874 and further short versions in 1907. Stopes's books often reprint earlier published articles. See the list in F. S. Boas, *Charlotte Carmichael Stopes, Some Aspects of Her Life and Work, Essays By Divers Hands: Being the Transactions of the Royal Society of Literature of the United Kingdom*, New Series vol. X, 1931.

5   See Laura E. Nym Mayhall, 'Defining Militancy: Radical Protest, the Constitutional Idiom, and Women's Suffrage in Britain, 1908–1909', *Journal of British Studies* 39 (2000), 340–71, 350–1.

6   *The Sphere of 'Man' in relation to that of 'Woman' in the Constitution* (London, 1907) p. 23, p. 38.

7   *Sphere of Man*, p. 11.

8 Her examples are mostly taken from the canon of famous educated women.

9 *Shakespeare's Industry* (London, 1916) p. 16.

10 Another 'forgotten' woman scholar, see *Oxford Dictionary of National Biography* (*ODNB*) http://www.oxforddnb.com. ezproxye.bham.ac.uk/view/article/34771

11 Vickery, p. 402. See also Jill Liddington, 'Era of Commemoration: Celebrating the Suffrage Centenary', *History Workshop Journal* (2005), 194–218.

12 14 November 1904. This group of letters has recently been identified and has not yet been completely catalogued.

13 The Japan connection came via her daughter Marie Stopes who had spent time there. Charlotte's husband, Henry, was an amateur geologist.

14 Anthea Trodd, 'The Conditions of Women's Writing' in *Women's Writing in English Britain 1900–1945* (1998), p. 44.

15 James Thomson, 'Fabian Society Founders' *ODNB* Reference group, see http://www.oxforddnb.com.ezproxye.bham.ac.uk/view/theme/98085

16 F. S. Boas, *Charlotte Carmichael Stopes*, p. 84. Helen Blackburn (1842–1903) was Secretary of the Central Committee of National Society for Women's Suffrage and, like Stopes, a woman of influence rather than means. See *ODNB* http://www.oxforddnb.com.ezproxye.bham.ac.uk/view/article/31905?docPos=1

17 See William St Clair, 'After the Reading Nation' in David McKitterick ed., *Cambridge History of the Book Volume 6, 1830–1914* (Cambridge, 2009), p. 724 for a comparison between payment for literary writing and governesses' wages.

18 Introduction to Charlotte Stopes, *Bacon and Shakespeare* (London, 1888).

19 The contact had come from Constance Wilde's co- membership of the Rational Dress Society.

20 Stephanie Green, 'The Serious Mrs Stopes, Gender, Writing and Scholarship in Late Victorian Britain', *Nineteenth Century Gender Studies* 5, 3 (2007), 27.

21 See Savage letters 20 July 1896 and 14 June 1911.

22 Introduction to *'Shakespeare's Environment* (London, 1918) p. xii.

23 For a history of the prize and a list of recipients, see http:// www.britac.ac.uk/about/medals/Rose_Mary_Crawshay_Prize. cfm

24 Savage letter 6 December 1914.

25 Their papers are co-located in the British Library and the LSE. Marie's story is in Ruth Hall, *Marie Stopes: A Biography* (London, 1977): for the transformation of Marie's name into the brand of 'Marie Stopes International'. See http:// en.wikipedia.org/wiki/Marie_Stopes_International

26 Ruth Hall, *Marie Stopes*, p. 75.

27 Ruth Hall, *Marie Stopes*, p. 212.

28 Eric Hobsbawm describes the 'silent decisions of armies of couples to limit the size of their families' for economic reasons in *The Age of Empire* (London, 1995) pp. 194–5.

29 Ruth Hall, *Marie Stopes,* p. 20.

30 Preface, *Burbage and Shakespeare's Stage* (London, 1913), p. xiii.

31 *Shakespeare's Family* (London, 1901) Preface, p. vi.

32 *'Burbage and Shakespeare's Stage'* (London, 1913), pp. 59–60.

33 Lanier, Douglas, 'Recasting the Plays: Homage Adaptation Parody', in *Shakespeare and Modern Popular Culture* (Oxford, 2002), pp. 82–109.

20

'Or was it Sh—p—re?': Shakespeare in the Manuscript of Virginia Woolf's *To the Lighthouse*

Reiko Oya
Keio University

*...when we speak names we deeply reverence to
ourselves we never speak them whole*

ORLANDO

While refraining from writing a full-length essay on Shakespeare, Virginia Woolf was preoccupied with the Elizabethan playwright throughout her career and scattered her novels and essays with references to his works. Even more interestingly, the novelist's manuscripts included many important Shakespearean allusions that would be deleted in the course of composition and are missing in the final versions. The following discussion traces Shakespeare's transient appearance in the holograph draft of Woolf's autobiographical novel, *To the Lighthouse* (1927),[1] to show the reciprocal relationship between the modernist writer's refashioning of the dramatist in her creative imagination and formation of her feminist and aesthetic agenda.

Woolf's 'feminine weakness'

In 1900, a 19-year-old Virginia Stephen expressed a sense of admiration and bewilderment that a reading of *Cymbeline* had evoked in a letter to her elder brother Thoby, then a student at Trinity College, Cambridge, and sought his guidance:

> ... I was quite upset! Really and truly I am now let in to [the] company of worshippers – though I still feel a little oppressed by his – greatness I suppose. I shall want a lecture when I see you; to clear up some points about the Plays. I mean about the characters. Why aren't they more human? Imogen and Posthumous and Cymbeline – I find them beyond me – Is this my feminine weakness in the upper region?[2]

Woolf explored her 'feminine weakness' in the face of the oppressive authority figures (Shakespeare and his present-day representative Thoby) further in an unfinished short story 'The Introduction' (1925). In this sequel to *Mrs Dalloway* (1925), the protagonist Lily Everit has just written a 'First rate' essay on the character of Dean Swift (just as Woolf herself had done in the year of the story's composition). The literary self-confidence of this aspiring writer is seriously shaken at Mrs Dalloway's party, however, where she is confronted with a 'young man just down from Oxford' who stands in 'direct descent from Shakespeare'.[3]

Two years later, Woolf's alter ego Lily Everit reincarnated

as the Post-Impressionistic painter Lily Briscoe in *To the Lighthouse*, a novel in three titled parts portraying the life of a large Victorian family on two days ten years apart. In the first section, 'The Window', Lily Briscoe is spending the summer with the Ramsays at their cottage on the Isle of Skye and encounters an unlikeable misogynist Charles Tansley, who whispers in her ear, 'Women can't paint, women can't write' (*TTL*, 45, 80). In the first draft, Woolf elaborated on the theme of male dominance and female subordination by making the woman painter wonder, 'Why, then, did one mind what he [i.e. Tansley] said ...<for being so> insignificant as he was!':

> O it's Shakespeare, she corrected herself – as a forgetful person entering <Hyde Park>, Regents Park, <might wonder why> & seeing the Park keeper was coming towards her menacingly; <they make on dogs must be on a lead;> might exclaim Oh / of course / I remember dogs must be on a lead! So Lily Briscoe remembered that <everyon man> has Shakespeare <behind him;> & women have not.
>
> (*TTLh*, 136)[4]

In the revisionary process, Woolf deleted this passage completely. She would examine the threat Shakespeare poses to women's artistic creativity once again in Chapter 3 of her influential feminist polemic, *A Room of One's Own* (1929), where an 'old gentleman, who is dead now, but was a bishop, I think', is repeatedly cited as declaring 'that it was impossible for any woman, past, present, or to come, to have the genius of Shakespeare' and that 'Cats do not go to heaven. Women cannot write the plays of Shakespeare'.[5] In *To the Lighthouse*, in the meanwhile, Woolf set out to explore a different import the Elizabethan playwright conveyed in her portrayal of her late parents Leslie and Julia Stephen, whose haunting memory the 1927 novel both preserved and laid to rest.

Posthumous fame and male anxiety

In 1895, immediately after the death of his beloved second wife, Leslie Stephen wrote an intimate memoir of their courtship and marriage for Julia's seven children. In it, he portrayed himself as 'a failure' as a philosopher ('I have scattered myself too much. I think that I had it in me to make something like a real contribution to philosophical or ethical thought. Unluckily, what with journalism and dictionary making, I have been a jack of all trades'). This renowned editor of the *Cornhill Magazine* (1871–81) and the *Dictionary of National Biography* (1882–91) reflected on the everlasting fame he might have attained by citing an anecdote about Alfred Tennyson as conveyed by Julia's aunt and pioneering photographer Julia Margaret Cameron:

> In one of the letters upon our engagement, Mrs Cameron asks, what is the value of literary fame? Tennyson, she says, had said that a man of genius might be lucky were he remembered for 1000 years; and what, as the psalmist asks, is a thousand years?... Had I – as I often reflect – no pretext for calling myself a failure, had I succeeded in my most ambitious dreams and surpassed all my contemporaries in my own line, what should I have done? I should have written a book or two which would have been admired by my own and perhaps the next generation.[6]

Woolf made use of, but also subtly revised, her father's self-portrayal to create the protagonist, Mr Ramsay, of *To the Lighthouse*.[7] Like the fictional persona of a dictionary editor, Mr Ramsay imagines intellectual progress as stretching in alphabetical order in which he is stuck at Q:

> But how many men in a thousand million men <press on to> /reach/ Z? One perhaps. And his fame lasts how long? Perhaps two thousand years. And what are two thousand

years <in the long> in the roll of the ages? <And> What
indeed? The very stones one kicks with the toe of ones boot
<have> / will / outlast<ed Plato.> Shakespeare. His little
light would shine, not very brightly for a year or two, &
then be <seen no more, &> merged in some bigger light, &
that in a bigger still. –

(*TTLh*, 68)[8]

As Leslie Stephen's 'my own line' was philosophy and ethics,
Woolf first named 'Plato' as an exemplary 'man of genius' and,
apparently by reckoning the age of the Greek philosopher,
changed '1000 years' to '2000 years'. She then deleted 'Plato'
and, changing the tense from present perfect to future, inserted
(inappropriately, considering her father's, and Mr Ramsay's,
moral philosophical aspirations) the name of 'Shakespeare'
instead. Now Shakespeare symbolizes the masculine desire
for everlasting fame and the insecurity it causes. Leslie
Stephen went on to speculate on the relevance of intellectual
endeavours to the progress of society:

But putting aside the very few great names, with whom I
could not in my wildest fancy compare myself, even the
best thinkers become obsolete in a brief time, and turn out
to have been superfluous. Putting my imaginary achievements at the best, they would have made no perceptible
difference to the world.

(*Mausoleum Book*, 96)

Again Woolf varied her father's argument with recourse to
Shakespeare, making Mr Ramsay wonder,

Whether that is to say if Shakespeare had never existed the
world would have differed very much from what it is today
– whether, then, the progress of civilisation depends upon
great men; whether the lot of the average human being is
<much> better now than it was in the time of the Phar[a]ohs?

(*TTLh*, 80)

The precarious relationship between 'the arts' and common life of the multitudes is scrutinized further in the final version, where Mr Ramsay says to himself,

> that the world exists for the average human being; that the arts are merely a decoration imposed on the top of human life; they do not express it. Nor is Shakespeare necessary to it.
>
> (*TTL*, 40)

Mr Ramsay cannot explain even to himself 'precisely why it was that he wanted to disparage Shakespeare' and come to the rescue of the obscure 'liftman in the Tube'. The conflict between the genius and the arts on the one hand and the nameless mortals and their lives on the other will be resolved in the final section of 'The Window', where yet again the Elizabethan playwright puts in a transient appearance.

Reading Shakespeare's *Sonnets*

In Chapter 19 of 'The Window', children and house guests have retired for the night. With her husband immersed in Walter Scott's *The Antiquary*, Mrs Ramsay looks over her knitting at the books on the little table and takes up 'an anthology of poems, & opened it <anywhere>, laying it on her knee':

> Never reading at all, except in this way, <she turned leaves>, turning leaves, climbing from this to that, she had not any <sense of> security whatever, or any knowledge even, but of names, but only <how the that the lines about the sonnets of Shakespeare> felt it a great relief; & <at the same time had> for she loved <to get at> the repose of the words; & <its> /the/ counterbalancing <of this one that she did feel, more & more> /the soft flowers/.
>
> (*TTLh*, 194)[9]

Shakespeare's *Sonnets* is mentioned once again in the manuscript, only to be likewise deleted later in the course of revision. Catching snatches of the Shakespearean poetry, Mrs Ramsay lapses into a dreamy reverie:

> She was rocking; she was <sa brooding; on the rhythm, in the> /stretched/ mesh <stretched tight> of Shakespeare's sonnets.
>
> (*TTLh*, 195)

Omitting to name the much admired Bard, 'The Window' foreshadowed the aesthetics of anonymity to be developed in Woolf's later novels and essays.[10] In *A Room of One's Own*, Woolf represents Shakespeare as the icon of superior male culture (Chapter 3) and then as the ideal model of the mentally androgynous writer (Chapter 6). On the other hand, in *Orlando* (1928), where the Bard makes a cameo appearance twice anonymously as 'a rather fat, rather shabby man' (8, 47) and then as an elusive 'Sh – p – re' (204), the novelist attends to 'the value of obscurity and the delight of having no name', thinking,

> how obscurity rids the mind of the irk of envy and spite; how it sets running in the veins the free waters of generosity and magnanimity; and allows giving and taking without thanks offered or praise given ... Shakespeare must have written like that, and the church builders built like that, anonymously, needing no thanking or naming...
>
> (*Orlando*, 63–4)

Woolf would expand on Shakespeare's 'sunny impersonality' on her visit to Stratford-upon-Avon in May 1934,[11] and, most substantially, in the unfinished introductory essay of *Reading at Random*, entitled 'Anon', written just before her death by suicide in 1941.[12] With the name of the sonneteer deleted, Mrs Ramsay's readerly act in the final version of 'The Window' already bears out Woolf's theory of anonymity. Mr Ramsay chooses to read Scott due to his concern about his own philosophical fame, for, as Mrs Ramsay observes, 'Charles Tansley had been saying ... that people don't read Scott any more. Then her husband thought, "That's what they'll say of me"; so he went and got one of those books' (*TTL*, 109). Mrs Ramsay is not interested in literary fame ('It didn't matter, any of it, she thought. A great man, a great book, fame – who could tell?'), and quite unconcerned about the author of the book she is going to read: she only 'turned and felt on the table beside her for a book', which turns out to be an anthology of poems and is not attributable to a single author, to begin with. Anticipating the title of Woolf's final literary project, Mrs Ramsay 'opened the book and began reading here and there *at random*, and as she did so she felt that she was climbing backwards, upwards, shoving her way up under petals that curved over her, so that she only knew this is white, or this is red. She did not know at first what the words meant at all' (*TTL*, 110–11, emphasis added). After skimming over 'The Sirens' Song' of William Browne of Tavistock, Mrs Ramsay luxuriates in the lines of Shakespeare's Sonnet 98:

> Mrs Ramsay raised her head and like a person in a light sleep seemed to say that if he wanted her to wake she would, she really would, but otherwise, might she go on sleeping, just a little longer, just a little longer? She was climbing up those branches, this way and that, laying hands on one flower and then another.
>   Nor praise the deep vermilion in the rose,
> she read, and so reading she was ascending, she felt, on to the top, on to the summit. How satisfying! How restful!
> (*TTL*, 112)

In the manuscript version, after reading Shakespeare's exquisite verse, Mrs Ramsay becomes averse to real-life conversation:

> She felt, especially when she had been reading poetry, <that how> /[start?]/ /[nothing?]/ little could be said, & <that>

not rightly; & she was coming to shrink from talk more & more...<who could say what she felt now?>

(*TTLh*, 196)

In the final version, the anonymous poem enables Mrs Ramsay to gather the day's ephemera into a perfect order:

All the odds and ends of the day stuck to this magnet; her mind felt swept, felt clean. And then there it was, suddenly entire shaped in her hands, beautiful and reasonable, clear and complete, the essence sucked out of life and held rounded here – the sonnet.

(*TTL*, 112)

The sonnet now belongs to Mrs Ramsay as much as it does to Shakespeare.

In 'Anon', Woolf regards the Elizabethan play as a collective art form, 'a common produce, written by one hand, but so moulded in transition that the author had no sense of property in it' ('Anon', 395). Men and women 'whose only reading had been the Bible or some old chronicle came out into the light of the present moment' in the Elizabethan playhouse:

They saw themselves splendidly dressed. They heard themselves saying out loud what they had never said yet. They heard their aspirations, their profanities, their ribaldries spoken for them in poetry.

('Anon', 395–6)

Portraying Mrs Ramsay's immersion into the unidentified Sonnet 98, Woolf shows that, like the play, the sonnet could also be a collective art form and could transform 'the odds and ends' of ordinary people into a 'beautiful and reasonable, clear and complete' lyric effusion.

Shakespeare makes the most elusive final appearance in the manuscript of the central sequence of *To the Lighthouse*, entitled 'Time Passes'. Woolf depicts a passage of ten years during which the First World War begins and ends and Mrs Ramsay passes away. Time ruins the Ramsays' summerhouse, prompting the narrator to muse on the futility of human endeavours and aspirations in the face of 'this fertility & insensibility of nature':

> Let the wind blow, let the poppy seed itself, & the carnation mate with the cabbage. Let the swallow build <on the works of Shakespeare; & the butterfly flaunt> in the drawing room, & the thistle thrust up the tiles /up/, & the butterfly sun itself on the faded chinzy<es> arm chairs. <Let the ch broken china be> & all <beaut> civilisation lie like broken china to be tangled over with <the> blackberries & grass.

> (*TTLh*, 228)

Symbolically, Woolf's deletion spares Shakespeare's works from the fate that befalls other human artefacts. Amid the ravages of time, the Elizabethan playwright attains immortality in *To the Lighthouse* precisely by being omitted and becoming an invisible, nameless Anon.

Notes

1   The manuscript of *To the Lighthouse* consists of two writing books and a folder containing loose pages. No other drafts, any typescripts or page proofs have been located. See Susan Dick's introduction to Virginia Woolf, *To the Lighthouse: The Original Holograph Draft*, transcribed and ed. Susan Dick (London, 1983), hereafter cited parenthetically as *TTLh*. I will indicate Woolf's deletions in the holograph by <>, and interlinear additions by //. References to the published version of *To the Lighthouse* are to the Hogarth collected edition (London, 1990), and will be cited as *TTL*. Unless otherwise specified, quotations from Woolf's novels are from this collection.

2   *Letters*, Nigel Nicolson and Joanne Trautmann (eds), 6 vols.
     (New York, 1975–1980), 1:45. References to Woolf's letters
     are to this edition.

3   'The Introduction', in Virginia Woolf, *Mrs Dalloway's Party: A
     Short Story Sequence*, ed. Stella McNichol (New York, 1973),
     pp. 38, 41–2 (3).

4   See also *TTLh*, 137, where the passage is reworked slightly.

5   Woolf, *A Room of One's Own and Three Guineas*, ed. Morag
     Shiach (Oxford, 1992), pp. 59–60, p. 62. References to *A
     Room* are to this edition. For the connection between *To the
     Lighthouse* and *A Room*, see Julia Briggs, 'Virginia Woolf
     Reads Shakespeare: Or, her Silence on Master William',
     Shakespeare Survey 58 (2006), 118–29.

6   Leslie Stephen, *Mausoleum Book*, ed. Alan Bell (Oxford,
     1977), p. 95.

7   Woolf wrote to her sister Vanessa Bell that she refrained from
     reading 'her [i.e. Julia's] letters or father's life' (*Letters*, 3:379),
     though it is unclear whether the 'life' refers to F. W. Maitland's
     biography of Leslie Stephen (1906) or to the *Mausoleum Book*.

8   See also *TTLh*, 67, where the number of years is changed from
     1,000 to 'two thousand', but Plato is still not mentioned.

9   For an analysis of the contrasting reading experience of Mr
     and Mrs Ramsay, see Jane Marcus, *Art and Anger: Reading
     Like a Woman* (Columbus, 1988), pp. 236–49.

10   For the place of Shakespeare in Woolf's aesthetics, see Christine
     Froula, 'Virginia Woolf as Shakespeare's Sister: Chapters
     in a Woman Writer's Autobiography', in Marianne Novy
     ed., *Women's Re-Visions of Shakespeare* (Urbana, 1990),
     pp. 123–42.

11   Woolf, *Diary*, ed. Anne Olivier Bell, 4 vols (London,
     1977–1984), 4: 219–20.

12   Woolf, 'Anon', in Brenda R. Silver ed., '"Anon" and "The
     Reader": Virginia Woolf's Last Essays', *Twentieth Century
     Literature 25* (1979), 356–441 (380–424). References to
     'Anon' are to this edition. For an extensive discussion of
     Woolf's conception of the anonymous Shakespeare, see also
     Beth C. Schwartz, 'Thinking Back Through Our Mothers:
     Virginia Woolf Reads Shakespeare', *ELH 58* (1991), 721–46.

PART THREE

Performance

21

The Vere Street Desdemona: *Othello* and the Theatrical Englishwoman, 1602–1660

Clare McManus

University of Roehampton

In 1996, Ann Thompson considered women's relationship to early modern theatre.[1] Inspired partly by Elizabeth Howe's *First English Actresses*, Thompson focused on the Restoration stage but argued for further research into the traditions of women's theatricality prior to 1660.[2] Seventeen years on, the early modern theatrical woman has become an established focus of critical interest.[3] The grip of the 'all-male stage' on the history of early modern theatre has loosened, and the criticism offers an implicit challenge to periodicity: the identification of a tradition of English women's performance in the century preceding the Restoration suggests that the Restoration actress is no longer a 'first', no longer an exception to a hitherto unbroken rule.

I will briefly explore the contribution of this research to our understanding both of the early modern dramatic canon and of women's participation in its formation. My focus will be Shakespeare's *Othello*, a play that recurs at important moments in the history of women's engagement with early modern theatre. It was performed throughout the seventeenth century: at Whitehall in 1604, at Oxford in 1610, in a Blackfriars revival in 1635, and – famously – on the early Restoration stage. Beginning with the latter, I will consider the place of *Othello* in the history of the early modern theatrical woman and her relationship to Shakespearean 'high tragedy'.

* * *

On 8 December 1660, an unnamed woman took to the stage of the Vere Street Theatre to play Desdemona in a production of *Othello*.[4] Though often depicted as a seismic moment in theatre history – the appearance of the first English actress – the reality is less pioneering. The lack of documentary evidence has given the production an air of backstreet mystery, exploited in Richard Eyre's 2004 film, *Stage Beauty*, but the glamour fades when we note Howe's evidence that both William Davenant and Thomas Killigrew already had women in their companies before December 1660. This anonymous woman (Howe's case for Anne Marshall hasn't been bettered) might be just *one* of the first Englishwomen to act a spoken part for a commercial playing company rather than the actual first.[5]

That said, she may well be the first Englishwoman to play Desdemona, prompting reflections on the play's relationship to the history of women in theatre. The Vere Street Desdemona was not the first woman to appear in a tragic role for an English audience – that distinction went to Catherine Coleman four years earlier in Davenant's 1656 *Siege of Rhodes* – but the unnamed actress is the first woman recorded as speaking rather than singing her tragic part.[6] This, then, is no sea change but the emergence of women's fuller membership of the playing companies as a development of earlier theatrical tradition. The choice of *Othello* and the dynamics of playing Desdemona, however, remain intriguing.

Thomas Jordan, in his prologue, first excites, then reassures, his audience:

> I come, unknown to any of the rest
> To tell you news, I saw the Lady drest;
> The Woman playes to day, mistake me not,
> No Man in Gown, or Page in Petty-Coat;
> A Woman to my knowledge[.][7]

For Jordan, theatrical judgement depends on sight, and in the last decades of the seventeenth century English theatre traded voyeuristically upon the 'ocular proof' of the woman's body. Equivalent clarity had been offered to audiences of Jacobean court masques who regularly saw elite female performers' exposed breasts and thus could judge these theatrical women against the transvestite boys who took female speaking roles in the same spectacles.[8] Shakespeare arguably exploits his own casting conditions: *Othello,* performed without women, constantly seeks to place women under scrutiny. Othello says he would 'see before I doubt, when I doubt, prove' (3.3.193) but, like the play, he is unable to keep the object of investigation in sight.[9] Sight, Evelyn Tribble reminds us, is 'fundamentally subject to manipulation and error', and she identifies Iago as an arch exploiter of this medium, 'recasting' the visual to suit his ends.[10] *Othello* investigates the absent woman who is 'called into being', in Jean E. Howard's formulation, 'by white paint, fabric, and pre-penned words', presenting us with a character who leaps from denotation to 'foregone conclusion' (3.3.430), believing too easily in representation.[11] Ocular proof of femininity may have been available in other theatrical forms – in masquing, song or medicine shows – but, as the slow unpinning of the boy playing Desdemona in 4.3 demonstrates, it was not available in the early Jacobean commercial playhouses. Othello finds himself caught in a radical uncertainty only exacerbated by the representational strategies of the Jacobean stage.

In December 1660, *Othello*'s focus on the domestic and sensational may have contributed to its selection. Certainly, the voyeuristic final scene and the sexualization of Desdemona's role, from her Senate speech in 1.3, to her banter with Iago in 2.1, to her passing recognition of Lodovico's attractions in 4.3, helped set the tone for the Restoration stage's treatment of female players. More directly, *Othello* emphasizes the risk of allowing women into public spaces. The play demarcates and then obscures the boundaries between the domestic and the political, a hazardous strategy the consequences of which are obvious not only in terms of plot but in the play's spatial organization of public and private. Narrowing its focus over the course of five acts towards the curtained space of the couple's bed, the play obsessively polices women's movements. Hence, Iago orders Emilia to 'Speak within doors' (4.2.146), for Bianca the fact that Cassio found a handkerchief in his chamber is proof that its owner is a 'minx' (4.1.152), while he takes her greeting to him on the 'sea-bank' as a marker of her promiscuity (4.1.133). There are sudden switches in the spatial dynamic, as when Cassio waits for Desdemona's return with Othello in 3.4, to be found by Bianca somewhere that, if not clearly indoors, is certainly within the court compound. 'What make you from home?' Cassio asks this new intruder (3.4.169), thrown by the switch from private to public space. Yet the play tests out the limits of female mobility, figuring social position in spatial terms. Desdemona is the daughter of a Venetian magnifico; she may not move as freely as her 'extravagant and wheeling stranger' of a husband (1.1.134), but she expects to use the freedoms of her birth to intercede between Othello and his suitors and she takes such freedoms until patriarchy closes them down. Women's relationship to the public realm is at issue in the play – emphatically so in the December 1660 production when the play's spatial dynamics echo and perhaps exaggerate the unknown actress's move into the public theatre.

I mention over-emphasis because this move in fact partially predates the Vere Street actress. Four years earlier, Catherine Coleman sung the part of Ianthe, another woman who accompanies her husband to a Mediterranean island threatened by the Ottomans only for him to wrongly accuse her of infidelity, in *The Siege of Rhodes*. Davenant and Shakespeare share a source, Knolles's *Generall Historie of the Turkes* (1603), and both texts are concerned with the liminal conflict zone of Mediterranean empire. Under the cover of a semi-private – and hence semi-public – performance, Coleman, daughter of the Jacobean court musician Alphonso Ferrabosco, became the first professional histrionic female singer to take to the English stage outside the masque.[12] Those watching the Vere Street actress play out Desdemona's death in the domestic interior of the bedchamber, only partially concealed by the bed and dressed – assuming faithfulness to the text – only in a shift, might have recognized the similar exposure of Catherine Coleman's body four years earlier. Ianthe first appears in a veil that she refuses to take off for anyone but her husband, declaring 'This Curtain opens only to his eyes' (*1 Siege*, 2.2.85) but her body is progressively exposed until in the fifth entry she is carried in wounded, like a female Cassio, 'in a Night-Gown and a Chair' (*1 Siege*, 5.3.0 SD). This loose shift of light material recalls its use for the boy actor of *Othello* 4.3 and 5.2 and perhaps recurred in Vere Street. These interactions would continue between the repeated performances of both texts in the early Restoration.[13] Killigrew's choice of *Othello* in winter 1660, though, exploits the King's Company's Shakespearean repertory and may have been designed to lure Davenant's pre-Restoration audience to his rival's company.

I propose that the choice of *Othello* reveals the extent to which Shakespeare embeds into his play traces of Jacobean female theatricality that were revivified when the Vere Street actress made her move into commercial, spoken performance. The Willow Song, Shakespeare's variation on an existing ballad, for instance, reflects the labour of female ballad sellers, Englishwomen who sang for money in alehouses and streets.[14]

Similarly, Shakespeare's 'super-subtle Venetian' (1.3.357) is inflected with the virtuosic flexibility of the Italian actress – part of the tradition Pamela Allen Brown has identified as 'the foreign diva played by skilled English boys' – or the performativity of the famous Venetian courtesan.[15]

Critics have sometimes found Desdemona's characterization confusingly sexualized. Distracting herself on the Cypriot dockside in 2.1 as she waits to hear if Othello is safe, Desdemona insists that Iago entertain her with jests. She herself explains that 'I do beguile / The thing I am by seeming otherwise' (2.1.122–3) and this, as much as Iago's later description of her – 'when she seemed to shake, and fear your looks, / She loved them most' (3.3.210–11) – may present an image of deceptive theatricality. If, however, we follow Brown's assertion that jests and shaming rituals provide women with 'cues and scripts, a range of positions from which to speak and act', then – despite her own fears for Othello – Desdemona draws on her social superiority to script a confrontation with Iago on behalf of her serving woman, Emilia.[16]

Iago begins by criticizing Emilia as garrulous and Desdemona insists that Iago expand his worn sententiae on themes that she herself will set. Her command, 'What wouldst thou write of me, if thou shouldst praise me?' (2.1.117–18), entraps Iago in a shaming display of linguistic ineptitude in order to mock him and protect his wife, as he tries and fails to entertain the courtly lady. Desdemona stands up for a wife about to be publicly shamed by her husband precisely because Emilia, a maid in the presence of her mistress, cannot stand up for herself. Iago has taken a slanderous liberty and Desdemona rescinds it by critiquing his articulation of this slander. When she calls a halt to Iago's failed display of wit and calls his 'old fond paradoxes' a 'most lame and impotent conclusion!' (2.1.138, 161), she completes what Brown calls the 'performances and shaming tactics used to combat slander and sexual assaults against women', publicly judging the ensign as she would the courtier.[17] Down at the docks, the elite woman scorns the alehouse and Iago is left raging in an aside against the courtly manners of both Cassio *and* Desdemona. This Desdemona is a more active, skilful character than critics suggest, and the boy who plays her cannot be fully judged in isolation but only in the context of women's theatricalized jesting in the world beyond the playhouses.

* * *

I conclude with a note on one of *Othello*'s future incarnations as annotated hypertext. I have recently edited both texts of the play for the *Norton Shakespeare*, and am, to the best of my knowledge, the ninth woman to edit *Othello*.[18] This number, at once revealingly low and surprisingly high, should perhaps not surprise us, since, when Ann Thompson surveyed the relationship between feminist theory and Shakespearean editing in 1997, she too could count her female contemporaries on two hands.[19] This situation has changed markedly, and this is in no little part due to the trailblazing work of Thompson herself as general editor of the Arden Shakespeare.

Like Samuel Johnson, though I suspect for different reasons, I found editing *Othello*'s final scene difficult going.[20] The repeated editorial scrutiny of the crescendo towards Desdemona's murder was gruelling and destroyed any lingering sense that the editorial process depends on detached objectivity. Recent Desdemonas, notably Zoë Tapper at Shakespeare's Globe in 2007, have fought for their lives, crystalizing the scene's distressing power and raising questions about feminism's role in the theatre, in teaching, and in inter-rogating the functions of tragedy and spectatorship.

Othello's final scene systematically clears the stage of its female characters as the action focuses intensely on its protag-onist. The staging of Emilia and Desdemona's corpses, however, poses challenges for the editor. What, for instance, should an editor do with Emilia's request, 'O lay me by my mistress' side' (5.2.235)? Some editors ignore this, adding a stage direction to remove her body at the end of the scene, excluding Emilia from the final tableau. Others insert a direction that she be moved to the bed to join Desdemona, emphasizing her role as another murdered wife and her mistress's compromised confidante. Another such moment arises when Othello addresses Desdemona's corpse:

> [to Desdemona] Now, how dost thou look now? O
> ill-starred wench,
> Pale as thy smock. When we shall meet at count
> This look of thine will hurl my soul from heaven
> And fiends will snatch at it.
>
> (5.2.266–9)[21]

The formulation of the inserted stage direction '[to Desdemona]' caused me to linger. Faced with the dissonance between character and corpse, with the extremity of Desdemona's objectification in 'monumental alabaster' (5.2.5), I questioned whether she could still be considered a dramatic character.[22] Might the direction better read 'to Desdemona's body', or some other yet unconsidered alternative? Othello's address raises questions about monumentalization, agency, corporeality and identity, and the relationship of actor to role. The actor's personation of the corpse requires skill and stamina and it is arguably here that the transference of agency from character to performer is effected.

That this potential resides in performance is suggested in an eye-witness account of the boy actor from 1610. Henry Jackson wrote of the King's Men that:

> not only through speaking but also through acting certain things, they moved (the audience) to tears. But truly the celebrated Desdemona, slain in our presence by her husband, although she pleaded her case very effectively throughout, yet moved (us) more after she was dead, when, lying on her bed, she entreated the pity of the spectators by her very countenance.[23]

This documentation of the boy actor's corporeal rhetoric has attracted critical attention for its gendered pronouns, proof of the boy's persuasiveness in playing the woman.[24] Strikingly, though, for Jackson the performance of Desdemona's stage life after her death forms the focal point of the final tableau, trumping Othello's suicide. Jackson's response shows how active is the enacting of Desdemona-as-corpse. Jackson's pleasure is gleaned from Desdemona's objectification – and perhaps that of the boy – but he points to the virtuosity of a performer who can plead, move and persuade with gesture, posture and face.

When so much of the difference between the Vere Street Desdemona and those who came before her resides in the fact that she spoke and was paid to speak, Jackson's distinction between speech and acting – i.e. gesture – indicates that speech was only one of many techniques available to the King's Men's virtuoso boy. In this light, the Vere Street Desdemona adopts speech as a continuum with two traditions, those of the theatrical boy and the theatrical woman.

Notes

1   Ann Thompson, 'Women / 'Women' and the Stage', in Helen
    Wilcox ed., *Women and Literature in Britain 1500–1700*
    (Cambridge, 1996), pp. 100–16.

2   Elizabeth Howe, *The First English Actresses: Women and
    Drama, 1660–1700* (Cambridge, 1992).

3   See the work of Sophie Tomlinson, M. A. Katritzky, Eric
    Nicholson, Bella Mirabella, Pamela Allen Brown, Peter Parolin,
    Clare McManus, Karen Britland, Hero Chalmers, James Stokes
    and Natasha Korda.

4   See Howe, p. 19; Judith Milhous and Robert D. Hume (eds),
    Roscius Anglicanus (London, 1987), pp. 19–20. Peter Holland
    gives the date as 11 December but doesn't cite his source:
    'William Shakespeare', *ODNB*.

5   Howe, pp. 23–4.

6   William Davenant, *The Siege of Rhodes*, ed. Ann-Mari
    Hedbäck (Uppsala, 1973). All references are from this edition.

7   Thomas Jordan, *A Royal Arbor of Loyal Poesie* (London,
    1664), p. 21.

8   Clare McManus, *Women on the Renaissance Stage*
    (Manchester, 2002), pp. 111–35.

9   William Shakespeare, *Othello*, ed. E. A. J. Honigmann
    (London, 1999). Unless noted otherwise, all references are
    from this edition.

10 Evelyn Tribble, 'Sight and Spectacle', in Farah Karim-Cooper
    and Tiffany Stern (eds), *Shakespeare's Theatres and the
    Effects of Performance* (London, 2013), pp. 237–52, p. 237,
    p. 250.

11 Jean E. Howard, 'Staging the Absent Woman: The Theatrical
    Evocation of Elizabeth Tudor in Heywood's *If You Know Not
    Me, You Know Nobody, Part I*', in Pamela Allen Brown and
    Peter Parolin (eds), *Women Players in England, 1500–1660*
    (Aldershot, 2005), pp. 263–80, p. 278.

12 See Hero Chalmers, *Royalist Women Writers, 1650–1689*
    (Oxford, 2004), pp. 17–21; Sophie Tomlinson, *Women on
    Stage in Stuart Drama* (Cambridge, 2005), p. 154; Karen
    Britland, *Drama at the Courts of Queen Henrietta Maria*
    (Cambridge, 2006), pp. 91–8.

13 *The Siege of Rhodes* played again in 1661 and at intervals until
    1677: Hedbäck, vii.

14 Bruce R. Smith, 'Female Impersonation in Early Modern
    Ballads', in Brown and Parolin, pp. 281–304.

15 Brown, '"Cattle of this colour": Boying the Diva in *As You
    Like It*' *Early Theatre* 15: 1 (2012), 145–66, 145.

16 Brown, *Better a Shrew Than a Sheep: Women, Drama, and the
    Culture of Jest in Early Modern England* (Ithaca, NY, 2003),
    p. 31.

17 Brown, *Shrew*, p. 9.

18 William Shakespeare, *Othello*, Quarto and Folio texts,
    ed. Clare McManus, in Stephen Greenblatt et al., *The
    Norton Shakespeare*, 3rd edn (New York, forthcoming). See

Andrew Murphy, *Shakespeare in Print* (Cambridge, 2003), Chronological Appendix.

19 Ann Thompson, 'Feminist Theory and the Editing of Shakespeare: *The Taming of the Shrew* Revisited', reprinted in Kate Chedgzoy, ed., *Shakespeare, Feminism and Gender* (Basingstoke, 2001), pp. 49–69, p. 52.

20 Johnson wrote that 'this dreadful scene … is not to be endured': cited in Michael Neill ed., *Othello* (Oxford, 2006), 8.

21 Othello, ed. McManus.

22 Alan Sinfield asked a similar question in a different context: *Faultlines: Cultural Materialism and the Politics of Dissident Reading* (Oxford, 1989), 52–79.

23 Translated in G. Blakemore Evans ed., *The Riverside Shakespeare* (Boston, 1974), 1852.

24 Stephen Orgel, *Impersonations: The Performance of Gender in Shakespeare's England* (Cambridge, 1996), p. 32.

22

Lady Forbes-Robertson's War Work: Gertrude Elliott and the Shakespeare Hut Performances, 1916–1919

Ailsa Grant Ferguson

National Theatre

When Gertrude Elliott, Lady Forbes-Robertson, took on her war work in 1916, she brought with her a career as both a star actress and an activist for women's suffrage. Her mission was to provide entertainments for thousands of soldiers on leave in London who found refuge in the Shakespeare Hut, a huge mock-Tudor bungalow in the heart of Bloomsbury. The Hut, erected to commemorate Shakespeare's Tercentenary in 1916, contained within its walls a purpose-built performance space where, under Elliott's management, some of the era's biggest theatrical stars performed. Elliott's work at the Hut bridged the gap between her leadership of 'women's theatre' as part of the suffrage movement and her pioneering theatrical management.

US-born Elliott became a leading light in the London theatre. In 1900, she married her leading man, the top British actor-manager, Johnston Forbes-Robertson, becoming Lady Forbes-Robertson on his knighthood in 1913. From the early 1900s, Elliott had also been a high-profile activist for women's suffrage as a co-founder, and then President, of the Actresses' Franchise League (AFL). When she took on the entertainments at the Shakespeare Hut, these two strands of her career came together into something entirely new. Her organizational leadership of the AFL merged with her Shakespearean interests and her broad network of contacts among the upper echelons of the London theatrical community. This intersection resulted in a prolific period of performance production in which Elliott burst forth as a theatrical 'leader' in her own right. Her passion for female empowerment had far from diluted, and her work at the Hut formed a fascinating period that led to her artistic and organizational independence as a performer and manager.

Elliott had always been close, through her husband's involvement, to the movement to provide a National Theatre for Great Britain. After decades of debate, the movement merged with the campaign for the monumental commemoration of Shakespeare in London to form the Shakespeare Memorial National Theatre (SMNT) committee in 1908 (while Elliott was busy founding the AFL). However, partly due to financial disagreements, partly to clashes over the nature and function of such a theatre, by 1914 the SMNT committee had got little way towards realizing the plan. With the 1916 Tercentenary of Shakespeare's death fast approaching, the SMNT speedily purchased a site in Bloomsbury with the plan of erecting a National Theatre to commemorate Shakespeare. Just months later, the outbreak of war necessarily put the plans into abeyance; the site stood empty until 1916. However, in March of the Tercentenary year Professor Israel Gollancz, Honorary Secretary of the SMNT, mooted an unexpected plan. He approached the YMCA with the idea that the site could be used, for the duration of the war, to house a soldiers' respite 'hut' in honour of Shakespeare.[1] The Shakespeare Hut, the grandest YMCA hut ever built, opened in August 1916 to instant success. The Hut was always to be commemorative; an emphasis on Shakespeare and performance was at the core of its operational ethos. It contained a large, purpose-built theatre space in need of a manager.

The first mention of Elliott's name in relation to the Hut's entertainments can be found in a letter from playwright Arthur Pinero to Gollancz, dated 30 May 1916: 'Lady Forbes-Robertson should be asked to act as Chairman … for the providing of entertainments at the Hut. She is, there is no need for me to tell you, a clever and energetic woman, and she would have, of course, the help of her husband'.[2] Clearly, Elliott did not require Forbes-Robertson's help. In 1916, she took on the role of Chairman of the Shakespeare Hut Entertainment Committee, and set about organizing an ambitious programme of stage entertainments for the troops. Elliott quickly engaged the voluntary services of a number of female theatre practitioners and formed a regular production partnership for the Hut's performances with Edith Craig. Craig, a noted director and suffragist and the daughter of Ellen Terry, was regular director of the Pioneer Players, a suffrage performance company. Elliott enlisted a number of other performers who had been involved in the AFL and Pioneer Players, including Terry, to direct and perform in her new Hut performances. While far from the agitprop productions supported by the pre-war AFL, Elliott's entertainments at the Hut would have been associated, by those in the theatre and suffrage communities, with their manager's high-profile involvement in the 'women's theatre' movement before the outbreak of war. The Hut's audiences, however, are likely to have had no such notion, since the Hut was built primarily for the use of Anzac soldiers.

Under Elliott's management, productions at the Hut were prolific. In addition to the regular entertainments that were usual for YMCA huts, the Shakespeare Hut included more formal weekly productions: a mixture of dramatic recitals, musical interludes and play extracts. In the style of pre-war suffrage productions, the performances' format was an eclectic mix of music, speech and drama in short 'sketches'.[3] This range of entertainments and Shakespearean-themed events led to a certain freedom from the designation of value to the Hut's stage as a performance space either for 'low' or 'high art', mirroring the eclecticism and 'the refusal to distinguish between ... the value of a play or a sketch, a raffle and a recitation' that was integral to suffrage performances.[4] The Hut became a place where new one-act plays and extracts from upcoming theatrical runs were performed, often before their release in commercial theatres. These were no amateur productions, contrary to the few cursory mentions the Hut has so far received in theatre history.[5] Rather, these productions were performed and directed by some of the most famous practitioners of the day: Ellen Terry, Ben Greet, Martin Harvey and Edith Craig, among others. Elliott set about making a real 'theatre' of the Hut, even procuring painted cloths for a backdrop to the stage,[6] a feature of Craig's production style.[7]

That Elliott staged impressive entertainments on a weekly basis is widely corroborated. In a diary entry for 24 March 1917, Forbes-Robertson's sister, Ida, writes, 'Gertrude [is] running [a] one act ... at Shakespear [sic] Hut ... Gertrude organises a concert every Saturday'.[8] Press references to Elliott's extensive 'war work' at the Hut suggest she was employed full time in arranging these productions. In a 1919 interview the *Oakland Tribune* reported, 'Her soldiers and sailors hut ... was the most popular in London. The hostess, herself, practically lived there ... She inducted every one of her friends of the stage, of the musical world, of the world of art and entertainment, into her service.'[9] The notion of women's 'war work', especially among the upper-middle and moneyed classes, was embodied in the Shakespeare Hut, which was staffed day to day by over three hundred female

volunteers. Its presentation of theatre and musical entertainments was perceived as the fruits of Elliott's patriotic war
work.

In 1908, inaugurating resolutions of the Actresses' Franchise
League had included 'that women claim the franchise as a
necessary protection for the workers under modern indus-
trial conditions, and maintain that by their labour they have
earned the right to this defence'.[10] Such rhetoric of 'work' and
'labour' was central to the AFL, and the wider discourse of the
British female suffrage movement, before the war. The transference of energy into 'war work' was commonplace among
many middle- and upper-class suffragists. The AFL specifically asserted performance as a form of labour, including
themselves in the 'workers' they aimed to represent; the notion
of performance as 'war work' is a small leap to make. In fact,
it could be argued that Elliott's work at the Hut, like the
concert parties at the Front organized by her AFL colleague
Lena Ashwell, served to legitimize female-led performance
and management. These women's productions, then, could
move from subversive to hegemonically acceptable, even
commendable, in the eyes of the public and the government.

However, to read these two distinct performance contexts
as a direct transfer of 'duties' from suffragism to straightforward wartime patriotism would be reductive. The content,
context, and audience of the Hut performances present an
entirely different case from those of the AFL and the Pioneer
Players. While AFL-backed performances were usually limited
to suffrage agitprop plays, the Hut's entertainments featured
a range of drama. The gaze to which the performers were
exposed was neither the spitting objections of the anti-suffrage
lobby nor the primed eyes of suffrage supporters. Nor indeed
were these performances for the critics, who were not invited.
The Shakespeare Hut performances were only open to Allied
servicemen in uniform and, at that, tended to have an even
more specific audience: Anzac soldiers.[11] These men probably
had no idea of the feminist background of the manager of
their Hut's stage. The entertainments were sanctioned by the

YMCA with the specific objective of keeping their men off the streets and wholesomely entertained. By stepping onto the stage at the Hut, women were expected (by the YMCA) to present an image of female virtue, talent, and warmth to a young audience of men, thousands of miles from home and days away from the Front.[12] Entertainments did include male performers, though they remained in the minority, and the management lay with Elliott. Indeed, press reports of the Hut's comforts back home in New Zealand frequently dwelt on the maternal or sisterly welcome at the Shakespeare: 'the ladies set a standard which has a distinctly elevating effect. The mothers and sisters of New Zealand men cannot thank them enough'.[13] The Hut's female identity, created by its middle-class volunteer war workers and female-led productions on stage, aligned it with this 'softer' view of England as mother to the Dominions of her Empire.

In addition to empowering female-led production in the sense of professional 'work', then, the Shakespeare Hut performances could be viewed as a means by which female-led wartime theatrical production became maternalized. The Hut performances were given to an almost entirely male audience of a very young average age, while the entertainments Elliott arranged often featured middle-aged women. Whether a maternalization of female performance is necessarily problematic for the trajectory of the rise of 'women's theatre' supported by the pre-war AFL is debatable. Elliott worked tirelessly at the Hut while also being the mother of four children, in addition to the maternal role lent to her by the press coverage of her care of the young Anzacs at the Hut, so she was a working, rather than a domestic, mother figure.

Yet the Junior Players, a regular group of performers at the Hut, are difficult to delineate within the Hut's maternal function. A troupe of often cross-dressed teenaged girls, the Junior Players provided some of the weekly performances at the Hut as well as taking part in its annual Shakespeare memorial galas. A rare example of the programme of one of the Players' performances, dated 27 July 1918, shows that they performed extracts from Bulwer Lytton's *Richelieu*, Boucicault's *The Shaughraun* and Shakespeare's *Henry V*.[14] Not only were the performers all girls, the Stage Manager and pianist were women. In this way, the Hut offered a space for younger actresses to perform; for example, the Hut helped launch the career of Fabia Drake, who performed there as a young teenager, was taken under the wing of Elliott, Craig, and the Hut's manager, Henry Brice,[15] and went on to become a successful actress and director.

In wartime, the association of Shakespeare with these female-led productions lent a different kind of patriotic legitimacy to its performances. Shakespeare's utilization by the authorities ranged from government recruitment posters featuring Shakespearean quotations to the supply of Shakespearean extracts sent out to men at the frontlines. Framed by textual choices that nodded to the very plays being widely quoted in war propaganda could align the Hut performances with a wartime patriotism. This effect is heightened by the 'foreignness' of its Anzac audiences who were not only new to the country but were 'Dominion' soldiers, many of whom had volunteered for service based on a particular view of a 'Merry Old England' that was their 'motherland' and required protection, 'the "home" we had heard of all our lives!'.[16] Shakespeare's invocation by war authorities was as part of this utopian England that was worth fighting for. However, in the Shakespeare Hut performances other themes emerge from the fragmented version of Shakespeare its stage presented. By piecing together parts of Shakespeare, the Hut performances did not necessarily create synecdochic representations of the plays from which the extracts were drawn nor simply present a patriotic message. Instead, fragments were pieced together to make a whole performance that suited the new cultural and entertainment space offered by the Hut.

A programme for one of the Hut's annual Shakespeare galas shows us the kind of larger- scale performance that took place there. Co-directed by Elliott and Craig, the gala included Forbes-Robertson performing a soliloquy from *Hamlet* and

Jacques' 'Seven Ages' speech, 'Shakespeare Songs' (Maud Warrender), an address by Gollancz, Terry as Portia, scenes from *Henry V* (Junior Players) and a range of other songs and extracts, including scenes from *King John*.[17] Here, in the politics of the production's fragmentation of Shakespearean texts, lies another challenge to the straightforward notion of a maternalized, politically benign, or patriotic version of female-led Shakespearean production. The connection between Elliott's work at the Hut and her support for suffragism prior to the war may be stronger than first appears. In this context, the programming focus on Shakespeare, both as performance and as commemoration, is crucial to the significance of the Hut in the context of gender politics and theatre, not least because Shakespeare was a strong presence in the suffrage movement's press and campaigns.[18] Before the war, Terry had listed Portia among the characters she perceived as Shakespeare's protosuffragettes.[19] Forbes-Robertson's portrayal of Hamlet was also renowned in the suffrage movement, as his presentation of the prince was seen as that of a 'reformer'.[20]

The space the Hut provided for female-led Shakespeare and modern performance formed a bridge between pre-war women's theatre and female-led production entering the mainstream without controversy. While before the war Elliott had been highly active and an organizational force in the AFL, she had yet to move into true independence from her husband in the context of her theatrical career. However, while still working at the Shakespeare Hut, Elliott produced her first self-managed production, *The Eyes of Youth*, in 1918, followed by *Come Out of the Kitchen* at the Strand. After the Hut closed its doors to Anzacs in 1919, she formed her own company and made successful tours of South Africa and, significantly, Australia and New Zealand in the early 1920s.[21] Her stardom in the Antipodes was of a very particular kind: she had gained widespread fame for her war work and was honoured in both countries during her tour. The *Brisbane Courier* reported that she was guest of honour at a formal tea, representing the female war worker abroad; the event was 'to show their appreciation of the war work done by Lady Forbes Robertson (Gertrude Elliott) and, indirectly, of the many other British women war workers'.[22] In New Zealand, she was presented with an award for her services to their country, in the form of a golden Tiki statuette.

The opportunity for female-led theatre presented by the legitimacy of female war work and situated within the unique performance venue created in the Hut bridged the gap between Elliott as organizational activist and as independent theatre producer in her own right, a step hugely difficult and unusual to take outside the 'women's theatre' niche of the pre-war years. Yet the Hut performances are not only significant for Elliott's own career and influence. The continuation of professional alliances that had strengthened through the AFL meant that Elliott's time managing the Hut was a time of freedom for women on its stage, at least in terms of managerial and directorial autonomy. As for Elliott's version of Shakespeare, the Hut had a stage where fragmenting and splicing, singing and joking were all welcome approaches to his texts. Inspired, perhaps, by suffrage performances, perhaps even by music hall and the large-scale galas that were becoming increasingly fashionable, Elliott's management of the Hut's stage was certainly unique. Terry's protosuffrage Portia and Forbes-Robertson's 'reformer' Hamlet met singers, musicians and teenaged crossdressers on the Hut's stage, presenting a female-led version of Shakespearean production that effortlessly crossed the boundaries of cultural forms.

Notes

1   National Theatre Archive SMNT2/1/12, letter from Basil Yeaxlee to Gollancz, 3 March 1916.

2   National Theatre Archive SMNT2/1/12.

3   Katherine Cockin, *Edith Craig: Dramatic Lives* (London: Cassell, 1998), p. 93.

4   Cockin (1998), p. 93.

5   'To mark the tercentenary year of Shakespeare's death, the [Shakespeare] Hut also hosted performances of extracts for the plays – which were given by amateurs'; see Michael Dobson, *Shakespeare and Amateur Performance: A Cultural History* (Cambridge, 2011), p. 92.

6   BL mss/125/1/6/Ellen Terry Archive Z3,258 Letter from Gertrude Forbes-Robertson to Edy Craig, 26 April 1917.

7   Cockin (1998), p. 123.

8   BL mss/additional/62699, Knight and Forbes-Robertson Papers vol. vi, 431.

9   *Oakland Tribune* (USA), 10 November 1919.

10 *Votes for Women* 24 December 1908.

11 Stated on all surviving posters and programmes from the Hut.

12 Secretary of the Hut, G. W. W. B. Hughes (NZYMCA), wrote to his wife frequently of the need for the distraction of 'good' women at the Hut to 'rescue our men from the harpies who infest the streets' (April 1918, from private collection, by kind permission of the Hughes family).

13 Wanganui Chronicle, 28 August 1917.

14 BL/125/25/2/Ellen Terry Archive/ET/D849.

15 BL mss/125/1/6/Ellen Terry Archive Z3.258 Letter: Gertrude Forbes-Robertson to Edy Craig, 26 April 1917.

16 C. A. L. Treadwell, *Recollections of an Amateur Soldier* (New Plymouth, NZ: Avery, 1936), p. 174.

17 BL/125/25/2/Ellen Terry Archive/ET/D439.

18 Susan Carlson, 'Politicizing Harley Granville Barker: Suffragists and Shakespeare', *New Theatre Quarterly* 22, 2 (2006), 122–40 (124).

19 'Shakespeare as Suffragist', *The Vote*, 29 July 1911.

20 E. S., 'Hamlet the Reformer: Mr Forbes-Robertson in His Greatest Part', *Votes for Women*, 4 April 1913.

21 Interview with Gertrude Elliott, *Sydney Morning Herald* (NSW: 1842 – 1954), Monday 25 June 1923.

22 *Brisbane Courier*, Friday, 16 May 1924.

23

Editing Olivier's *Hamlet*: An Interview with Helga Keller

Gordon McMullan
King's College London

in memoriam HK, 1921–2013

It is a truism of contemporary Shakespeare criticism that no play can ever be a 'solo' creation, that all plays are collaborative enterprises, and critics readily acknowledge that this collaborative principle is equally true of films. Yet we habitually refer to the film of a given play as, say, 'Zeffirelli's' or 'Luhrmann's'. In so doing, not only do we, by implication, endorse the filmic auteur, but we may also at times, in not addressing the role of the film-making team as a whole, elide certain collective aspects of the creative process. This short interview with a key member of the team for two foundational Shakespeare films – *Hamlet* and *Richard III*, directed by and starring Laurence Olivier – suggests the enhancement of understanding that can be gained by attending to the creative work of others beside the auteur.

In 1939, an eighteen-year-old German-Jewish refugee, Helga Keller, arrived in London with no money but with a little training in commercial art.[1] Within seven years, by a combination of luck and talent, she had become – as Helga Cranston – the film editor for Olivier's *Hamlet;* later, she reprised that role for *Richard III.* Keller's recollections focus on the process of creation of the *Hamlet* film, offering insights into the planning and execution of the production, and on the role of the editor in the mid-century British film industry. They vividly relate one woman's unique professional engagement in the making of Shakespeare in the mid-twentieth century.[2]

On becoming Olivier's editor

I didn't choose to become a film editor.

I came to England in 1939, and worked as a cook and cleaner in Victoria. I met Maurice Cranston – we were both orphans in the storm – and we lived together; he worked for the Peace Pledge Union, and we went to meetings with Middleton Murry and Vera Brittain. I started working for a cartoon studio, but got thrown out for complaining to the union about the pittance we were paid. I found a job with another animation company, but they got an order from the Admiralty, and I wasn't British enough: everyone was scared of fifth columnists, and they clapped German refugees, German Jews included, into camps on the Isle of Man. Maurice was then working at Bloomsbury House, the central clearing station for Jewish refugees, and he met somebody who had been a film editor in Czechoslovakia and persuaded him to take me on as his assistant. He was a real sadist. In the cutting room, film is very sharp; I ended the first week with bloody hands because he was just impossible, so I had my eye on getting away, and I found a job at Denham Studios with an outfit that was putting English dialogue onto Eisenstein's *Alexander Nevsky*. I learned how to cut soundtrack: it was still the brown magnetic film, 35mm, and I made joins and rewound. In those days there was no way of learning a trade except by doing it. I suppose I had an eye for it. I had a good feeling for rhythm, a talent I never knew existed; I used to envisage the rhythm of a scene, run a blank piece of white film through the Moviola, and do this 'da-di-dum-da-di-da-da-di-dum', and fix the cuts to what I had been humming.

My first job as editor was on a film called *Daybreak* which was a mess – I recut the material several times – and the producer, Sydney Box, brought in Reginald Beck, a superb editor, to make another version of the film, and I worked with Reggie and we got on very well; he always said, 'We argue, Helga, but you argue on the side of the angels'. I learnt a lot about editing from him. He had been technical adviser to Olivier on *Henry V*, and Olivier relied on him very much. But then Reggie left, and Box lost interest in the film, and I sat in the cutting room because they paid me, though I was freezing to death – there was no electricity in that winter of 1945 – and then one day the Studio Manager from Denham Studios phoned me and said, 'Helga, please come next week; we want you to cut Olivier's *Hamlet*', and I put the receiver down thinking I hadn't heard right because I hadn't even finished one film at this point.

On editing *Hamlet*

I went to Denham Studios, and it was the first time I saw Olivier in person. He was doing a test of the Ghost scene. He had the idea that the Ghost would be in negative, so he was made up in negative, black face, white lips, in a white nightgown, and he had a battery hidden in his shirt with a connection to a little lightbulb in his mouth. He had recorded the voice, his own voice, and played it back slowly, and that was the voice of his father, and he was trying to synchronize this negative Ghost to the voice of his father, and we saw it in rushes, and it was terrible, just terrible. The Ghost scenes gave him a lot of trouble, because he wanted them to be special. Before I worked on the film, I had been to Paris with my uncle and had seen Jean-Louis Barrault in *Hamlet*; he did a Hamlet almost in mime, draping himself beautifully in self-conscious poses on the stage. But his ghost scenes were fantastic. He had a very effective sound that imitated the heartbeat, using an electronic instrument called an *Ondes Martenot*. Olivier asked Barrault's permission to use it on his *Hamlet*: he had the *Ondes Martenot* flown over and used that sound, shaving hair from his chest so that he could record his own heartbeat. It's his own heart that you hear as the picture goes in and out of focus, and the voice is his own voice, but recorded from his chest so that the sound of the lips would not be heard.

We used a lot of opticals in *Hamlet*, and effects to make the speech very unreal, and this is a purely technical task of the editor: you have different strips of film, and you have to give instructions to a laboratory where to synchronize, where to fade in, where to fade out, whether to give a lot of light or less light, and so on: very complex. In those days to do the dissolves you had to make a duplicate negative, and you were always aware of the effect, because it suddenly got more grainy; a digital image can be reproduced identically, but you couldn't reproduce the image unchanged back then.

When I saw the *Hamlet* script, I was surprised at how precise the descriptions were of every camera position, every move. *Hamlet* was not a film where you had a lot of leeway as editor, as you usually have in a film where they shoot a master scene from a medium distance and then close-ups, and then you put it all together so that it flows. *Hamlet* was shot in long takes because the dialogue was more important almost than the film itself, and it was very important that the cutting wouldn't detract from the audience's understanding of the speeches. You had these long takes, and then you suddenly had to cut – and to cut is a complete distraction, a displacement of the eye of the audience, so instead of being far away, suddenly you are close up or vice versa, so as editor you became intensely conscious of the cuts. I worked a lot on each cut to ensure that it was absolutely in the right place, and I must say I feel very happy now when I see *Hamlet* and I know a cut is coming and I say 'I must spot the cut', and very often I don't see it because I made it in the right place and it comes and I don't notice it.

There is a scene where Hamlet pushes the Queen onto the bed – the scene where he kills Polonius – but in one shot you see him from behind, with his back to the camera, pushing the Queen onto the bed; in another shot, you will see him, shooting towards him, pushing her. Now there the editor would decide whether he will cut in the middle of the action or let the Queen be pushed and see Hamlet's face and then go to the shot of the Queen only when she recovers from her incredible surprise of having been pushed by her son in such a violent fashion: these are things that an editor will feel. Before an actor will speak, there is a sort of development on his face – it's a reaction – and you would never cut to the actor with the immediate sound of his voice; you will always give him a few frames to see this moment, which of course is the essence of acting, that he is absolutely believable though he hasn't said anything yet, but you see it in his eyes and the way the face is set.

Despite the very pre-planned nature of the script, there was one moment towards the end of shooting that stands out, one for which I got a lot of back-slapping from Olivier. He had visualized the scene after 'Get thee to a nunnery' as the experience of somebody on a winding staircase running up and getting faster and faster and then out above the sea, at which point, high on a turret, he finally speaks 'To be or not to be'. The special effects department had built a circular staircase and had a camera on a metal pole that went along the staircase, but the movement cancelled out the visual effect of the staircase and they couldn't capture it as Olivier hoped. They worked on it and worked on it, and it was quite expensive, and eventually Olivier said, 'Forget about it'. But one day I thought, my God, I have an idea; there were lots of takes that started with the camera panning across empty stairs and then finding actors in the distance, and I wondered what would happen if I made a loop of one of these shots panning across the stairs. So I made a loop and, lo and behold, I had the movement to make the stairs look like they were winding. Later I doctored it a lot with slow shots and faster shots and sped it up by taking frames out of it. But when I showed the first version to Larry, he was ecstatic – as was I, since I had made a creative contribution over and above the usual process of cutting and assembling.

On editing *Richard III*

For *Richard III,* before we started shooting in the studio, we were in Spain shooting the battle, and we were having a script conference because after 'A horse, a horse, my kingdom for a horse' there was a plan for Stanley to ride to Plantagenet to hand him the crown – at the end of the battle the crown is kicked by a horse under a bush, and then Stanley lifts it and rides with it – and already Richard had died several deaths during that battle, and in my – I can't say foolishness, but you can see how much at home I was – I said, 'Larry, you know, you will have to be terribly careful because once Richard is dead and the crown's been kicked, people will be reaching for their umbrellas and raincoats'. He was not amused. He looked at me with those grey eyes, those grey critical eyes, and he said to me, 'Really, darling?' and everybody looked at me, and I felt, my God, why didn't I keep my mouth shut. Yet the next day we were planning the shooting and I was walking in the field and Larry was riding his horse, and he came up to me and said, 'I've been thinking about what you said yesterday, but you see, darling, I want to have a feeling of the continuation of the royal succession, and for me it is very important that Stanley takes the crown to that fool Plantagenet and gives it to him, and that's why think I want to have that scene in the picture'. You must see how generous he was; I had said something to really upset him, and he could have just dismissed it, but didn't do that because he felt that I really meant what I said and had thought about it.

On the director-editor relationship

Not so much has been written about the relationship between the director and the editor. Yet the role of the editor is different from the rest of the crew. The editor is the first real audience of the film and the first critic, because the director will watch the actor or will watch whether what he wanted has come over, but the evaluation of the film's overall effect is with a good editor – and also the dramatic line and value of the scene, which very often is disappointing, or a scene which seemed without any real action or drama suddenly, because it is slightly enigmatic, becomes a very telling piece of film, and it is these decisions or thoughts on the film that a good editor will be able to give to the director. One of the editor's greatest contributions is to make a rough cut, the first assembly of the material, according to how he thinks it should go, and quite often he surprises the director, because there will be a different emphasis on certain things, so the rough cut is the first version of the film and a basis for continuous discussions. The director may not like it, and it'll go back and forth a good deal until eventually there is a version that the director agrees to. The editor will sometimes, without knowing, go quite against the grain of what the director wanted, because he will suddenly discover a dramatic value in a shot that the director thought had already had its screen life, because every shot has its screen life: beyond a certain point, it cannot contribute, and sometimes by holding onto a shot, you get a certain distancing of the audience from what is going on, and sometimes by cutting before that, you'll get a sudden wakening-up of the audience.

On being a woman in the film business in the 1940s

You ask about being a woman in the film business in England in the 1940s and 1950s. There were a few, a very few, women editors at that point, but it's strange – when I think back to that time, I used to sit in conferences and technical discussions and I never felt that I was a woman amongst seven men discussing film quality and certain colour values and so on. I simply didn't feel it.

Everybody said, 'I am sure you were in love with Olivier', because he was handsome. I worked with him cheek-to-cheek on the Moviola; lots of people would have envied that. And there were moments that wouldn't happen now. We had a press showing of *Hamlet*, and there was no place in the projection theatre, so I sat on his lap for two hours and everybody said 'My God'. But I think he was a typical product of British public school, without much knowledge of what to do with women. I remember I had very long hair and I had it all twisted up, and one morning I got up too late and came in with my hair down, and he said, 'Helga, immediately go and put your hair up. What are you going to do? Turn the heads of the whole crew? And distract them?'

I have always said that I had never had reason to be a feminist, because I'd never suffered from discrimination. It was only when I started to direct documentary films for government officials in Israel in the 1950s – they all knew how to direct, they all knew how to edit, and I was only a woman – and there I felt what it was to be one of these dumb creatures for the first time. How did I deal with it? I put my foot down with them. I just thought it was very funny, you know, because it made me realize in retrospect how I had never suffered from it when I was working professionally up to that point.

I have always been quite certain that my opinions were worth as much as any man's.

Notes

1 Helga Keller, who was born in Darmstadt, Germany, in 1921, was a film editor, director and art historian. She moved to Israel in the late 1950s and taught at the University of Tel Aviv. She published several books, including *Kunstpioniere in Eretz Israel* (Berlin, 2008) and a memoir, *Farbig in Moll: Darmstadt-Berlin, 1933–1939* (Darmstadt, 1996). She died on 1 March 2013.

2 This interview has been edited from conversations between Helga Keller and the editor in 2007 and 2010, the latter conducted via videolink before an audience at a conference, 'Olivier's Shakespeare: Violence and Memory', London Shakespeare Centre, King's College London, October 2010. The editor would like to record his gratitude to Sheila MacLean for her painstaking transcription of the tapes.

24

Trusting the Words: Patsy Rodenburg, Laurence Olivier and the Women of *Richard III*

Trudi Darby

King's College London

Patsy Rodenburg is well known as one of the most distinguished voice coaches in international theatre, but for some thirty years she has also been Head of Voice at the Guildhall School of Music and Drama. In 2011 she directed her final year students in a production of *Richard III* at the Bridewell Theatre, in London. It was a production about which she had been thinking for several years, and had tried out earlier in workshops with senior actors in New York.[1] It gave her the scope to demonstrate the fundamental principles of her practice: that actors and directors should trust the text and speak it well.[2] For Rodenburg, this meant keeping the shape of the play intact (albeit some 900 lines had to be cut) and, in particular, keeping the adult female characters – Lady Anne,

Queen Elizabeth, the Duchess of York, Queen Margaret – and their scenes.

I want here to compare Rodenburg's work with one of the few productions that can truly be called iconic: Laurence Olivier's 1955 film *Richard III*. I do so not in any sense that one approach is 'correct' and another 'wrong;' rather, I hope to demonstrate the infinite adaptability of the Shakespearean text – conscious that, as James J. Marino writes, 'Early modern plays were never finished; they were merely sent to the printers.'[3] The comparison shows the development in Shakespearean performance over the half-century or so between the two productions, much of it attributable to Rodenburg's influence.

As the opening credits acknowledge, Olivier's film included 'interpolations' by David Garrick and Colley Cibber. He introduced the silent character of Jane Shore (Pamela Brown), and he cut characters, including Queen Margaret. These interventions were not frivolous but were justified by his views on how to direct: 'If you are going to cut a Shakespeare play, there is only one thing to do – lift out scenes. If you cut the lines down merely to keep all the characters in, you end up with a mass of short ends.'[4]

Olivier based the film on his successful stage production, which had opened in London in 1944 and later toured to Australia. As has been widely acknowledged, this film was close to the theatrical presentation, so much so that the cinematographer, Otto Heller, was initially asked to reproduce theatrical lighting effects and the stage blocking was sometimes preserved.[5] On the whole, the stage cast including John Gielgud (Clarence) and Ralph Richardson (Buckingham) was retained, but there was one significant change: instead of Vivien Leigh, who had played Lady Anne in London and on tour, Olivier cast a relative newcomer, Claire Bloom. Bloom, in her memoir *Leaving a Doll's House*, states that Olivier's approach to her was completely unexpected.[6] However, by 1954 Leigh was beginning to gain a reputation for unreliability, and the young Claire Bloom was 'insurable' as Vivien Leigh was not.[7]

Olivier saw *Richard III* as being a play entirely about Richard; thus, like Garrick, Cibber, and the great actors of the nineteenth century, the play was a vehicle for the lead actor. Acts 1 and 2 were viewed as being mostly exposition and in need of drastic reorganization. 'To start with it's a very long play,' Olivier told Roger Manvell in 1955. 'It's not until the little Princes come on that the story forms that nice river sweep, going swiftly to its conclusion from about half way through the play. The first part up until that moment is an absolute delta of plot and pre-supposed foreknowledge of events.'[8]

This approach influenced how Olivier directed and performed the scene in which Richard, at this point still Duke of Gloucester, woos Anne to be his wife (1.2 in Shakespeare's play,[9] Chapter 2 on DVD). The scene opens with Anne following a small procession carrying a bier on which is a body – of Henry VI in the play but here implied, through clever cutting of Anne's speech, to be that of her husband, Henry's son. Both characters have been killed by Richard in the backstory. As Anne weeps over the 'Pale ashes of the house of Lancaster' (1.2.6), Richard approaches and begins his advance. Anne resists Richard at first, but gradually Richard disarms her, admits that he killed her husband and father-in-law but claims he was driven to it by her beauty. He gives Anne his sword and offers to let her kill him; she hesitates; eventually, Anne succumbs to his rhetoric and agrees, guardedly, to accept his ring. The scene is one of great power, and the audacity of his success surprises even Richard: 'Was ever woman in this humour wooed?' (1.2.230).

In Olivier's staging, this long scene is interrupted at 1.2.114, when Richard says to Anne that he is fit for 'Your bedchamber'. The stage direction from 1.2.147, '*She spits at him*' is brought forward to this point, Anne leaves with the body and Richard speaks a line brought forward from 1.2.232: 'I'll have her, but I will not keep her long.' Then he moves on to intercept his brother Clarence on his way to the Tower, in a scene displaced from 1.1.41–117. After this interchange, the camera takes us again to Anne, now praying at a tomb (presumably her husband's) in a cloister, and Richard resumes his wooing, until Anne accepts his ring. As well as re-ordering the action, Olivier cut many lines from the scene, both from Richard's role and Anne's. As Olivier said, it is a long play and cuts were inevitable.[10] The effect, however, is to shorten Anne's resistance to Richard and the time it takes for him to 'turn' her; the camera closes in on her as she takes the ring and gives undue prominence to the jewellery, as if this is what has finally won her. Between the first and second stages of the wooing (Chapters 2 and 3 on DVD) she has changed from a dark gown and elaborate headdress to a white gown and loose hair, quite virginal in appearance. Among the lines that Anne has lost are some of her most vehement repulses of Richard: 'Dost grant me, hedgehog?' (1.2.104); 'Black night o'ershade thy day, and death thy life' (1.2.134). Also cut is the moment when the corpse's wounds bleed in Richard's presence, indicating him as the murderer. Changing the identity of the corpse she mourns from her father-in-law to her husband also serves to give even more force to the boldness of Richard's wooing and to make her yielding seem reprehensible.

Olivier's Anne is a fragile medieval beauty who is mesmerized by Richard. In this she is not alone, as Manvell noted: 'For the purposes of this production everyone whom Gloucester overthrows has at least the appearance of helplessness.'[11] Claire Bloom caught the character to perfection, and in casting her, Olivier picked up on a quality that she was able to bring to the part at this moment in her life. She says of herself, 'I was lonely, sad, and when I started to work on *Richard III* I was extremely vulnerable ... I was, at the same time, very unsure of myself, and desperately anxious about the future ... to play opposite [Olivier] was like being caught in an electric current.'[12] This vulnerability and uncertainty about the future is inherent in her portrayal of Anne caught in Richard's magnetism.

As we have seen, Olivier saw *Richard III* as centred on Richard and coming to life only with the introduction of the

Princes in the Tower at 2.4. For Patsy Rodenburg, however, the structure of the play depends on the scenes with the women: Anne (Alex Clatworthy), Elizabeth (Kae Yukawa), Margaret (Marianne Tees), and the Duchess of York (Constance Cha). The scenes with Margaret, 1.3 and 4.4, are the pillars holding up the arch of the play's movement. She sees the women in *Richard III* as survivors: witnesses to the horrors of war. Margaret is the only character to speak in every one of the four plays – the three parts of *Henry VI* and *Richard III* – which make up this tetralogy, and the story of the Wars of the Roses is as much Margaret's story as anyone else's. This point was made by Jane Howell in her production of *Richard III* for the BBC TV Shakespeare series. After Richmond has spoken the last line, the camera moves over corpses, first close in and then gradually pulling back to show a pyramid of bloodied bodies; at the top is Margaret, who is laughing as she holds the dead Richard.

Not only did Rodenburg retain the female roles, she also added one. Shakespeare creates two roles, the Keeper of the Tower and Brakenbury, which in performance are sometimes combined, sometimes doubled by the same actor, sometimes played as two characters by two actors. Rodenburg was clear that she wanted one role, so that the character could be seen to develop, and she cast it as a woman (Rachael Deering). This was a production set in contemporary London and, in an age which has seen women at the head of the Security Services (as well as playing M in James Bond movies), this was a credible portrayal. Brakenbury begins in 1.1 as the polite bureaucrat escorting Clarence to the Tower and, when she interrupts Richard's conversation with him, showing due deference to her master's brothers – 'I beseech your graces both to pardon me' (1.1.84) – but insistent. In 4.1 she performs the same duty, preventing Anne, Elizabeth, and the Duchess from visiting the Princes in the Tower: 'By your patience, / I may not suffer you to visit them' (4.1.15–16). In fact, as she reports her instructions, Richard III repeats his dead brother's earlier command:

His majesty [Edward IV] hath straitly given in charge
That no man shall have private conference,
Of what degree soever, with your brother.

(1.1.85–7)

I may not suffer you to visit them.
The King [Richard III] hath strictly charged the contrary.

(4.1.16–17)

Brakenbury's speech is the first indication for Elizabeth that
'the King' is no longer her son Edward. Under Rosenburg's
direction, Brakenbury visibly empathized with Elizabeth and
comforted her; the gesture emphasized that for all its high
politics, this is a play about a family which has seen too much
grief. As the play progressed, Brakenbury became one of the
women's party.

By giving the women's scenes their original scope, Rodenburg
highlighted the building blocks of the play's structure. There is
a strong symmetry in the action, most obviously in Margaret's
speeches. At 1.3.187–302 she curses Edward IV, Elizabeth,
Prince Edward, Rivers, Dorset, Hastings, Richard; when she
returns at 4.4, her curses have come to fruition and her lines
explicitly point up how the second half of the play mirrors
the first:

I called thee then vain flourish of my fortune;
I called thee then, poor shadow, painted queen,
Decline all this, and see what now thou art.

(4.4.82–3, 97)

These speeches are stylized, a vocal representation of the turn
of the wheel of fortune, yet Rodenburg also imbues them with
a warmth and domesticity. This is a queen defeated in battle,
about to leave her adopted country for ever; but it is also the
family elder who has watched the younger generation making
all the mistakes that she did. Her litany of death, in which

Elizabeth and the Duchess join, is all of family members: 'I had an Edward ... I had an husband ...Thou hadst an Edward ... Thou hadst a Richard ... I had a Richard ... I had a Rutland ...Thou hadst a Clarence ...' (4.4.40–6). And whose fault is it? Her relative the Duchess's, who brought Richard into the world and did not control him: 'From forth the kennel of thy womb hath crept / A hell-hound' (4.4.47–8). For all its artfulness, the scene is full of intimacy and humanity; for Rodenburg, Richard may be – is – a monster, but with a family like this, can we really be surprised? Shakespeare provides a sliver of explanation for even the most evil of men.

This is not to suggest that Rodenburg turned *Richard III* into a domestic tragedy, but to demonstrate the depth and insight of the play which emerges when the women's parts are taken at face value. Shakespeare gave seven scenes to the women's roles (excluding the Ghosts of 5.3): 1.2 (Anne), 1.3 (Elizabeth, Margaret); 2.1 (Elizabeth); 2.2 (Duchess, Elizabeth); 2.4 (Elizabeth, Duchess); 4.1 (Elizabeth, Duchess, Anne); 4.4 (Margaret, Elizabeth, Duchess). Act 3, in which there are no women, is the Act in which Richard manoeuvres his way to the throne, with the bustle of meetings with the Lord Mayor, arranging councils – all the plotting that goes with staging a coup. It is the centre of the play and the keystone of the arch of Richard's story, for which the women's scenes provide the support. Rodenburg made cuts here, but still retained all the narrative.

Richard III has an unusually high number of female speaking parts for a Shakespearean play, as well as four children,[13] and none of the female roles is necessary for the progress of the plot. Yet, Rodenburg says, 'playwrights craft better roles for the boy-players' than for grown men because they have to spell everything out – nothing can be left to assumption. And the women in *Richard III* are closely observed when they are away from the male characters. Rodenburg sees 4.1 as a scene in which 'the women gather to bear witness.' Here, the two Princes are housed in the Tower and their mother Elizabeth, grandmother Duchess, and aunt Anne have come to see them but are turned away. In their hearts, they know that the Princes have been killed. In preparing the actors for this scene, Rodenburg told them about incidents in India in which local women would gather outside a house where they thought a dowry-killing had taken place, and bang pots and pans to show that they knew what had happened: to bear witness. This is the effect she was looking for here. Similarly, in the lines in 4.4 discussed above, the women are giving voice to the names of the dead to keep them present. Again, the women are the living witnesses to the slain.

Rodenburg argues that the other women learn from Margaret. Although Elizabeth asks Margaret, 'teach me how to curse mine enemies' (4.4.117), Margaret's lesson to her is how to stop Richard's plans: 'Margaret gives the women courage.' At 538 lines, 4.4 is the longest scene in the play. It begins with Margaret's dialogue with Elizabeth and the Duchess, then introduces Richard and his entourage, and moves into a reprise of 1.2 (Anne is now dead) with Richard trying to persuade Elizabeth to let him marry her daughter. But his rhetoric no longer works. Schooled by Margaret, Elizabeth fights back. In Rodenburg's words, 'Elizabeth is literally fighting for the life of her child', and all the grief for the death of her sons is channelled into anger. In her production, the actors literally fought, using the energy from the lines and the space from an uncluttered stage space in a frightening, intensely physical, scene. Elizabeth eventually seems to give way but, unlike Anne, she is using Richard's deviousness against him. By Act 5 she has betrothed her daughter to Richard's opponent Richmond. Rodenburg argues that Elizabeth's resistance has shaken Richard: he has lost his confidence, and will lose the battle.

Rodenburg's vision of the women in *Richard III* is, then, very different from the tradition in which Olivier was playing. She is quick to say that she could only direct the play in this way because she had an exceptionally generous actor playing Richard (Kurt Egyiawan). Olivier's production came at the end of the era of the great star system of actors. Although it is now much-studied and its filmic qualities appreciated, as

Russell Jackson says, 'Olivier's film of *Richard III* was more of a terminus than a turning point.'[14] Rodenburg's practice is defined by a belief in ensemble playing and connexion to the text.[15] It is her faith in Shakespeare's playwriting skills that enables her to bring out both the intricacies and the overarching vision of a play such as *Richard III*. And what she is teaching her students is, above all else, to trust the words.

Notes

1   Personal information in conversation with the author, as is all material relating to this production; interview at the Guildhall School, 11 December 2012.

2   Patsy Rodenburg, *Speaking Shakespeare* (London, 2002), esp. pp. 1–16.

3   James J. Marino, *Owning Shakespeare. The King's Men and Their Intellectual Property* (Philadelphia: University of Pennsylvania Press), 2011, p. 74.

4   Roger Manvell, *Shakespeare and the Film* (New York, 1971), p. 48.

5   Barbara Freedmann, 'Critical Junctures in Shakespeare Screen History' in *The Cambridge Companion to Shakespeare on Film*, ed. Russell Jackson (Cambridge 2007), pp. 56–8.

6   Claire Bloom, *Leaving a Doll's House. A Memoir* (London 1996), p. 94.

7   Russell Jackson, 'Olivier's Film of *Richard III*: A Legend of the Crown – Among Other Stories' in Sarah Hatchuel and Nathalie Vienne-Guerrin (eds), *Shakespeare on Screen. Richard III*, (Rouen, 2005), p. 235.

8   Manvell, p. 48.

9   All citations from William Shakespeare, *King Richard III*, ed. James R. Siemon, The Arden Shakespeare, 3rd edn. (London, 2009).

10   The BBC Shakespeare production, which is not cut, runs 239 minutes.

11   Manvell, p. 50.

12   Bloom, p. 94.

13   Elizabeth's two sons Edward and York, and Clarence's son and daughter. Rodenburg cut Clarence's children.

14   Jackson, p. 240.

15   Podcast 1 December 2010 at https://itunes.apple.com/gb/podcast/guildhall-school-events-podcast/id332579993 [accessed 30 December 2012].

25

Peggy of Anjou

Russ McDonald

Goldsmiths, University of London

'Of course', said the lofty, superannuated scholar to me during the interval of a recent performance of Beckett's *Happy Days,* 'I saw Peggy'. That phrase has become a kind of byword for my theatrical belatedness: I never saw Peggy Ashcroft on the stage. Knowing only her work in film and television, I set out to explore the nature of her theatrical talent, concentrating on her performance as Margaret in *The Wars of the Roses.* Devised by John Barton and Peter Hall for the Royal Shakespeare Company, this adaptation of Shakespeare's first tetralogy into three parts, *Henry VI, Edward IV,* and *Richard III,* was performed first at Stratford-upon-Avon in the summer of 1963, transplanted to London that winter, repeated along with the second tetralogy in the centenary celebrations of 1964, and filmed expressly for television and broadcast by the BBC in the winter of 1965.

Two topics will occupy my attention. The first is the vital contribution that Ashcroft's participation in this ambitious project made to the legitimization of the Royal Shakespeare Company. This moment in theatre history will be familiar to some readers, but given that exactly fifty years have passed, it seems appropriate to reflect again upon the instability of the company in those early days and to reiterate, in a book on Women Making Shakespeare, the constructive effect of Ashcroft's participation on-stage and off. The second half of the essay scrutinizes a portion of her performance as Margaret of Anjou. This topic, too, is not unknown to theatre historians. But Shakespearean performance criticism was relatively undeveloped in the mid-1960s, and the journalistic reviews, although laudatory and often helpful, fail to provide an adequate account of her achievement. The recent availability of the BBC film, both in the RSC archives and on YouTube, offers an opportunity to examine Ashcroft's Margaret in detail and prompts me to notice and enlarge upon some qualities that make the characterization so exceptional. I shall concentrate particularly on the Molehill Scene, the moment in the second play in which Queen Margaret, her forces having captured the Duke of York, taunts and then stabs him.[1] It should be heartening to certain readers, and appropriate in a book honouring a retiring colleague, that Peggy Ashcroft, at fifty-five, was too old to do what she did in *The Wars of the Roses*. The improbability is part of her triumph and one of the keys to the success of the project at large.

Making a company

The authority that Ashcroft commanded in the English theatre was invaluable to Peter Hall's efforts to convert the haphazard Stratford programme into the Royal Shakespeare Company, to attract a stable group of actors with three-year contracts, to create a London base, and to secure public funding. She was the first performer he asked, and she instantly agreed. According to Hall, 'that we had one of the undisputed leaders of the profession endorsing the whole scheme meant that other actors, other directors followed. The creation of the RSC owes a great deal to her presence'.[2] Her ongoing contribution was critical given the shaky beginnings of the company. The first three years were not as bright as its subsequent triumphs might suggest, and apart from a couple of extraordinary productions – e.g. Michael Elliott's direction of Vanessa Redgrave in *As You Like It* and the Peter Brook / Paul Scofield *King Lear* – the initial seasons hardly amounted to a string of hits.

Ashcroft's cultural sovereignty also assisted Hall in his scheme to obtain government funding for the company. This was a pressing concern in the early 1960s – witness the programme for the Aldwych performances of *The Wars of the Roses* in the winter of 1963–4. Placed in a central position, along with the cast list, a textual note, and other such necessary business, is a sidebar making a frank demand for state subsidy.

> Why does a company playing to such massive audiences need subsidising? The system of presenting plays in repertoire … is very expensive … On the continent it has been accepted for years that this sort of theatre needs heavy State subsidy … But the idea of such a company is new to this country.

The ambition, energy, and imagination exhibited by Hall and his forces in those early years – *The Wars of the Roses* being a primary illustration – helped to attract government funding and thus to stabilize the company. Ashcroft's role, in several senses, was crucial.

The narrative of how the project came into being is well known. Hall and Barton since their days at Cambridge had wanted to find a way of mounting the early history plays, but remained doubtful about commercial viability. Hall had more than once approached Peter Brook, but when he countered with the proposal that Hall himself stage them, Hall invited Barton to prepare a script; assigned John Bury to create a distinctive, workable design; cast – after Ashcroft

– many young actors who had emerged in the company, e.g. Ian Holm, Janet Suzman, David Warner; prepared to begin rehearsals; watched his marriage to Leslie Caron disintegrate; and promptly suffered a nervous collapse. Ashcroft was engaged personally in the rescue operation, summoning Brook from Paris to provide support, advising that return to work was the road to health, and equipping the rehearsal studio with a chaise longue and an attending physician. Ashcroft, it is said, also suggested the idea of performing all three parts on one marathon day, which was done five times that season. The opening, slightly delayed, took place in Stratford in July 1963, the first two plays in one day. Bernard Levin declared it 'a landmark and beacon in the post-war English theatre and a triumphant vindication of Mr Hall's policy'.[3]

Making a character

The overriding fact about Ashcroft's performance is her range, mostly of age, but also of emotion. Her Margaret, according to Philip Hope-Wallace,

> skipped onto the Aldwych stage, a lightfooted, ginger, sub-deb sub-bitch at about 11:35 a.m. and was last seen, a bedraggled crone with glittering eye, rambling and cussing with undiminished fury 11 hours later, having grown before our eyes into a vexed and contumacious queen, a battle-axe and a maniac monster of rage and cruelty.[4]

The transitions were aided by the costumer and wig-maker. As the young Princess, she wears long hair streaming down her back from a gold circlet on the head; as Henry's young queen her hair is plaited into side circles, like Princess Leia in *Star Wars;* on the battlefield her head is hidden under chain mail; and in *Richard III* the coiffure is a gray fright wig, teased and out of control.

An essential feature is her voice. The formidable Kenneth Tynan had frequently hectored Ashcroft in print for her 'Kensington vowels', code, probably, for old-fashioned acting that he sought to replace, and in 1958 had complained that 'there is not in her soul the iron' required by a character she played. But he thought her Margaret 'balefully persuasive'.[5] In creating the French princess, AKA the 'she-wolf of France', Ashcroft manipulated the pitch of her voice, deploying a higher, lighter tone in the early scenes and lowering the tonal range practically to a female baritone for the deposed lunatic. For an actress famous for vocal sweetness, a purr which suited many of her West End characters and which audiences expected, such baritonal pitch and the fierceness of utterance made a strong impression. Repeated modulation proved taxing, however, given the schedule of performances. As she explained in an early interview, 'What is sometimes worrying is when I play an old woman at night and then the young girl the next day. The voice is lower for the old woman. Overnight it retains its depth, and that has to be watched'.[6]

The other celebrated aspect of her speech, dominant throughout, was the affectation of a French 'r', or rather a conversion of the English 'r' into a 'w'. Ashcroft devised the trick as a signal of her Gallic heritage, a way of emphasizing her isolation from the English court; and as her sojourn in England continues, the tic diminishes slightly, as presumably she becomes more at home and more practiced at English. At the dress rehearsal, Peter Hall advised her that while the accent had allowed her to imagine the character at first, she no longer needed it, but she retained it anyway, and it became one of the hallmarks of her performance. Her deformation of the 'r' is striking at her first entrance, the encounter with Suffolk who, considering her suitability for marriage to King Henry, vows to approve the union and to take her for his mistress. It is a flirtatious exchange, much of its sexy humour deriving from her play with the noun 'ransom' ('wansom'), which she speaks in three successive lines and then revisits with a wink at the audience on 'random' ('He talks at wandom; sure, the man is mad').

The Molehill Scene (Scene 36 in the Barton script; 1.4 of *3 Henry VI*) is certainly a showpiece for her extraordinary talents, but more than that it is an epitome of the whole, in which Ashcroft conveys the complexity of the role perhaps more persuasively than anywhere else in the script. Throughout the cycle she contributes many cherishable moments, to be sure: the scene in which she must conceal from Henry her glee at her having disposed of the faithful Duke Humphrey, or the contest of lamentation with Queen Elizabeth and the Duchess of Gloucester in *Richard III*. But in the Molehill Scene we witness both the extent of her violent malice and early intimations of her capacity to be injured. Her sexual and political scheming and her disloyalty to Henry manifest themselves early in the show, but the duel with York exposes her bloodthirstiness, her triumphant glee at being able to terrorize her enemy with the bloody napkin, the ghastly relic of infanticide.

It is a commonplace that great acting differs from good in that the supreme performer is as committed when silent as when speaking. Here Ashcroft's interactions with York and responses to his meltdown attest to the completeness of her characterization. His curse is lengthy, and throughout the cinematic close-ups mostly focus on the speaker, but we see enough of Margaret's reaction to feel the brute power, the practically psychotic ruthlessness with which she treats the enemy. There is a frankness in her relish at York's suffering, as when she demands visible and aural evidence of his misery: 'Stamp, rave and fret, that I may sing and dance'. But, surprisingly, she reacts to his curse with an unwonted vulnerability. As he assaults her verbally, she initially gestures to him with inverted palms and beckoning fingers, as if to say 'come on, give me your worst', and as he gains traction she seems to intone a high-pitched *vocalize* over his lament, as if his emotional outburst were arousing her, the wordless hum something like a hysterical version of the familiar laugh.

Just previously Sinden, responding to her concluding insults ('O, 'tis a fault too, too unpardonable'), had begun to emit a low moan beneath her words. Without overstating, we might describe the contest as suggesting fierce sexual engagement, a struggle between two forceful, passionate beasts. Her ironic disgust at his contumely also expresses itself in a gleeful cackle; but as York builds to his curse, weeping, howling over the murder of young Rutland ('That face of his the hungry cannibals / Would not have touched'), Margaret's hysterical joy, so her face suggests, is gradually converted to anxiety, perhaps even latent sympathy. We see, and it may be that she feels, intimations of the horror she will know when she watches her own boy stabbed by York's 'mess of sons' in Scene 51. By the end of his attack she is reeling, and Exeter's sympathy for the doomed father's pain, a compassionate response that Margaret brusquely dismisses, patently represents a displacement of her own emotional damage.[7]

The verbal skills for which Ashcroft was famous account for her power in the scene and are audible in both the audiotape and the televised version. (One hears slight differences between the two performances, but her delivery of most lines is similar.) The overriding quality is her capacity for conveying the meaning of the verse. Having identified and absorbed those poetic and grammatical turns that shape the content of a phrase, a sentence, or a passage, she is able to highlight the trope and thus clarify the sense for the auditor. Repetitions sound especially juicy because she uses them semiotically, usually to mock her victim:

What, was it you that would be England's King?
Was't you that revell'd in our parliament [...]

Having placed the mock crown on his head – an especially grotesque moment, since York's battered head is bloody and the crown now nothing but crumpled paper – she ceremoniously introduces him, hammering the repetitions with ironic force:

Ay, marry, sir, now looks he like a King!
Ay, *this is he* [pause] that took King Henry's *chair*;
And *this is he* [pause] was his adopted *heir*.

This sensitivity to the rhetorical substructure bespeaks her instinct for the musicality of the verse, a gift that reviewers had been applauding for decades. Her attention to vital consonants and vowels animates line after line (note particularly the *m* and *l* sounds in 'Come, make him stand upon this molehill here'), and she unequivocally endorses the Peter Hall principle of verse speaking: although most lines are end-stopped, characteristic of early Shakespeare, even those that are not receive a slight pause at the end. All these techniques acknowledge and delight in the artificiality of the text while at the same time promoting its meaning.

One of her favourite devices is modulation of pitch. At this mid-point in the cycle she mostly sustains a medium register, something between the higher reaches of the girlish princess and the darker depths of the vengeful crone. There is, moreover, an unusual degree of steel in the sound, surprising in one famous for 'the moonlit softness of her voice'.[8] This medium range allows her to achieve emphasis, surprise, and other such effects. But the most telling manipulations of pitch are the quiet leaps into the upper register: the lift on 'England's **King**?'; the squeak on 'And made a [tiny pause] **pweachment** of his high descent'; the gleefully high 'valiant **cwook**-back pwodigy'; the high giggle on '**Alas**, poor York'; and especially the ascent in the arching phrase 'York cannot speak, **unless he wear a cwown**'. Descent into the lower register is less frequent but is sometimes combined with an emptying of the tone (see below) and usually signals a logical shift.

She also introduces shifts in pace and volume. Most of these lines are delivered at a moderate tempo, since there is a stentorian quality to her taunting of York, but variations occur. She takes a ritard on 'Where are your mess of sons to back you now?', and sometimes she races forward, as on 'Why art thou patient, man? thou shouldst be mad; / And I to make thee mad, do mock thee thus'. She also makes brilliant use of short stops, as in 'Or, with the west, [pause] where [pause] is your darling, [pause] Wutland?' The three words that open her first three speeches, the imperatives 'Yield' and 'Come' followed by the ironic 'What', are relatively high-pitched but come straight from the diaphragm, almost shouted, thus establishing her merciless command. Occasionally she suddenly drops the volume, as in her revelation of Rutland's murder: 'Look, [basso] **York**, I stain'd this napkin ...' Lowered volume imparts extra venom to the question, 'But how is it that great Plantagenet / Is crown'd so soon, and broke his solemn oath?' Especially effective is the quietly spoken word combined with an altered timbre, as in two related instances of 'where':

> **Where** are your mess of sons to back you now ...
> Or, with the rest, **where** is your darling Rutland [...]

The adverb is almost whispered, but with greater spookiness because bleached of tone. This is another of Margaret's vicious weapons: her delivery implies suspense, surprise, and irony, teasing the listener with the horror to come.

This 120-line scene is only a small part of a huge work, and my reading has scarcely covered its many strengths, some of them authorial, some directorial. One Shakespearean detail that Hall emphasizes is the chiasmic function of the napkin: Margaret gives the bloody cloth to York to wipe away his tears; some fifty lines later he returns it to her, having used his tears to wipe away Rutland's blood. Similarly, the bloodstain on her mouth is chilling. One guarantor of the power of the scene is the talent of Donald Sinden as her victim. The two actors seem to have inspired each other to greater levels of savagery. At the dress rehearsal, as they met in the wings, exhausted, just after their vicious confrontation, Ashcroft turned to Sinden and said 'You were best'; his reply was 'But you were funniest'.[9]

Notes

1   My analysis is based chiefly on two documents: 1) an audio clip of part of the scene from the British Library's anthology, *Essential Shakespeare Live*; 2) a videotape of the BBC's televised version, held in the archives of the Shakespeare Centre in Stratford-upon-Avon.
    http://www.youtube.com/watch?v=vrXGG45zrm0&list=PL90CCB99663A5A0DA continuing at http://www.youtube.com/watch?v=rSI6j3-HpeA. I wish to express my gratitude to Patricia Tatspaugh, Carol Chillington Rutter, and Russell Jackson for their help in preparing this piece.

2   Quoted in Michael Billington, *Peggy Ashcroft* (London: Mandarin, 1988), p. 183.

3   *Daily Mail,* 23 July 1963.

4   *The Guardian,* 13 January 1964.

5   The lack of 'iron' is found in a review of *Shadow of Heroes,* the praise of her Margaret in his review of the first two plays in their Stratford run: they are printed in *Tynan Right and Left* (London: Longman, 1967), p. 7 and p. 142.

6   *Daily Mail,* 19 August 1963.

7   Barton and Hall have reassigned Northumberland's lines to Exeter.

8   Kenneth Tynan, *Evening Standard*, 30 June 1953.

9   Billington, p. 202.

26

Women Playing Hamlet on the Spanish Stage

José Manuel González
University of Alicante

Studies of female Shakespearean performance are practically non-existent in Spain, despite the fact women have been part of Spanish theatre since medieval times. Their presence on the public stage has remained a problematic and complex issue for different reasons. The controversy about the morality of comedies in Spain during the last decades of the sixteenth century had an immediate and adverse impact on women acting professionally, yet actresses nevertheless soon conquered the Spanish stage: women were first allowed to perform in plays in 1587, but they had to wait until 4 October 1772 to play Shakespeare. The first Spanish woman in a Shakespearean role was Catalina Tordesillas, who performed Gertrude in a *Hamlet* staged at the Corral del Príncipe Theatre in Madrid.

Since that time, a particular challenge for Spanish actresses – perhaps unexpectedly – has been the playing not of Gertrude but of Hamlet. The Hamlets of Gloria Torres, Margarita Xirgu,

Nuria Espert, and Blanca Portillo have made valuable contributions to the construction and transformation of modern theatre in Spain from the beginning of the twentieth century up to the present. The iconoclasm and alleged femininity of Hamlet – Hamlet himself sees his inaction and verbosity as womanish, of course (2.2.517–21) – have fascinated Spanish actresses at different times. They have played Hamlet because they sought to exploit 'what was seen as a feminine ability to convey the interiority of the character and to do justice to Hamlet's romantic sensitivity'.[1] Delacroix had emphasized the same gender ambiguity in his studies of 1835, in which his model for Hamlet was Marguerite Pierret, and Zuloaga depicted Blanca Barrymore dressed as the Prince while posing in front of the Segovia Alcázar in 1924. In this essay I will offer accounts of four actresses who have played Hamlet on the Spanish stage – Sarah Bernhardt, Margarita Xirgu, Nuria Espert, and Blanca Portillo – for the benefit of scholars and theatre practitioners unfamiliar with the history of Shakespeare in Spain, showing how they introduced new ways for acting and producing a female Spanish Hamlet at different times and under particular conditions.

Sarah Bernhardt: 'Masters, you are all welcome'

Sarah Bernhardt was the first female Hamlet to appear on the Spanish stage. Like that of Hamlet, the life of the French actress (born Rosine Bernard, 1844–1923) remains a mystery. It is perhaps the mystique surrounding her that ensured her success and the continuous interest in her life and work. During her lifetime *Hamlet* was the most frequently staged play in France. She had previously taken part in a production of *King Lear* as a young actress and had also been Ophelia at the Théâtre de la Porte Saint-Martin in 1886, but her female Hamlet was undoubtedly her most acclaimed and famous role. Although Sarah Siddons is reputed to have been the first established actress to play Hamlet in 1776, Sarah Bernhardt took on the role of the Prince first in Paris, where she was also filmed in a silent movie as Hamlet during the scene of the duel, and then in London, New York and Madrid, playing a daring and innovative Hamlet and showing his androgynous side. It was not a successful performance, not least because the production 'in fifteen scenes with musical interludes lasted almost five hours'.[2]

Before playing Hamlet in Madrid in 1899, Bernhardt had been Gilberta in *Frou-Frou* and Margarita in *La dame aux camélias*. These were outstanding performances; audiences bowed to the simplicity of her style. But her Hamlet raised greater expectation among the public. It was unusual at the time for a woman to undertake such a paradigmatic and complex male role, yet there was a unanimously positive response to her acting. Spectators applauded warmly – as they had not done in her previous performances – and congratulated her on such moving and wonderful acting. It was made clear that the diva '[m]oved and persuaded in her characterization of Hamlet'.[3] Bernhardt thus became the inspiration for a series of subsequent Spanish actresses taking on the role.

Margarita Xirgu: 'Our state to be disjoint and out of frame'

Margarita Xirgu (1888–1969) has been most often compared with Sarah Bernhardt, as she was to repeat much of Bernhardt's success in the theatre. She was not the first Spanish-born actress to play Hamlet on the Spanish stage, as there is evidence, though scant, that Gloria Torres, the leading actress in Salvador Martínez's company, also played the role of Hamlet before the Spanish Civil War which effectively marked the end of an era in Spanish theatre.[4] But performances never stopped completely despite adverse conditions. Probably the only production of *Hamlet* between 1936 and 1939 was that of Salvador Soler and Milagros Leal staged at the Eslava Theatre while soldiers were fighting some miles away.[5] Xirgu was on tour in Latin America with her company at the outbreak of the Civil War. The political situation and her Republican commitment made her stay in America until her death. While she thus dominated the Spanish theatre only until 1936, her haunting presence was felt throughout the whole century. She became a symbol of Catalan culture and of the Republic in exile, promoting the staging of plays that could not be seen in Spain because of Francoist censorship.

Xirgu was not only an accomplished actress, but also a reputed director and theatre manager. She typically played the role of bold, aggressive heroines. José Alsina considered her 'a great modern actress, different from the rest, highly individualistic, sensitive, cerebral'.[6] She showed a particular ability to play with silence and to use her hands in her performances, drawing inspiration from El Greco's and Velázquez's paintings for her acting and productions. From the beginning, there was a subversive tone in the roles and performances she chose to stage, ranging from Oscar Wilde's *Salome* (1910), which sparked a public response so violent that the theatre closed to avoid further trouble, to Galdós's *Santa Juana de Castilla* (1918), written especially for her, and Bernard Shaw's *Saint Joan* (1924) as well as Lorca's *Yerma* (1934), *Bodas de sangre* (1935) and *La casa de Bernarda Alba* (1945). She enjoyed a close friendship with Lorca until his tragic shooting in August 1936; he wrote the poem 'If I leave, I love you more/ If I stay, I love you the same' for her. She has been considered his 'muse', and her inspiration and influence appear to have shaped Lorca's theatrical art, as shown in the opera *Ainadamar* that was presented at the Teatro Real in Madrid on 8 July 2012 and that opened when Margarita Xirgu was stepping onto the stage for what would be her last performance of Lorca's *Mariana Pineda*.

For Xirgu the actor was as important as the author, and had become a primary instance of the importance to the audience of the lead actor as she confesses to Domènec Guansé, '[y]ou go to the theatre not just to be familiar with Shakespeare's *Hamlet* but to see the play performed by Zacconi, Talhma or Sarah Bernhardt'.[7] Xirgu's Shakespearean roles were few, but significant: '*Macbeth*, staged while in exile, as a study of the execution of dictatorial power, the fear of the erotic feminine and the frayed ties of the family unit; *A Midsummer Night's Dream*, Lorca's favourite Shakespearean work, whose intertextual traces linger in *Comedia sin título*; and *Hamlet*, a mercurial feminization of the agonized prince'.[8] In 1950 she also directed and produced *Romeo and Juliet*, working with a translation by Marcelino Menéndez y Pelayo. Her interest in *Hamlet* started when she performed *Electra*, fearing that her voice would not be good enough to convey Hamlet's philosophical tone. But considering that the productions she had seen were too conventional and not true to the spirit of the Prince, she projected a transvestite Hamlet that would be, she believed, natural and spontaneous. Jacinto Benavente, the Spanish Nobel prize winner in 1922, encouraged her to take on the role, since playing Hamlet was always an honour reserved for the best actors.

From that moment, performing Hamlet became an obsession for Xirgu. She decided to go to England to learn more about how to stage *Hamlet*, and in the summer of 1933 went to Stratford, accompanied by Benavente, to see performances of the play and discovered first hand that it was possible to stage *Hamlet* with a level of simplicity that she had not previously experienced. Her own *Hamlet* production took place at the Teatro Odeón in Buenos Aires in 1938, with Amelia de la Torre as Ophelia and a translation by Gregorio Martínez Sierra and María Lejárraga. Even her own company had issues with Xirgu's taking on the role of Hamlet herself: the actor Pedro López Lagar suddenly left the company due to his disappointment at not being allowed to perform the role of the Prince. Xirgu's Hamlet dramatized an angry rivalry with his dead father, which was played as overtly Oedipal;

sexual ambiguity was also a salient feature of the Hamlet/
Ophelia encounters and of the Gertrude/Hamlet relationship.
The production thus became in a way a radical reworking
of Bernhardt's Hamlet, triggering an unexpectedly positive
response in young spectators.

Nuria Espert: 'Come, give us a taste of your quality, come, a passionate speech'

Nuria Espert has done everything in the theatre. She has
been actress, theatre and opera manager and director, and
translator. Espert's career first took off at the age of nineteen
when she received a standing ovation at the Grec Theater
in Barcelona for her role in *Medea* in 1954. Since then, her
acting has been controversial. During Franco's regime she
performed polemical dramatists like Genet, O'Neill, Sartre,
Bretch, Arrabal and Lorca. Her production of *La casa de
Bernarda Alba* in 1985 at the Lyric Theatre Hammersmith in
London, with Glenda Jackson as Bernarda and Joan Plowright
as Poncia, was an unprecedented success, bringing her international acclaim and recognition. Her choices of role located
her within a developing tradition: like Bernhardt and Xirgu,
for instance, she played Salome.

For Espert, staging Shakespeare was much more than just
performing a text: it was, she said, 'as if one were doing
something that existed from the beginning of the universe'.[9]
Her love affair with Shakespeare began when she performed
Juliet in 1953; two years later she produced *The Comedy of
Errors* and played a minor role in *Julius Caesar*. Eight years
later – after performing *Medea* – she decided to play Hamlet.
Despite the pressure of the circumstances – this was a very
busy time in her career – it was a very rewarding experience
as she could show the 'pleasure [she] had had to bother and

provoke'.[10] Playing Hamlet came naturally to her and made her more mature as an actress.

Hamlet was produced by Armando Moreno, her husband, with translation by Nicolás González Ruiz. It had its premiere at the open air Teatre Grec in Barcelona in 1960. Sigfrido Burmann's scenery used the old moat and walls of Montjuich to give the impression of a huge castle: the set included battlements, platforms, and a throne room. Espert's choice to play Hamlet when she was just twenty-four was controversial, even scandalous.[11] Spectators seem to have been shocked by her performance, for which she kept her hair long so as 'to highlight the homosexual dimension of Hamlet's relationships, and more precisely, an inability to come to terms with his own sexuality',[12] and they reacted vocally, as Espert started to say 'Less than kin', the audience began booing, and at the end of the first half there was both bawling and applause. The provocative nature of her performance, her costume choices, and the deliberately anachronistic nature of the production, merging different historical periods, seem to have split the audience between acclamation and opposition. Perhaps the failure of her Hamlet was due to imitation as she tried to reproduce Hamlet roles of past productions, like those of Bernhardt and Olivier.

Later she was expected to produce *Macbeth*, with Luis Buñuel as director, but he finally declined the offer due to bad health. She also played the roles of Prospero and Ariel in her own production of *The Tempest* on 23 May 1983 at the Romea Theatre in Barcelona with the Catalan translation by Josep Maria de Sagarra and directed by Jorge Lavelli. Playing Prospero and Ariel was a challenge for her, as she had to look for new ways of being both at the same time. The problem was finally solved by making Ariel a reflected image in a mirror. In 2010, she starred in a one-actress show as she played all the parts in Miguel del Arco's adaptation of Shakespeare's long narrative poem *The Rape of Lucrece*. She was able to show the villainy, doubt, ferocity, and desperation of Tarquin as well as the innocence, unbearable pain and ultimate strength of Lucrece. The production was certainly the culmination of her career as one of the best Spanish actresses of all time.

Blanca Portillo: To be a man or/and a woman – that is the question

Like Xirgu and Espert, Blanca Portillo has been an actress, director and theatre manager. She has also taken part in two Pedro Almodóvar films, *Volver* (2006), as Agustina, and *Los abrazos rotos* (2009), as Judit García. *Hamlet* was neither her first Shakespeare play as she had been Hermione in *The Winter's Tale* in 1992, nor her first male role, as she had been the inquisitor Brother Emilio Bocanegra in the film *Alatriste* (2006) and had played Segismund in Helena Pimenta's adaptation of Calderón's *La vida es sueño* (2012). But Tomaz Pandur's *Hamlet* was a paradigmatic production, where Blanca Portillo became the centre of the dramatic action.

The performance, which lasted for four hours, had its premiere on 12 February 2009 at El Matadero Theatre in Madrid. The theatrical space, designed by Numen, was full of puddles. The location was Denmark, and the court of Elsinore was an island about to submerge in a sea of mirrors, with catwalks and huge curtains hanging from above that moved like waves among the islands. There was an astonishing atmosphere of suspicion, such as when Hamlet encountered the Ghost (Asier Etxeandia) in a bar. He was there by Hamlet's side to listen and guide him while the other characters hid behind curtains to spy. Curtains replaced walls in Elsinore. Lively action and violence were omnipresent from the beginning, such as when Portillo appeared hitting a boxing bag with all her fury. Hamlet was no longer a melancholic character but an athlete trying to take his revenge on those who had brought mourning and disaster to Elsinore. Hamlet was living in constant turmoil, as he was forced to choose between passion and reason, between violence and melancholy, between the feminine and the masculine. Here, Hamlet was a woman who had been educated as a man. But what the production made clear was that Hamlet was beyond gender determinacy, as shown in the famous monologue 'To be or not to be', delivered by Portillo in complete nakedness, ending in a beautiful image of Narcissus contemplating his reflection in the water. Hamlet's sexual ambiguity mirrors the times, when we see how gender roles are so unstable.

In this way the presence of a modern Hamlet on the Spanish stage has been largely due to the contribution of Spanish actresses daring to challenge such a paradigmatic male role by looking for alternative ways of making a different Hamlet alive for Spanish spectators. They sought to exploit his ambiguity so as to present a radical reading of his complex and troubled interiority that became a source of creativity and inspiration in their own performances. Spanish female Hamlets have opened up new forms of acting and producing *Hamlet*, showing possibilities for theatrical experimentation ahead of their times. Women performing Hamlet on the Spanish stage have also reflected the temper of the times and offered lively voices of dissent. Xirgu and Espert functioned as emblematic political opposition during Franco's regime. They emphasized Hamlet's aggressive and provocative part beyond the standard traditional stereotype of the philosophical Prince, and they suggested that women are as well equipped as men to convey the emotional depth of the tragic hero and to bring out – in ways that male actors have not done – Hamlet's enormous capacity for love beyond gender determinacy, which is constantly baffled and frustrated in the play. Spanish actresses performing Hamlet have proved that solitude, despair, melancholy, ethical doubts about revenge, and a sense of betrayed love are qualities that transcend gender barriers. Instead of impersonating maleness, they have shown how Hamlet's thwarted love is nothing but a desperate desire to communicate, as seen in Portillo's production. Their performances have facilitated the discovery of meaningful aspects of Hamlet's 'mysterious' character that were unknown to Spanish audiences. As Xirgu's, Espert's, and Portillo's female Hamlets become history, we look forward to seeing more such performances in years to come.

Notes

1   Ann Thompson and Neil Taylor, *Hamlet* (Plymouth, 1996), p. 44.

2   Tony Howard, *Women as Hamlet. Performance and Interpretation in Theatre, Film and Fiction* (Cambridge, 2007), p. 101.

3   *El Imparcial*, 6 November 1899.

4   Rafael Portillo and Mercedes Salvador, 'Spanish Productions of *Hamlet* in the Twentieth Century', in A. Luis Pujante and Ton Hoenselaars (eds), *Four Hundred Years of Shakespeare in Europe* (Newark, DE, 2003), p. 188.

5   César Oliva, *El teatro desde 1936* (Madrid: Alhambra, 1989), p. 24.

6   José Alsina in *Mundo Gráfico* 1914. Cited in Antonina Rodrigo, *Margarita Xirgu y su teatro* (Barcelona 1974), p. 95.

7   Domènec Guansé, 'Toda una vida', in Cuadernos *El Público* 36:46.

8   María Delgado, '*Other' Spanish Theatres. Erasure and Inscription on the Twentieth Century Spanish Stage* (Manchester, 2003), p. 61.

9   José Manuel González, 'Entrevista a Nuria Espert', *Shakespeare en España: Crítica, traducciones y representaciones* (Zaragoza, 1993), p. 416.

10   González, p. 414.

11   Nuria Espert and Marcos Ordoñez, *De aire y fuego. Memorias* (Madrid, 2002), p. 66.

12   Keith Gregor, *Shakespeare in the Spanish Theatre. 1772 to the Present* (London, 2010), p. 96.

27

Re-making Katherina: Julia Marlowe and *The Taming of the Shrew*

Elizabeth Schafer
Royal Holloway, University of London

In *Women Reading Shakespeare 1660–1900*, Ann Thompson and Sasha Roberts contend that 'by re-examining our notion of the genres of Shakespeare criticism we can rediscover the work of women reading Shakespeare'.[2] This essay responds to the challenge issued by Thompson and Roberts, and focuses on two examples of a much neglected genre – the prompt copy – in order to analyse how Julia Marlowe (1865–1950) read Shakespeare. Marlowe's prompt copies provide detailed evidence of how this actress researched, interrogated, and then performed in Shakespeare's plays and her *Shrew* prompt copies provide vivid evidence of how Marlowe attempted to re-make Katherina.

Marlowe had a remarkable career, lasting several decades, as a leading Shakespearian actress. Despite many opportunities to make money in commercial theatre, Marlowe prioritized playing Shakespeare:[2] she performed in comedy

– Beatrice, Viola, Imogen, Portia, Rosalind, and Katherina –
and tragedy – Juliet, Ophelia, Lady Macbeth, and Cleopatra.[3]
Marlowe was forty when she started playing Katherina in
1905 and her Petruchio was E. H. Sothern, the man who
would become Marlowe's second husband in 1911. As an
actor manager, sometimes working alongside Sothern, and
sometimes working independently, Marlowe enjoyed considerable autonomy for much of her career. But what really
marks Marlowe out as extraordinary is her work as theatre
maker, what would now be called a dramaturg: Marlowe
researched her productions; she edited her own texts for
performance; she devised stage business. After she retired,
Marlowe archived her work, trying to ensure it would be
possible for future generations to appreciate the re-making of
Shakespeare's heroines that she accomplished.

At the beginning of the twentieth century, in the United States,
the Katherina of Ada Rehan reigned supreme.[4] Augustin Daly's
long running and magnificently upholstered 1887 production,
starring Rehan, cut vulgarity, minimized farce and dignified
Katherina. But in 1905 Marlowe threw down the gauntlet,
challenging and explicitly critiquing Rehan's queenly shrew.[5]
Marlowe contended, in performance and in print, that *The
Shrew* should be robustly farcical. Marlowe's Katherina was
'vehement and pungent' (Russell, p. 334); she was 'consistent,
human, likeable' and she had 'a clever, persisting, indomitable,
coil-springed, feminine mind' (Russell, p. 335). Marlowe's
performance suggested that Katherina 'was merely biding her
time until she could reassert her dominion', and the end of
Shakespeare's play was the beginning of 'the taming of the
tamer' (Russell, p. 337). By the standards of her day, Marlowe's
campaign to remake Katherina was feminist.

There is some evidence to suggest that Marlowe might
have been interested in the cause of early twentieth-century
feminism. In 1893 Marlowe addressed the Woman's Congress
of the Chicago World's Fair on the subject of 'Woman's
Work on the Stage'. In this speech she celebrated women's
achievements in the theatre as well as their 'Courage and

perseverance' and their 'executive ability'.[6] Marlowe was friends with Susan B. Anthony (1820–1906), the suffragist and abolitionist. She was also a very close friend of Charles Edward Russell (1860–1941), a 'sober, serious and passionate social crusader', anticapitalist, a determined 'muckraker', the son of an abolitionist and, in 1909, one of the founders of the National Association for the Advancement of Coloured People.[7] Marlowe and Russell met in 1888 (Russell, p. 136); once Marlowe and Sothern were married, they spent most summers in Europe with Russell and his second wife, Theresa Herschel, 'an ardent feminist' who was 'active in the women's movement' (Miraldi, p. 204). The friendships between these two couples appear to have been close and although Russell tried and 'failed' to 'convince Marlowe to become involved in social issues' (Miraldi, p. 301 n.1), it seems likely that Marlowe and Theresa Herschel Russell, the 'ardent feminist' would have discussed Katherina.

In 1926 Charles Russell wrote an authorized biography of Marlowe, which constructs her as a never say die heroine of great and talent and tenacity, who succeeds against the odds. Russell only refers obliquely to the fact that from the late 1890s, he advised Marlowe on business matters, particularly investments in war bonds (Russell, p. 264) and the Stock Market (Miraldi, p. 205). However, these investments were critical: they made Marlowe a wealthy woman, one who could afford to take risks in the theatre.[8] If reviewers and audiences disliked Marlowe's Katherina, preferring the status quo of Rehan's imperious shrew, Marlowe would not go bankrupt.

One unexpected feature of Russell's biography is his emphasis on Marlowe's careful preparation of her prompt copies. Russell states that

[h]er way was to take a page of text and paste it upon a page of a blank book much larger. Then, with insatiable care, she marked every emphasis and covered all the marginal space with minute annotations as to meaning, purpose, business, intonation, gesture. On each role, she

spent months and sometimes years of diligent study and
patient review before she was willing to essay it; reading the
commentators, weighing the meanings, testing emphases,
fitting the character into its times and background, putting
Rolfe by the side of Theobald and White by Steevens, until,
at last, the competent mistress of the full significance of the
role as a definite creation in arts, she walked upon the stage
to delineate it.[9]

While such predetermined direction would be anathema to
many theatre practitioners today, Marlowe's acknowledgement
of scholarship, and how it can feed into theatre, is noteworthy.[10]
Russell also pinpoints the summer of 1905 as the moment
when Marlowe worked on the prompt copy for *Shrew*, along
with *The Merchant of Venice* (Russell, p. 333).

Although Marlowe's *Shrew* was not popular with some
critics, particularly those who were devotees of Daly, the show
ran for two weeks in New York to 'crowded houses' (Russell,
346). It then

continued in the Sothern-Marlowe repertoire for twenty
years, was repeated and repeated in New York and every
other important city in (the US), drew to each performance a capacity house, and so far as Shakespeare is
concerned, established new bounds of popular favour
(Russell, p. 352).[11]

Marlowe's *Shrew* changed a great deal over the decades:
sometimes it used a full pictorial set; after the First World
War it tended to be more bare-boards. Some changes – such
as delaying Katherina's first entry until 2.1 – may have had
more to do with Marlowe's decreasing stamina and ill health
over the years than with critical interpretation. But the prompt
copies clearly indicate that Marlowe cut the text, rearranged
lines and interpolated business in order to remake Katherina's
relationship with Petruchio and, in particular, to qualify
Katherina's final submission.

It is important to note, from a bibliographic point of view, that the term 'prompt copy' in relation to the Sothern and Marlowe productions is an inclusive term that covers a wide range of kinds of text.[12] These include: souvenir copies such as the records made by Lark Taylor, an actor with Sothern and Marlowe's company;[13] preparation copies; part books; lighting plots; typescripts; touring prompt copies; instructions to carpenters; the working prompt copy used by stage managers, such as Frederick Kaufman, to run a show. Some prompt copies appear to take the reader very close to Marlowe's performance; for example, *Twelfth Night* 58 has 'Lines marked for stresses by Miss Marlowe' (Shattuck, p. 481).[14] Collating all the extant prompt copies of the Sothern/Marlowe *Shrew* would create an information overload, so I will focus here on two contrasting *Shrew* prompt copies, labelled by Shattuck as 47 and 48. *Shrew* 47 is a souvenir prompt copy donated to the Folger in 1934 by Francis S. T. Powell. It has Powell's handwritten notes on a published text of *The Shrew*; Powell stage managed the Sothern/ Marlowe production, was intimately familiar with it, and was helped in reconstructing the prompt copy by another Sothern/ Marlowe stage manager, Frederick S. Kaufman.[15] *Shrew* 47 documents the five-act, fuller version of the Sothern/Marlowe production whereas *Shrew* 48 records details of the four act version, which opened at Baptista's first speech. *Shrew* 48 is a typescript and has very full information on lighting, prop lists, music, etc. Shattuck (p. 442) identifies it as a Kaufman prompt copy.

The *Shrew* 47 and 48 prompt copies testify that Sothern's Petruchio seized every opportunity to signal that he was completely smitten by the fiery charms of Katherina, something which gave her a significant power base; thus, in 5.2, when Petruchio demands in a 'Commanding tone' that Katherina should fetch Bianca and the Widow, there is a moment of renegotiation: 'when he continues' with this 'Commanding tone', Katherina 'looks at him and they exchange an understanding glance and he adopts a softer tone' (*Shrew* 48, p. 18). After Katherina throws her cap underfoot, 'Petruchio picks up cap and gives it to Katherina' (*Shrew* 48, p. 19). Nevertheless, on hearing Petruchio's demand that she lecture on 'duty', Marlowe's Katherina 'protestingly falls on stool" (*Shrew* 48, p. 19) even though Sothern's Petruchio 'pats his money pouch' when Lucentio complains he has lost 'a hundred crowns since supper-time', presumably, to signal to Katherina that money is at stake (*Shrew* 48, p. 19). After Katherina places her hand on the floor, Petruchio 'seizes her hand, and places his own on floor. She places her foot on his hand' (*Shrew* 47, n.p.). Finally Katherina 'holds up her dress and he takes gold he has won and pours all of it into her lap as .....CURTAINS CLOSE' (*Shrew* 48, p. 21). Marlowe thus qualifies the submission speech radically as firstly Katherina is invited to join forces with her husband to make money and appears to accept, and secondly Petruchio abjects himself by placing his hand upon the floor, allowing Katherina to tread on his foot before he hands over the proceeds of the wager to her.

For modern feminists such stage business might appear to be band-aiding. However, Marlowe's fighting defence of her production in the face of criticism, especially by Daly's apologists, a defence first published in the *Evening Telegram*, has to be read as feminist. Marlowe claims that she has gone back to Shakespeare, which, for her, means the Folio text, 'the real text of Shakespeare devoid of the conventionalities and traditions with which it has been encumbered for years' (Russell, p. 343). The Folio is also the source of Marlowe's commitment to farce; the text demands characters strike each other and productions which omit such business are 'misconceptions, perversions, and un-Shakespearean "Shrews"' (Russell, p. 344).[16] Marlowe cites contemporary critics – Fleay, Ward, Furnival, and Furness (Russell, p. 343) – to bolster her argument and denounces the use of 'incongruous austerity' in 'recent productions' which approached *The Shrew* 'as if it were of a classically comic fiber comparable in dignity and grace to "As You Like It" or to "Twelfth Night"' (Russell, p. 342). Marlowe claims *The Shrew* is an 'Elizabethan farce comedy' (Russell, p. 342), and 'the subdued, dignified, restrained interpretation of the play', that Daly had popularized, is wrong. Marlowe states her Katherina 'was tamed not so much by physical overbearance' as by her amusement at the 'practical joker' Petruchio (Russell, p. 344). Marlowe concedes that Shakespeare's roles are open to many different interpretations but 'I must play according to my own conviction, not by another's' (Russell, p. 345). Twenty years after Marlowe's direct, possibly shrewish, defence of her artistic choices, Russell decided – presumably with Marlowe's blessing – to reprint Marlowe's article in his 1926 biography. Both Marlowe and Sothern were then retired, looking back over their careers and actively seeking to ensure their achievements were not forgotten. Sothern had published an autobiography in 1917, *My Remembrances: The Melancholy Tale of "Me"*, and he was planning to write *Julia Marlowe's Story*.[17] Sothern and Marlowe had also, in 1922, cut a series of 78 rpm records featuring famous Shakespearian speeches; these records include two sequences from *The Shrew*.[18] One *Shrew* recording is easily accessible via an elegant, online installation, which marries the sound track of the first meeting between Marlowe's Katherina and Sothern's Petruchio with stills of Marlowe.[19] Marlowe's famous contralto voice occasionally 'sing[s]' by modern standards of performance, but Katherina's resistance to Petruchio can be heard in a series of incoherent noises of astonishment and protest. The second recording – Katherina's advice to women – departs radically from the business indicated by Marlowe's prompt copies;[20] however, Marlowe's interpretation – that Petruchio arouses Katherina's sense of humour (Russell, p. 334) – is still very clear. The sequence cuts 5.2 from line 99 onwards, sometimes rather awkwardly, in order to fashion a duet that includes the throwing down of Katherina's cap. When Petruchio issues his cap throwing order, Katherina reacts by laughing as if she is very amused. She delivers the advice to women speech uncut, rendering Marlowe the star and Sothern the support act in this recording, and Petruchio's response, 'Why, there's a wench. Come on, and kiss me, Kate' is followed by a series of exaggerated kissing sounds, and much laughter: Petruchio laughs in a slightly pirate-king style and Katherina in a much higher key. Marlowe's Katherina and Sothern's Petruchio are playing an amusing game and are having great fun. Thus while the Victor recordings present an adaptation of what is documented in the prompt copies as Marlowe's stage performance, the audio performances still complement the overall interpretation of *The Shrew* that the prompt copies offer; for Marlowe, *The Shrew* should be full of laughs and, at the end, Katherina is unbowed, amused and actually in control.

Marlowe valued her prompt copies and tried to ensure they survived by donating them to archives.[21] While prompt copies need to be theorized, and questions asked about their provenance, use, and their status as evidence in constructing performance histories, Marlowe's indubitably offer theatrically pragmatic insights into her readings of Shakespeare's plays, both the plays that she and Sothern produced and the plays, such as *Measure for Measure* and *The Tempest*, that they planned to produce but didn't. Her prompt copies also offer a useful corrective to reviews, which with the increasing availability of newspapers online, risk becoming dominant sources in performance histories simply because they are so accessible. What the *Shrew* prompt copies indicate, for me, is that Marlowe was not only a star actress but also a remarkable dramaturg; she was tenacious in her resistance to the dignified Katherina, popularized by Daly's production; determined in her qualification of what Katherina's submission meant; and energetic in promoting her reading – in performance, in print and via a sound recording – of Katherina. Marlowe found playfulness, fun and laughter in the *Shrew*; it may be hard now to laugh at the jokes she enjoyed, but Marlowe's resilience in promulgating her remaking of Katherina deserves respect.

Notes

1   Ann Thompson and Sasha Roberts (eds), *Women Reading Shakespeare 1660–1900: An Anthology of Criticism* (Manchester, 1997), p. 7.

2   John D. Barry, in *Julia Marlowe*, Sock and Buskin Biographies (Boston, 1899?), records Marlowe's 'determination to become a Shaksperian (sic) actress' (19).

3   Marlowe also played Hal to the Hotspur of her then husband, Robert Taber, in *1 Henry IV* but it was not a success. Photograph in Barry (opposite p. 56).

4   For more on *The Shrew*'s performance history in this period, see Elizabeth Schafer, *The Taming of the Shrew*, Shakespeare in Production (Cambridge, 2002), pp. 15–22.

5   Daly waged a vendetta against Marlowe for years. See Charles Edward Russell, *Julia Marlowe: Her Life and Art* (New York and London, 1926), Chapter XIV, 'The Fight with Augustin Daly'.

6   Marlowe, Julia, 'Woman's Work on the Stage', read before the Woman's Congress of the Chicago world's Fair, Wednesday 17 May 1893, reproduced in Russell, pp. 551–6 (554).

7   Miraldi, Robert, *The Pen is Mightier: The Muckraking Life of Charles Edward Russell* (Basingstoke, 2003), p. 204.

8   For the last thirty years of her life, Marlowe lived at the New York Plaza Hotel (*Chicago Daily Tribune*, 13 November 1950). For risk taking see Patty S. Derrick, 'Julia Marlowe's Imogen: Modern Identity, Victorian Style' *Theatre History Studies* 31 (2011), pp. 90–117, on the costly failure of the lavishly mounted 1923 Sothern/Marlowe *Cymbeline*.

9   Russell xxi. More information on Marlowe's methods appears on p. 151.

10 Barry, writing in 1899, states that Marlowe and her then husband, Robert Taber, 'prepared a stage version of their own, after studying those made by Mr Hackett and Mrs Inchbold' (*sic*) (Barry, p. 61).

11 Marlowe finally retired from the stage in 1924 although ill health had been an increasing challenge from 1914 on. See

Forrest Izard, *Heroines of the Modern Stage* (New York, 1915), p. 316.

12   Charles Shattuck, in *The Shakespeare Promptbooks: A Descriptive Catalogue* (Urbana, IL, 1965), lists 13 prompt copies for the Sothern/Marlowe *Shrew*. His 'Introduction' acknowledges the wide range of 'marked copies' he lists under the heading 'promptbook' (5).

13   Lark Taylor also appeared in Daly's production and some of the business he records seems to be Daly's rather than Sothern and Marlowe's.

14   All references to individual prompt copies use the numbers employed by Shattuck.

15   Prefatory comments to *Shrew* 47 state that 'The manuscript was made by Francis T. S. Powell, Stage Manager, with assistance of Frederick Kaufman, Assistant Stage Manager.'

16   Somewhat inconsistently, Marlowe rejects the 'spurious' (Russell, p. 343) Induction, which Daly's production played.

17   See E. H. Sothern, *My Remembrances: The Melancholy Tale of 'Me'* (London, 1917), and *Julia Marlowe's Story*, ed. Fairfax Downey (New York, 1954). Marlowe delayed publication of *Julia Marlowe's Story* until after her death. The book is dedicated to Russell, and Sothern writes in the first person as if he is Marlowe. The text was edited after Marlowe's death by Fairfax Downey. There is very little on *The Shrew* in either of Sothern's memoirs.

18   The Victor Records catalogue lists the wooing scene as 74704 and Katherina's advice to women as 74705.

19   See http://www.youtube.com/watch?v=OaxdIHU6V3k and http://shakespeare.berkeley.edu/Shakespeare/index.php?option=com_content&view=article&id=148&Itemid=100008

20   I would like to thank Stephen Dryden of the British Library's Sound Archives for help in accessing this recording.

21   Most Sothern/Marlowe prompt copies were deposited in the New York Public Library, the Museum of the City of New York, and the Folger Library.

28

Class, Identity, and Comic Choice: Bill Alexander's *The Taming of the Shrew*

Iska Alter

Hofstra University

Although a critical commonplace in discussions of the play, let us nevertheless begin with what purports to be most obvious about *The Taming of the Shrew*: its gender politics, which it is alleged must inevitably determine the methodology of dramatic action necessary to bring Shakespeare's problematic comedy to the stage. Whatever the historical circumstances governing theatrical choice and audience response, whether read with sympathy, grudging acceptance, or bitter hostility, there can be little doubt, so the argument goes, that meaning in the staged or printed text is solely generated by the skirmishes of heterosexual warfare.

What seems less obvious, however, is the extent to which the contentious forces of patriarchy, female assertiveness, and woman's wonted obedience, whose centrality to *The Shrew*'s comedic substance is irreducible, drives the play's representational energies (to a greater or lesser degree) to one of two increasingly conventionalized paradigms. The first theatrical formula to become apparent seems to have been farce in which Kate's behaviour and Petruchio's actions are translated into slapstick, swagger, and knockabout two stooges' physicality. One version of this model is played out by Elizabeth Taylor and Richard Burton in Franco Zeffirelli's 1967 film offering the audience a view of the playwright's characters through the scrim of the couples' own raucous celebrity, establishing, as Barbara Hodgdon observes, a brash 'aura of immediacy and authenticity'.[1] The other pattern, and perhaps the increasingly dominant performative mode since the 1960s and the emergence of strongly inflected feminist critiques of the play, is that of bleak sardonic irony, nearer tragedy than comedy wherein Katherina is browbeaten (or worse still, brainwashed, as some insist) by a brutish, violent Petruchio into dull, compliant servitude. Tina Packer, in a more recent variant of Katherina as the iconic subjugated female that is part of her continuously evolving production, *Women of Will,* begins with three disturbing, if by now, narrow, readings of Kate's final submission, first as 'a mad, manic prisoner gasping for life'; then as 'a cooing sexy geisha'; and, at the last, as a 'broken-backed figure of depressed resignation'.[2]

But even as disapproving critics would rather exile *The Taming of the Shrew* to some theatrical Ultima Thule, far away from the vulnerable, too easily influenced spectators, or as disappointed reviewers would prefer another pratfalling adaptation of Shakespeare's *Punch and Judy Show,* scholars have been exploring the relative complexity of this early comedy. The disruptive tensions of *The Shrew*'s tripartite design – the Sly frame, the shrew taming main plot, and the Bianca subplot uncomfortably jostling one another – and the sometimes contradictory claims of comic authority enforced by local, folkloric, and Italianate sources call into equal question issues of identity and class as well as those of gender relations.

Given the insistent, even deliberate simplifications embedded in and the result of its production history, how then can director, company, actors introduce into performance variant and reconsidered *Shrews*? What theatrical choices can be made to enact a more complicated view of what constitutes the comic action of *The Taming of the Shrew*? In 1980, Jonathan Miller offered just such an alternative (which received a mixed critical reception, to be sure) for the televised BBC-Time/ Life Shakespeare series. This counter-*Shrew* was shaped by what Miller presumed to be sixteenth- and seventeenth-century Reformation notions of taming/training/education, particularly for women, the corollary, but no less difficult, development of a coherent, stable self, and the problematic construction of a viable social/communal identity. In order to achieve such a comic embourgeoisement, the director's Petruchio employs actual and symbolic mirrors, including his own exaggerated, even shrewish[3] conduct, to permit Katherina to see herself as others do. By the end of Miller's revisionary exercise, Kate has successfully and publicly humiliated the 'good' Bianca (who is the shrew now, the viewer is asked to consider); husband and wife, acting as coequal partners, have acquired in 'good' bourgeois fashion, additional financial capital, a reward for self-consciously performing the culture's definition of normative conjugal roles; and the audience is presented with a demonstration of the new fashioned 'good' companionate marriage. Sexual politics is important only insofar as gender provides a context through which character and spectator alike are instructed in the processes by which the civilities of middle class life come into existence.

If the interpolated hymn socializing the self-satisfactions of the bourgeois family freezes the last moments of Miller's comic reading into holier-than-thou sanctimony, very nearly erasing the production's transformational energy, then Bill Alexander's 1992 *The Taming of The Shrew* for the Royal Shakespeare Company is more unsettling still, especially for the many reviewers anticipating the broad humour of stage tradition,[4] because it incorporates into its intricate and volatile mix the disorderly anxieties of class. Indeed, Peter Holland is almost persuaded by Alexander's interpretation that 'the play is ... about class and that male subjugation of women is only an example of masters' oppression of servants'.[5] Alexander achieves this sense of subversive disquiet in a variety of ways, but primarily by reimagining and restoring the Christopher Sly frame to the performance text, by fully integrating the newly configured and modernized Induction into the play's action, and finally, by deploying these now elaborate patterns of incident and event across symbolically marked and organized stage space.

One might argue that these alterations do Shakespeare a disservice (although the playwright has been subjected to such 'betrayals' with few compunctions for several hundred years), or that the scope of the adaptation is too extreme, the rewriting too extensive, and the additions too intrusive. (This is Peter Holland's complaint, although he readily admits the general effectiveness of an Induction which must be taken 'seriously as a response to the inner play'.[6]) But in a directorial programme note, Alexander justifies his refashioned text in which Lord, Huntsmen, Servants, and Page become contemporary aristocrats – Lord Simon Llewellyn, his brother Rupert, the Honourable Hugo Daly-Young and Peter Sinclair, Lady Sarah Ormsby, and Mrs. Ruth Banks-Ellis – as a clarifying return to original intention:

> The text spoken by Christopher Sly, Lord Simon and the Warwickshire characters is adapted from the 1594 Quarto text, *The Taming of a Shrew* ... the overall structure, in terms of the relationship of the Sly story to the Shrew story, represent[ing] Shakespeare's thematic intention. This production follows the structure of the Quarto text while remaining faithful to the 1623 Folio text for the story itself. Although it can never be proved, I believe ... that this restores the full scheme of the play.[7]

While Peter Holland (once again) regards the phrase 'adapted from' as disingenuous[8], and many of the popular theatre critics dismissed Alexander's revisions as 'tiresomely modish',[9] or the newly minted dialogue as 'rock bottom',[10] how different in sentiment and belief is Simon's blunt, sneering 'How beastly. Look at him lying there like a pig. How foul!'[11] from the Lord's resonant 'O monstrous beast, how like a swine he lies! / Grim death, how foul and loathsome is thine image!'[12]

There is no doubt that the director's recreated upper-class characters are presented as an arrogant, complacent, thoroughly unpleasant lot. Lord Simon is drawn as a particularly disagreeable of barely contained male aggression, more brutal and vicious than his lordly sixteenth-century counterpart, especially toward his younger sibling (who is first introduced in the early minutes of the Induction as prey in a mock foxhunt and then feminized as Sly's wife at Simon's unbrookable insistence), his women (Lady Sarah is abused if she does not obey), and his drunk 'who needs teaching a lesson. We'll mess around with his mind a bit, OK'?[13] But all seem to possess the impenetrable certitude of a class used to wielding authority with few restrictions on their impulses and appetites. However, his actors, employed to give a private performance to self-indulgent, rich young men and women, will prove to be their undoing and our education. Notwithstanding their assigned functions as aristocratic possessions, these shape shifters, by the very nature of their profession, carry with them destabilizing energies that will, at least momentarily, dissolve the fixities of class and character.

The choice to tease out, elaborate, and intensify the latent class antagonisms present in both *The Shrew*'s incomplete frame and *A Shrew*'s more fully developed Induction allows Alexander to construct out of the problematic encounters among the aristocrats, Sly, the actors, the roles the actors inhabit, and the roles the aristocrats are asked to assume a series of multiplying and reflexive theatrical narratives, a dramatic hall of mirrors in which the ambiguities if social identity and selfhood are reflected for the various audiences on stage and in the playhouse.

It is therefore not unexpected that the language, gestures, and disposition of power that appear among the upper class company are writ large in the performance of the comedy called *The Taming of the Shrew*. But the complex theatricality of Alexander's production also suggests that the actor, whose only name is that of the character he plays – Petruchio – might also embody yet another version of mastery, intimidating the aristocrats (no professionals they) impressed into the cast of the inner *Shrew* play to portray Petruchio's household servants, just as he, in the character of Petruchio, intimidates and overwhelms his Kate.

Do the members of the on-stage audience, who themselves have created, directed, and participated in the drama of Christopher Sly's metamorphosis recognize the performance of their own behaviour in the actions of Kate and Petruchio, Lucentio and Bianca, Tranio and Grumio? Does Alexander's tangled/entangling stagecraft force the members of that other audience – the spectators seated comfortably in a darkened theatre waiting to be entertained – to acknowledge their parts in the dynamics which increasingly blur the distinctions between the role and the reality?

These unsettling questions are enacted on a stage landscape that will reinforce and enhance the productions affective insta-bility. The play begins on a nearly bare stage in front of the pub from which the drunken Sly is unceremoniously exiled. If it is a space momentarily emptied of physical markers which separate, isolate, and organize, an apparently level, albeit a transient, playing field as it were, it soon will contain for a brief time the working class Sly, the company of aristocrats, and a troupe of jobbing actors hired by Lord Simon Llewellyn to entertain his mates and his minions for the evening. Each carries in and on the body easily recognizable signs of his/her position within the hierarchy of class which forms the social context for all subsequent action.

When the scaffolding is raised to show the audience an expensively dressed interior and a bare forestage (the performance area allocated for the actors), the now divided topography of the entire stage with its variety of material indicators clearly incorporates greater complexity of movement and meaning. The upstage living room and the stripped downstage, providing an easy visual equivalent of class division, are separated by a small step, a slight rise which functions as a theatrical threshold, a liminal space where worlds of aristocrat and actor meet.

Initially, the territory *cum* class partition is rigidly maintained: the golden girls and boys remain in their well-appointed luxury, the actors restricted to their forestage working space. But over the course of the performance of *The Taming of the Shrew*, this strict spatial segregation disintegrates as actor and aristocrat move with increasing ease back and forth over the threshold/boundary: actors enter through the rear door of the living room approaching their stage through the aristocratic company, share space on the sofas with their patrons, stand comfortably next to Ruth or Peter or Hugo while the aristocrats step downstage to join the actors as participating extras in the comedy.

The most powerful moment for this viewer (and I saw the production twice, once in Stratford, once in London) during which the tangled threads at last coalesce to form a visible design (even if that design resembles a set of Chinese boxes) occurs precisely at that point in 4.1.80ff. when Ruth, Simon, and Sarah, recruited to play servants, enter another country. Suddenly they are émigrés, displaced persons in a society they do not know, and more important, that they do not control, whose scripts they have not mastered, and where authority resides elsewhere.

Inadequate to their tasks, neither competent actors nor competent servants (even with text in hand), they become objects to the players just as the players had been objects to the aristocrats. When Emily Watson playing Ruth playing Nathaniel is unable to function, Anton Lesser as the actor playing Petruchio slaps her, the sound echoing across the stage and into the audience. The slap stuns and silences – the world quite suddenly has turned upside down.

But to whom is the punishment addressed and by whom is power expressed? Is the explosion of temper 'real' or 'feigned'? Is Petruchio angry at Nathaniel? Is the player teaching Mrs Ruth Banks-Ellis a lesson about a community in which she is powerless? Exactly what lesson is being taught? In a single theatrical gesture, the unfixed relational nature of personal and social identity is exposed, the barriers (or should one say the barricades) of class seem to topple and all – actors, aristocrats, and we who watch – are thrust into that liminal borderland where boundaries are rendered permeable and the certainties which supposedly govern the self and the world dissolve.

However the instant passes, and a presumed revolution does not seem to have happened. The performance goes on to its conclusion as Katherina's final speech recalls into being the old hierarchies. But if conventions are restored, things are not quite the same. Rupert gently returns Christopher Sly to his place under the pub sign; Ruth Banks-Ellis has been liberated by her experience with shape-shifting, role-playing, and performance; and Lady Sarah Ormsby leaves Lord Simon standing alone in a darkening room. Perhaps the revolutions have occurred, after all.

But the play is not yet over. As Sly awakens, enchanted and baffled 'by the best dream that ever I had in all my life',[14] ready now to tame **his** wife, the players renter, their power hidden beneath street clothes, merely ordinary, and a flicker of recognition passes between them. Or does it?

One final observation in this production, those who are in some way abused by any system's need for hierarchy, order and acquiescence (and there are always victims in the administration of power) – the worker (Christopher Sly), the women (Lady Sarah Ormsby, Ruth Banks-Ellis, Katherina Minola), the vulnerable young (Rupert Llewellyn) – are allowed to retain bits of their humanity and our sympathy the longest. Make of that what you will.

Notes

1   'Spectacular Bodies: Acting + Cinema + Shakespeare', *A Concise Companion to Shakespeare on Screen*, ed. Diana E. Henderson (Oxford, 2006), p. 106. I would also like to suggest that the directorial exploitation of his stars' notoriety and the filmgoers' inescapable awareness of the autobiographical complementarity may unwittingly create a cinematic frame, analogous to the Induction of the Shakespearean original.

2   Ben Brantley, 'Shakespeare's Mighty Sorority,' *The New York Times*, 3 February 2013.

3   It is worth noting here that according to the *Oxford English Dictionary* the earliest definition of **shrew** still extent in the sixteenth century refers to male misbehaviour: 'A wicked, evil-disposed, or malignant man; a mischievous or vexatious person; a rascal, villain.'

4   The majority of reviewers from Benedict Nightingale in *The Times* to Charles Spencer, Irving Wardle, and Kenneth Hurren, among others, miss Alexander's point and purpose, preferring traditional *Shrews* wherever possible.

5   *English Shakespeares: Shakespeare on the English Stage in the 1990s* (Cambridge, 1997), p. 129.

6   Ibid.

7   Programme for the RSC production of *The Taming of the Shrew*, 1992, unpaginated.

8   Holland, op. cit., p. 129

9   Charles Spencer, *Daily Telegraph*, 3 April 1992, quoted in *Theatre Record*, 24 March–7 April 1992 vol. XII (1992), p. 419.

10 Irving Wardle, *Independent on Sunday*, 5 April 1994, quoted in *Theatre Record*, op. cit., p. 420

11 'Induction', typescript, RSC production, *The Taming of the Shrew*, p. 4. I would like to thank Professor Michael Warren for his copy of 'The Induction'.

12 William Shakespeare, *The Taming of the Shrew*, 'Induction',

ll. 30–1, The New Cambridge Shakespeare, ed. Ann Thompson (Cambridge, 1984; reprinted 1985, 1988, 1995), p. 48.

13 'Induction', typescript, op. cit., p. 4.

14 'Induction', unpaginated.

29

Re-creating Katherina: *The Taming of the Shrew* at Shakespeare's Globe

Farah Karim-Cooper
Shakespeare's Globe

During one of Globe Education's Setting-the-Scene lectures on *The Taming of the Shrew* in the summer of 2012, Ann Thompson lamented the fact that, editorially speaking, the play had largely been ignored by women. To a rapt audience she remarked that she was the first woman to edit the play in the 1980s and that the next time a woman edited the play was 2010, noting wryly that the latter, Barbara Hodgdon's Arden edition, was in fact commissioned by her as one of the General Editors of Arden 3. While it may be true that its female editors are few and far between, the performance of the play since 1660 has required female actors to engage directly with the complex social questions about the status of women. Shakespeare's *The Taming of the Shrew* is perhaps one of the most problematic plays for a modern reader and playgoer. Holly A. Crocker observes that its stage history 'speaks to the near impossibility of representing submissive femininity', that the domination of Katherina's will and her apparent submission at the end form a disturbing, though unsurprising, resolution to the play.[1]

I offer no answers here to the questions feminist critics might ask about this play: Was Shakespeare a misogynist? Did Shakespeare believe in the social and domestic subordination of women? Is Katherina's final speech ironic? To me, such questions are complicated by our lack of knowledge about how Shakespeare's company might have staged the play. Indeed, as Thompson suggests, there is no textual evidence of the original performances: 'Neither surviving text,' she notes, 'seems wholly to preserve the play as it was performed before the closing of the theatre'.[2] I am not sure, in any case, that these are the most productive questions to ask in response to such a socially and culturally complex comedy. Nevertheless, throughout the 400-year history of its performance, *Shrew* has provoked such questions. Modern performers must negotiate between the play's radically enforced 'domestication' of women and our current expectations of their theatrical representation. What can be problematic is the propensity of modern theatre companies, however, to interpret the relationship between Katherina and Petruchio as equal or mutual. I suggest that this propensity is largely due to the actors' impulse to make sense of the narrative trajectory and psychological development of character. Character motivation, long outmoded as an analytical model for literary criticism, remains absolutely central to an actor's process.

In addition to character, genre establishes for theatre companies the ways key relationships and thus the play could work in performance. *Shrew*'s generic framework is comedy, and it is marketed as an enjoyable experience. But simple enjoyment as a response to this play can be problematic. Too often, Emily Detmer concludes, to 'enjoy the comedy of the play, readers and viewers must work to see domestic violence, and, at the same time, justify its use'.[3] This crux – enjoyment requiring the justification of violence – is precisely what acting companies must overcome. There are, from time to time, productions that counteract the presupposition that a light comedic interpretation of physical abuse as farcical relaxes audiences and thus enables enjoyment, and they might do so by over-punctuating the violence inherent in the play. The controversial all-male Propeller production in 2007 (revived in 2013) is a good example of such theatrical interventions. The male performers could throw each other around a lot more than would be usual had women played the female parts, and they could therefore highlight physically the mental abuse the play espouses. *The New York Times* review stated that 'the show refuses to let you root for Petruchio', that Simon Scardifield's Katherina won audience's affections and so:

> Clinging wanly to her Petruchio, the Kate of the concluding scenes has become a textbook case of Stockholm syndrome. And the laughter among the audience, so hearty in the show's first half, fades into guilty silence.[4]

Brantley's observation indicates that the audience's complex and mixed response might be appropriate for the twenty-first century: laughter, then guilt. Equally, it suggests that Propeller's production, through the use of overt physicality, enabled audiences to interrogate the problems in this comedy.

Significantly, the sensation of enjoyment has come to characterize the experience of attending plays in the reconstructed Globe Theatre; controversially, at times, it is a response induced even during some tragedies and problem comedies that have been performed there since 1997, often provoking dismay from critics towards the Globe groundlings. In a playhouse that is so evocative of the past and that is in frequent danger of replicating, through historically informed productions, long outmoded ideologies, what type of Katherina and what type of Petruchio should we expect to encounter in a production of *Shrew* there? So for the rest of this essay I will consider the Globe's 2012 production, looking in particular (through discussion with its lead actor, Samantha

Spiro) at the ways in which, practically and ideologically, the construction and development of her character might be used to alleviate anxieties provoked by the play's seeming investment in female subordination and domestic violence. The Globe's *Shrew* reminded audiences that the play is a comedy and that, in many places, it is meant to be funny, whether or not the humour is palatable now. Katherina's exaggerated violent anger was unleashed with comic vigour but, given the comedic emphasis in her performance, the Globe's Katherina (Spiro) also had to work to balance the laughs with a sincere portrayal of her experience of cruelty.

Constructing Katherina for a modern Globe audience

In this production, a conflated version of the Quarto and Folio texts was staged in 'Renaissance Style' dress.[5] Directed by Toby Frow, the production confronted the issues that might bother a modern audience. As Spiro said herself, 'I wanted to embrace all the problems; I didn't want to shy away'.[6] I asked how she reconciled some of the play's more disturbing aspects, and in particular the concept of 'taming' a woman:

I haven't played the part before. I feel as though it's been on my radar and it's a part that I've wanted to play. I've always been aware that lots of actors have avoided it and, when they have played it, have really tried to 'fix' this play and make it work for a modern audience. So I think the first thing I wanted to do, when I was offered it, was find out when it was set, because, for me, it is incredibly difficult post-feminism. So I was relieved, first of all, that it was set in its own context.[7]

As Spiro acknowledges, the company and director showed great interest in and came to depend upon the play's social contexts. During rehearsals they asked the Globe Research team to contextualize the taming theme; thus research and lectures about the position of women in early modern Europe, humoral psychology and medicine, contemporary 'taming' methodologies, the relationships within family structures, domestic abuse and the anti-violence reforms in early- modern England informed the process through which both Spiro and Simon Paisley Day (Petruchio) came to grips with their characters and their relationship to each other. Unearthing the historical context and acknowledging the Globe Theatre's own evocation of pastness helped to circumvent the play's problems. Embedded in its own moment, the play can be 'enjoyed' objectively, the past acting as a kind of fourth wall between the performers, their audience and the text's difficult themes.

However, while this is what the production seemed to do, it is not actually what was intended and, certainly, both the past and the present contributed to the meaning. In addition to taking on the historical conditions in which Katherina was written, Spiro also developed a psychological back story, infusing Kate's character with bitterness towards her sister and father and developing for Petruchio feelings of love and devotion as the play progresses. Seeing the play as primarily a love story, both Spiro and Paisley Day found common ground, and thus interpreted the demonstrations of cruelty as mutually affecting, devastating yet reformative:

> Simon Paisley Day [Petruchio] and Toby Frow [Director] were both coming from the point of view that this was about two broken people that go on a journey and both end up together having fallen in love; they are playing the society as opposed to Kate playing Petruccio in any way.[8]

When Paisley Day's Petruchio saw Katherina for the first time, he could maximize the Globe's outdoor conditions, in which the actor and audience are equally lit, indicating through facial expression that she was the most beautiful woman he had ever seen. Such a reaction was meant to reveal more vulnerability in Petruchio than his prior remarks that he, 'will board her, though she chide as loud / As thunder when the clouds in autumn crack' (1.2.95–5) would seem to indicate.[9] Spiro's Katherina did the same thing upon seeing Petruchio for the first time. Thus, love at first sight, usually associated with *Romeo and Juliet*, was appropriated for the relationship being constructed as fundamentally loving and equal. It also delighted the Globe audience, who enjoyed their privileged access to a hidden truth: Katherina and Petruchio love each other. Some feminist critics might argue that this approach is problematic. As Detmer concludes, such an interpretation suggests Stockholm syndrome as the only explanation for Katherina's wholehearted submission not only to Petruchio but to the very idea of being in love with him: 'alternating coercive threats and kindness [as Petruchio does] sets up a situation where victims actively look for ways to please rather than upset their captors'.[10] Seeing Katherina as Petruchio's captive is plausible: she is taken away from her surroundings, starved and deprived of sleep. However, Spiro suggests that in spite of their emphasis on the comic elements of their relationship, she and Paisley Day were keen not to deny the inherent cruelty in the play:

> There is cruelty ... she feels the cruelty [but] ... he feels the cruelty too and they both learn from it. He [Paisley Day] felt that it was very important that Petruccio also doesn't sleep, also doesn't eat, so that he's exhausted by the time we get to 'the sun and the moon'; he goes on a similar journey.[11]

Hodgdon reminds us that this concept characterized Julie Taymor's interpretation in a production for New York Theatre for a New Audience in 1988: 'Stressing the other characters' conventionality, her staging set Katherina and Petruchio off against them, playing the erotic excitement of their intellectual compatibility and their shared delight in games as leading to a mutual equality'.[12] The question that arises here is whether or not a sense of mutual equality is really what is at stake in this play. A production of *The Shrew* requires acknowledgement of the dark cruelty within its comic framework. Spiro discusses possible comic interpretations:

> [w]hen we were investigating the play, we didn't want to limit the depth of what Petruccio does to Katherina. But also it is a comedy; you can do lots of different versions of comedy; there are some versions that try and balance both. Then there are some versions that are very, very dark and you find yourself laughing because you feel uncomfortable. There are not three versions of comedy, but three ways to do this play and I think we have sort of hit it in the middle. Obviously, we were not aiming for mediocrity, and I hope we have been able to make the audience laugh, but really show that there is cruelty.[13]

Still the company's desire to balance comedy with cruelty seems unachievable without acknowledging the progressive deterioration of Katherina's will and the assertion of Petruchio's. If Katherina is to be given dignity, Crocker suggests, 'Petruchio's challenge ... is to animate a legitimate subject whose identity is comprehensive in relation to his own character but whose virtue is believable outside the context in which he presents her'.[14] The loving glance the 'lovers' shoot each other in the Globe's production might underscore the 'mutual equality' between them (if everyone in the audience notices it), but what happens when the final gesture is performed? How can this most famous – and most contentious – moment demonstrate 'mutual equality'? Spiro says:

> I certainly felt very strongly that in the moment she's realizing these thoughts; it's not preconceived. I think everything is fresh and new for her and she is a woman that has newly fallen desperately in love. The size of that

emotion is overwhelming for her and she would lay down her life for him. The gesture came out very instinctively in rehearsal and I still feel it every night so strongly ... it's total devotion, total giving of herself to him, and I think she feels it back in bucket loads from him as well.[15]

The play's final moments have also been interpreted as an act of defiance, at least within an early modern context. Sixteenth-century ideal wives were indeed obedient, but they were silent too, something Katherina refuses to be. By all accounts, speech is the one consistent feature of her character from beginning to end. Using language that polarizes the two sisters, Tranio says, 'Mark'd you not how her sister / Began to scold and raise up such a storm / That mortal ears might hardly endure the din' (1.1.170–2). Melinda Spencer argues that given the bridal ritual the gesture connotes and her lengthy, rhetorically apt speech, 'her compliance is presented as a role she must play in order to get what she wants, as well as a role necessary for social stability'.[16] This is not a sign of submission, according to Spencer, it is performance. Spiro would disagree: a reconciliation with female subordination can be achieved by playing the scene lovingly. But she does see Shakespeare interrogating early-modern courtship rituals that construct false hierarchies between men and women that are immediately reversed upon marriage.

Thus, for Spiro, Shakespeare's social scrutiny occurs throughout the play. All the suitors are questionable, and Bianca's performance as 'mistress' is highly suspect. In the wedding scene, Spiro says that Katherina is,

a woman hoping she's going to be swept off her feet. And that's not what we want to necessarily say as feminists; but I wasn't afraid of that either, of a deep longing that she dared not think that he might just come along and save her from this world and take her off on his horse. And then he turns up on Grumio! You know?! That's the humour. And so for me, it's those contrasts that Shakespeare has written so brilliantly, a woman desperate to be taken off by a knight in shining armour and then this is what really happens. This is reality.[17]

Shakespeare is no doubt scrutinizing cultural rituals around courtship, marriage, and love. Perhaps there is scope for imagining the Kate-Petruchio relationship as a great love story. Regardless of whether a theatre company emphasizes love, comedy, or cruelty, the play's cultivation of mental abuse and occasional torture will never quite be acceptable to a modern sensibility. Spiro, perhaps one of the most energized, clever yet vulnerable Katherinas I have seen, plays an idealistic scenario with her Petruchio. But I admire her faith in love and in Shakespeare: she discovered a deep and mutual love between the couple and still managed to find the feminist in Shakespeare, something we are all trying to do.

Notes

1   Holly A. Crocker, 'Affective Resistance: Performing Passivity and Playing A-Part in *The Taming of the Shrew*', *Shakespeare Quarterly* 54, 2 (Summer, 2003), pp. 142–59, (142).

2   Ann Thompson ed., introduction, *The Taming of the Shrew*, The New Cambridge Shakespeare (Cambridge, 1984), p. 3.

3   Emily Detmer, 'Civilizing Subordination: Domestic Violence and *The Taming of the Shrew*', *Shakespeare Quarterly* 48, 3 (Autumn 1997): 273–94, 274.

4   Ben Brantley, 'Be it Padua or Illyria, Boys will be Boistrous', *New York Times* Theater Review, 20 March 2007 theater2. nytimes.com/2007/03/20/theater/reviews/20brantley.html (accessed 20 January 2013).

5   'Renaissance style' is indicated in publicity material denoting that a production will be set in the early modern period, but without deploying 'original practices'. See Carson and Karim-Cooper, *Shakespeare's Globe: A Theatrical Experiment*

(Cambridge, 2008) for a discussion of 'original practices' as a specific Globe performance practice.

6   Farah Karim-Cooper interview with Samantha Spiro, August 2012.

7   Spiro interview, August 2012.

8   Spiro interview, August 2012.

9   William Shakespeare, *The Taming of the Shrew*, ed. Barbara Hodgdon, The Arden Shakespeare, 3rd edn. (London, 2010).

10   Detmer, p. 286.

11   Spiro interview, August 2012.

12   Hodgdon, p. 128.

13   Spiro Interview, August 2012.

14   Crocker, p. 142.

15   Spiro interview, August 2012.

16   Melinda Spencer, 'Kate's Forward Humor: Historicizing Affect in *The Taming of the Shrew*', *South Atlantic Review* 69,1 (Winter, 2004), 61–84, 78.

17   Spiro interview, August 2012.

30

Ms-directing Shakespeare at the Globe to Globe Festival, 2012

Sonia Massai
King's College London

The Globe to Globe Festival showcased thirty-seven productions in thirty-seven languages at Shakespeare's Globe during the World Shakespeare Festival in 2012. Only five of these productions were directed or co-directed by women. Such a low figure sadly confirms that women theatre directors are still less likely to direct Shakespeare than their male counterparts – as Elizabeth Schafer pointed out in 1998, when she first used the wry term 'ms-directing' as a riposte to those who viewed productions directed by women as somehow intrinsically 'misguided' and 'misdirected'.[1] Although proportionally under-represented, the women directors whose work was included in the Globe to Globe Festival made a significant contribution to this event, which turned out to be the highlight of the World Shakespeare Festival as a whole. Productions directed by women ranged from Maja Kleczewska's Polish

Macbeth, where rape and infanticide, rather than regicide, epitomized the horrors ushered in by moral and political disorder, to Rachel House's Maori *Troilus and Cressida*, a stunning celebration of the indigenous language, culture and performative traditions of New Zealand. Less obviously controversial or uncompromisingly local, but more subtly ground-breaking in several respects, was Daniel Goldman and Sarah Norman's *The Merry Wives of Windsor*, a collaboration between Bitter Pill and the Theatre Company of Kenya. My interest in this production lies in its interestingly hybrid, intercultural qualities, which effectively neutralize the risk of reducing not only non-Western cultures but also women directors of Shakespeare to mere markers of an essential otherness.[2]

Goldman and Norman's production of *The Merry Wives of Windsor* was fast paced and extremely entertaining. They cut exchanges generally omitted in performance, including William's Latin lesson at the beginning of Act IV. They also relied heavily on physical comedy and on repetition, which is already central to the structure of Shakespeare's play, where, most memorably, Anne Page has three suitors and Falstaff is subjected to three humiliating acts of retribution aimed at purging his sexual and financial greed. In Goldman and Norman's production, which followed the received text of the play quite closely, repetition informed several new comic routines. Slender, for example, became increasingly frustrated in the opening scene, calling out for his servant Simple three times before the latter came rushing on to the stage. Seconds later Anne entered the gallery above the main stage and Slender gestured for his servant to move off and give them some privacy. Simple, his eyes sheepishly fixed on his master's face, took three steps sideways, prompted each time by Slender's thundering looks, until he ended up balancing dangerously on the edge of the stage. The audience roared with laughter when after a well-timed pause, Slender stared at Simple impatiently one last time, and the latter, played by a diminutive young actor (Eric Wanyama), had no choice but to jump awkwardly into the yard. Slender went on to entertain Anne by miming Sackerson the bear (1.1.175) and did not realize that, halfway through his routine, Anne slipped out and was replaced by a bemused but congenial Page, who eventually invited him to join his other dinner guests indoors. Goldman and Norman skilfully guided the audience's response through this opening sequence by casting three actors in the role of temporary spectators, with Anne Page and her father in the gallery above the main stage and Simple in the yard. The opening act set the tone for the rest of this production, which was impeccably acted and directed throughout and was generally very well received, with one reviewer aptly describing it as 'visually intoxicating'.[3]

This thoroughly enjoyable production came across as strangely familiar, despite the fact that it was performed entirely in Swahili by a Kenyan cast and despite the recurrent use of traditional songs to punctuate changes of setting and of traditional tribal masks and dancing in the last scene, when Shakespeare's fairies were reimagined within the context of East African folklore. Emma Cox, for example, noted that '[w]hile it felt a long way from Merrie England, this Swahili production … stuck to fairly conventional, recognizable means of attracting laughs … and tapped into … tradition[s] of English comedy, clearly familiar to a London audience'.[4] The production seemed even more familiar to those who had seen Christopher Luscombe's 2008 Globe production or its revival in 2010. The Kenyans moved equally seamlessly on the main stage, the upper stage, and the yard and interacted often and confidently with the audience. Two members of the audience were, for example, enlisted to push the buck basket off stage, once a fat-suited, flamboyant, and unusually young Falstaff had somersaulted into it to hide from Ford. More crucially, both companies distanced themselves from darker interpretations of the play, which became popular on both page and stage in the second half of the twentieth-century.[5] Some reviewers compared both productions to popular sit-coms. Maddy Costa in *The Guardian* took her cue

from the programme of the Globe production and compared
Ford to Basil Fawlty from *Fawlty Towers*.[6] Similarly, the
Kenyan production, with its 'feisty, wickedly funny women',
their 'pretty grand households in a wealthy neighbourhood'
and '[a] gaggle of flawed men, jealous or lecherous, who have
in common their desire for, and their failure to outsmart, the
local ladies' reminded Sarah Olive of '*Desperate Housewives*,
or any other such American comedy-drama where secrets and
lies, truths, and untruths, are spun out and revealed by groups
of female friends'.[7]

The surprising familiarity of the Kenyan production was
probably, at least partly, the product of the potentially
problematic division of labour between two British-trained
directors and the Kenyan actors, who were trained not only
to feel at home on the Globe stage but also to personate
their characters through rehearsal techniques and exercises
that were unfamiliar to them. In an interview conducted
during their brief residence at the Globe, Sharon Nanjosi,
who played Sir Hugh Evans, Anne Page, Pistol and Robert,
and Joshua Ogutu, who played Page, Nym, and Mistress
Quickly, described their physical training and the detailed
profiling of their characters, which they were required to
discuss in rehearsal, as a novel and challenging experience.[8]
Even the extensive use of doubling (eight actors played
twenty characters, the only exception being Mrisho Mpoto,
who played Falstaff alone) did not interfere with the actors'
personation of their characters as consistently recognizable
types, if not necessarily psychologically realistic individuals.

Despite similarities with recent stagings of the play as a
festive romp, this production was marked by a sustained
attempt to negotiate, rather than to erase or neutralize,
cultural difference. Significant in this respect was the opening
sequence. All companies invited to take part in the Festival
were issued with basic guidelines, ranging from the running
time (not to exceed two hours plus a fifteen-minute interval),
to the use of small props and no sets. Other guidelines proved
more problematic, including the ban on English even for

companies who regularly perform Shakespeare in English both
in their home countries and on tour and the ban on flags or
any other signifiers of national identity that might antagonize
communities in conflict over land or political independence.
Blatantly contravening the organizers' brief, the actor playing
Mistress Page, Chichi Seii, stepped onto the main stage,
invited the seating members of the audience to stand up, and
sang the Kenyan national anthem beautifully and solemnly,
thus occupying for a few minutes the powerful position of
prologue, a key vehicle for addressing the audience directly
before the fictive world of the play is fully established. Seii cut
a striking, elegant figure against the backdrop of the Globe
stage, where prologues and epilogues would originally be
delivered not only by members of all male companies but also
almost exclusively by male characters; as Rosalind reminds us
at the end of *As You Like It*, 'It is not the fashion to see the
lady the epilogue; but it is no more unhandsome than to see
the lord the prologue' (5.4.197–9).[9] Even when women actors
were first allowed to perform on the public stage, they were
not generally expected to address their audiences directly. On
the few occasions when they did, their lines stressed the exceptional quality of their role. Mrs Nell, for example, donning
'an Amazonian habit' at the revival of Ben Jonson's *Catiline*
at the Theatre Royal in 1669, saluted her audience as follows:
'A *Woman's Prologue*! / *This is vent'rous News*; / *But we, a*
Poet *wanting, Crav'd a Muse*'.[10] Though no longer familiar to
modern audiences, the roles of the prologue and the epilogue
still have unique resonance of the Globe stage, especially as
the actors who address the audience walk downstage and
stand in a spot which is close to the centre of the theatre.
Other actors, always male, greeted the audience, often in
English, during the Globe to Globe Festival, but Seii made a
different type of statement: by singing the Kenyan anthem,
five decades after Kenya gained political independence from
British rule, Seii was claiming a confident and affirmative voice
for her people as she and her fellow actors were preparing to
re-present Shakespeare in Swahili on the Globe stage.

Given the collaborative nature of this production, the decision to open it with the Kenyan national anthem did not seem driven purely by nationalist sentimentalism. National identity is extremely fraught in modern-day Kenya, mostly because Kenya, like the majority of African countries, became a 'post-tribal' state following the Berlin Conference of 1884–5, when, as Kole Omotoso has eloquently put it, 'Africa was delimited and mapped as a place of modern states with no consideration of tribal borders and cultural differences'.[11] Ethnic difference often underlies political conflict, which in turns leads to outbursts of civil unrest. The violent clashes that followed the last presidential election in Kenya in 2007 were symptomatic of such tensions; in 2012 all Kenyans would have been aware of the possibility of the reigniting of such violence in the build-up to the next election in spring 2013. Rather than pushing to the fore a nationalist agenda, Seii's spell-binding recitation of the national anthem accented the power of Swahili as a vehicle through which not only Shakespeare but also cultural and political identities in modern-day Kenya can be reimagined. The singing of the national anthem at the beginning of this production pre-empted the risk of reducing the foreignness of the language for non-Swahili members of the audience to an incidental, aesthetic feature of an otherwise familiar play.

Even those features that were registered as familiar and conventional by British critics and reviewers – the doubling of characters and a regular interaction between the actors and the audience – were in fact also specifically meant to appeal to Kenyan audiences because they reflect local theatrical styles and concerns.[12] Regular interaction with the audience is for example intrinsic to the type of popular theatre championed in Kenya by Ngugi wa Thiong'o since the 1970s. As Ciaruni Chesaina and Evan Mwangi explain, Ngugi revived traditional dramatic forms to critique the neocolonial quality of public institutions, including the elitarian ethos that informed the Kenya National Theatre, which, first founded before Kenya reached independence, continued to be 'European in orientation' afterwards.[13] In Ngugi's model of popular theatre 'democratic values are expressed through action in which the audience and the actor participate actively in the theatrical production'.[14] Similarly, the extensive use of doubling in Goldman and Norman's production did not simply aim to revive one of the main staging conventions in Shakespeare's theatre. In fact, the most prominent and memorable use of this convention, which involved the casting of one actor, Neville Sanganyi, to play all of Anne's suitors, Slender, Dr Caius, and Fenton, foregrounded the motif of arranged marriages as a resonant issue among Kenyans. By representing the suitors as ultimately interchangeable, this production suggested that the comic resolution depended more on Anne's ability to choose her husband, independently of his qualities or the arguably disinterested nature of his attachment to Anne, than on the fulfilment of a romantic interest in the subplot. Interestingly, while British reviewers remarked on Sanganyi's virtuoso performance of three key roles, only Kenyan reviewers have singled out Anne's predicament and Page's opposition to Fenton because '[t]he gentleman is of no having' (3.2.64–5), since Goldman and Norman's production has started to tour Kenya.[15] More generally, the fact that this production has appealed to British and to Kenyan audiences for different reasons is a testament to its sustained and ultimately successful effort to put the play and the traditions and conventions associated with Shakespeare's theatre into a productive dialogue with contemporary forms of theatrical performance in Kenya and with issues that have social and cultural currency among Kenyan audiences.

The collaboration between Goldman and Norman was also significant in light of the enduring disparity in the numbers of male and female directors currently working on Shakespeare, both at a national level in Britain and at international events, like the Globe to Globe Festival. Norman first directed a version of *The Merry Wives of Windsor* in Shona in 2009. This earlier production was conceived and performed at the Oval House Theatre in South London, a key venue for intercultural

experiments with Shakespeare involving local diasporic artists
and communities, especially of African origins. It was then
revived, later in 2009, at HIFA, the Harare International
Festival of the Arts. When the Festival organizers expressed
an interest in her work, Norman restarted working on *The
Merry Wives of Windsor* with a different company, in a
different language, and with a new co-director.[16] The collaborative impulse that prompted Norman to seek new partners in
preparation for the Globe to Globe Festival has clearly paid
off. Not only has her Swahili version of *Merry Wives* proved
immensely popular, both in London and in Kenya, but it
has also eluded categorization as 'Ms-directed Shakespeare',
thanks to Norman's collaboration with Goldman and with
Theatre Company Kenya. Less optimistically, though, I was
disappointed to find that, by the time this production returned
to Kenya and started to tour in East Africa and India,
Norman's contribution as initiator and co-director of the
version staged in London during the Festival had started to
disappear from reviews and press releases. While changes in
the crediting of Norman's contribution to this production
were undoubtedly benign – Norman has recently redirected
her artistic and professional efforts towards non-theatrical
projects – one can only hope to see more, not less, of Norman
in future projects involving intercultural experiments with
Shakespeare on stage.

   Last, but not least, I should like to stress that Norman
and Goldman's collaboration with Theatre Company Kenya
reflects an exciting new tendency to 'Africanize' Shakespeare
and 'spaces associated with European theatre' in Kenya,
which first started in the 1990s.[17] Theatre Company Kenya,
which was founded in 2000, create original Kenyan-based
performances but also use Swahili as a vehicle to appropriate
and localize classical texts drawn from a worldwide theatrical repertory, within which Shakespeare enjoys a prominent
role. Goldman and Norman's co-production with Theatre
Company Kenya fulfilled one of the main objectives of this
new breed of theatre artists in Kenya, who strive to close the

so far gaping distance between neocolonial forms of insti-
tutionalized theatrical entertainment, aimed only at wealthy
minorities in Nairobi, where the Kenya National Theatre
has been based since it first opened in 1950, and the popular
theatre promoted by leading theatre theorists, writers and
practitioners like Ngugi wa Thiong'o. I certainly left the Globe
Theatre, after its opening at the Festival on 25 April 2012,
feeling that this production of *The Merry Wives of Windsor*
had confidently and joyfully pointed the way towards refresh-
ingly productive collaborations across gender and cultural
divides.[18]

Notes

1   Elizabeth Schafer, *Ms-Directing Shakespeare: Women Direct
     Shakespeare* (London, 1998), p. 6.

2   The other productions directed by women at the Globe to
     Globe Festival were Corinne Jaber's *The Comedy of Errors*,
     performed in Dari Persian by Roy-e-Sabs, an Afghani company
     based in Kabul, and Paula Garfield's *Love's Labours Lost*,
     performed by Deafinitely Theatre in British Sign Language.

3   Andrew Gilchrist, *The Guardian*, 27 April 2012.

4   Emma Cox, 'The girl defies': A Kenyan *Merry Wives of
     Windsor*, in Susan Bennett and Christie Carson (eds),
     Shakespeare Beyond English: A Global Experiment
     (Cambridge, forthcoming 2013) pp. 53–66.

5   The darker undertones of the final scene, where Falstaff can
     be represented as victim and scapegoat and his public shaming
     as symbolic emasculation, became central to the approach of
     some late-twentieth-century critics and directors, including
     Terry Hands, who directed the play for the RSC in 1968, and
     Jeanne Addison Roberts in her seminal study, *Shakespeare's
     English Comedy: 'The Merry Wives of Windsor' in Context*
     (Lincoln, NE, 1979). Roberts relied on Northrop Frye's ritual
     interpretation of comedy and her work in turn affected critics
     such as Nancy Cotton (cf. 'Castrating (W)itches: Impotence

and Magic in *The Merry Wives of Windsor*' in *Shakespeare Quarterly* 38, 3 (1987), 320–6), who links the play's representation of masculinity to anxieties about cuckoldry as symbolic castration that are reinforced by Falstaff's ritual bashing.

6   Maddy Costa, *The Guardian*, 20 August 2010

7   Sarah Olive, review of *Merry Wives of Windsor*, in Paul Edmondson, Paul Prescott and Erin Sullivan eds, *Year of Shakespeare: Re-Living the World Shakespeare Festival* (London, 2013), pp. 133–5.

8   A recording of this interview can be found at http:// soundcloud.com/globe-education/tracks?page=2

9   See also the anonymous play *Every Woman in her Humour* (1609; STC 25948), where the boy actor playing '*Flauia as a Prologue*' remarks: 'a she prologue is as rare as an Vsurers Almes' (A2r).

10   Ben Jonson, *Catiline*, 1669 (WING J1008), A3 ll. 6–7.

11   Kole Omotoso, 'Concepts of history and theatre in Africa', in Kole Omotoso ed., *The History of Theatre in Africa* (Cambridge: Cambridge University Press, 2004), 1–12:11.

12   Keith Pearson, managing director of Theatre Company Kenya, private correspondence.

13   Ciaruni Chesaina and Evan Mwangi, 'Kenya', in Omotoso (2004), pp. 206–32, p. 219, p. 221.

14   Ibid., p. 227.

15   Joel Magu, *The Star*, 10 January 2013, http://www.the-star. co.ke/news/article-102278/wanawake-wa-heri-wa-winsa-great-masterpiece.

16   Keith Pearson, managing director of Theatre Company Kenya, private correspondence.

17   Chesaina and Mwangi, in Omotoso, 229.

18   I would like to thank Patricia Tatspaugh, as well as the volume editors, for reading earlier drafts of this essay.

31

Sexing up Goneril: Feminism and Fetishization in Contemporary *King Lear* Performance

Kevin A. Quarmby

Oxford College of Emory University

In April 2007, just prior to its opening Press Night, Trevor Nunn's RSC Stratford *King Lear* suffered an unexpected mishap. The production's Goneril, Frances Barber, broke her leg while cycling. Her accident left the RSC in a quandary. Do they 'open' with the official understudy, Melanie Jessop, stepping into Goneril's role, or do they delay Press Night and risk the raised eyebrows of suspicious theatre critics? As one commentator noted at the time, 'it's the understudy's dream [...] or nightmare':

> Twenty-four hours ago [Jessop] was Second Gloucester Servant, handing Edmund a glass of wine. Now she's Goneril.
> (Hopkins, 'Anecdote')[1]

The RSC's response to this change in Gonerils was calculated if not predictable. The Press Night of *Lear* was delayed six weeks to allow Barber's recovery. Jessop acted as stopgap daughter to Ian McKellen's Lear before returning to her minor role in the play.[2]

When Barber did eventually resume playing, *Lear* received its 'delayed critical plaudits'.[3] Nevertheless, Barber's return prompted a Leader comment in *The Guardian* that asked readers to 'spare a thought' for understudies like Jessop, who do 'most of the shows but [receive] none of the critical accolades' (*Guardian*). Similarly, Susannah Clapp of *The Observer* notes that, 'though the public had been paying full price for tickets,' they were unaware that the production was 'deemed not to be ready for critics' because Jessop had 'apparently never rehearsed with McKellen (why not?).'[4] Clapp's parenthetical question is understandable in the context of one not directly associated with theatre practice. In reality, understudies seldom if ever benefit from rehearsal with the principal actors. Understudy rehearsals traditionally begin *after* Press Night, once rehearsal room experimentation has ended. By then, the director has 'blocked' the play (decided precise onstage positions for the cast and properties), such 'blocking' being recorded for nightly reproduction to guarantee actors (and understudies) 'hit' pre-set lighting states. The presence of McKellen, Barber, or any other principal actor at an understudy rehearsal is unprecedented.

The RSC does, however, impose additional requirements on its understudies. As one 2007 employee confirms, the 'bulk' of RSC understudy rehearsals might occur 'after the main show has opened', but understudies also rehearse 'during the main rehearsal' period.[5] In addition, RSC understudies are expected 'to be on their lines [to have memorized their parts] very early on just in case', and to be 'present in the [rehearsal] room during all of the main blocking generally.' This was the case with Nunn's *Lear*. The RSC's unusual foresight (and its privileged finances that accommodate mirror casting) ensured that Barber's last-minute misfortune did not affect

Lear's performance schedule. Nevertheless, Jessop's readiness to 'take over such a substantial role with less than six hours' notice' is impressive, though her efforts were denied critical recognition (Hopkins). Jessop's Goneril remains therefore an apocryphized theatrical anomaly.

In itself, this anecdote might appear an insignificant footnote to theatre history were it not for the critical issues it highlights. The male 'star-centricity' of Nunn's *Lear*, evidenced by the RSC's much advertised 'reunion' of Nunn and McKellen, might account for the 'traditionally, conservatively, commercially staged world tour' that followed (Hopkins). Even so, it was the loss of Barber's Goneril that most affected the play's star-centric promotional identity. Without Barber in her allotted role, this *Lear* seemed, to the RSC publicity machine at least, incomplete. Such prioritizing of Goneril might appear surprising in the light of Valerie Wayne's 1991 collection of essays, *The Matter of Difference*, which includes Ann Thompson's wryly titled essay, 'Are there any women in *King Lear*?'[6] Thompson's question highlights the apparent disappearance of Goneril and Regan from late twentieth-century criticism. Nonetheless, as this chapter suggests, it also heralded alternative critical analyses that invited revisionist reinterpretations of Goneril and Regan. In tandem, productions either anticipated, paralleled, or (in some instances) consciously manifested this shift in critical focus, with the Barber/Jessop anecdote providing final tangible proof that, in the theatrical context, there are indeed 'women in *King Lear*'.

The disappearance of Goneril and Regan from 1980s scholarly debate is blamed in part, Thompson argues, on the phallocentricity of new historicist and cultural materialist criticism. These relatively new (in 1991) practices demonstrate a 'preoccupation with institutional forms of absolute male power [that] represents a drive for "mastery" which goes beyond the text' (Thompson, p. 118). Predominantly male new historicist and cultural materialist critics, who seemingly ignored 'the specific oppression of women within social and political structures,' were obviously at fault (p. 127).

Thompson's dismay at the masculinization of new historicist criticism is accompanied by a disappointment with feminist critics who appear 'reluctant to allow that men as well as women are ideologically inscribed in the past as well as in the present' (p. 127). By focusing on the perceived misogyny of Shakespeare, feminist critics stood accused of reifying the concepts of 'polarization' and mutual exclusivity into the critical canon, which in turn compounded the disappearance of Goneril and Regan from scholarly discourse (p. 127). This, despite Thompson's call for feminist critics not simply to 'give up on *King Lear*': 'we must not be content to turn our backs on such a powerful text' (p. 127). Feminists, new historicists, and cultural materialists unknowingly collaborate, so Thompson implies, in materializing Albany's Act V dismissive command. The recently empowered widower might call to 'Produce [Goneril and Regan's] bodies' (*KL* 5.3.229), only to 'cover their faces' (*KL* 5.3.240), but 1980s critical gender divisions went further in erasing these women entirely from the play.

In the years since Thompson's essay, Goneril and Regan have gained an alternative status as political victims rather than misogynized aberrations. Such politicization is accompanied, however, by an apparent over-sexualization of Goneril and Regan in performance. This foregrounding of the sisters as sexual predators seems counter to their serious re-examination in a feminist context. Nevertheless, their sexuality also highlights the dramatic currency of the characters as fetishized commodities for twenty-first century stage consumption. This shift in theatrical status, from unseen entity to sexualized commodity, offers the most convincing explanation for the star-status concern of the RSC, with the loss of Barber's legendary sensuality sufficient to delay opening night for nearly six weeks.[7] What Thompson calls the 'drive for "mastery"' of new historicist criticism seems uncomfortably manifested in the predominantly masculinized theatre industry, in which primarily male directors and producers seem preoccupied with 'star-centricity' and sexualization, rather than characterful performance.

A 1988 essay by John Turner highlights a peculiarly British reason for the critical neglect of Goneril and Regan, one potentially lost on an American audience.[8] When asking if critics like Turner are 'conspiring to erase women' from *Lear*, or if they are 'simply noticing the extent to which Shakespeare has already done so' (p. 122), Thompson quotes Turner's description of Goneril and Regan as 'the Wicked Sisters, the Ugly Sisters' (Turner, p. 111). Derived from the British pantomime tradition of Christmas children's entertainment, this localized reference projects a dismissive trope of humorous malice onto Goneril and Regan's personalities. By associating them with the Ugly Sisters – pantomime villains traditionally played by outrageously unconvincing female impersonators – Lear's daughters become inconsequential ciphers, more at home in vaudeville entertainment than Shakespearean tragedy.

The relegation of Goneril and Regan to the role of comedy fiends, by critics who seem intent on erasing these 'sea-monsters' from serious study, highlights a growing divide between literary and performance studies of Shakespeare. Nevertheless, this divide also invites study of the sisters as twentieth- and twenty-first century performance constructs, in analyses that combine the best of new historicist and feminist critical rigour. By way of example, Carol Chillington Rutter's 1997 essay, 'Eel Pie and Ugly Sisters in *King Lear*', offers performance inspired evidence that reinvigorates serious study of the sisters, even if it too bears the mark of pantomime analogy.[9] Rutter observes the generic similarity between the sisters' deviance, as 'imagined in *sexualized* metaphors', and concludes that these characters conform to a universal Shakespearean 'nexus of ideas', whereby male 'transgression may be sexual, may be political, but man's sexual transgression is always politicized':

> Female transgression is *only* sexual, is *always* sexualized. Even when a woman acts politically, the act is imagined sexually.
>
> (Rutter, p. 197)

The uncomfortable truth of Shakespearean social politics, whereby 'men who betray men' are called 'traitors,' and 'women who betray men' are called 'whores,' underscores Rutter's appraisal of Lear's daughters as sexualized, as opposed to wilfully sexual, transgressors (p. 197).

Rutter's comments confirm the value of performance criticism in offering alternative readings of Goneril and Regan, which in turn invite contextual acceptance, rather than condemnation based on anachronistic bias and Ugly Sister ciphering. Significantly, in the light of the RSC's Press Night postponement, Rutter views the overbearing predominance of male directors as a colluding factor in such misogynistic posturing (p. 175). For example, Peter Brook's 1962 film presents the on-screen suicide of Irene Worth's Goneril; swaying and creaking in leather-bound frenzy, Goneril dashes out her brains on a nearby rock with the intensity of a Marlovian Bajaseth. Although Brook's interpretation furnishes Goneril with a dramatic exit in keeping with Worth's malevolent portrayal, it also removes her corpse from the bleak closing scenes. The demotion of the dead sisters to unseen offstage referents is more stark in Jonathan Miller's 1982 BBC production, in which Albany's command, 'Produce the bodies, be they alive or dead' (5.3.229), is immediately followed by Edmund's dying speech, 'I pant for life' (5.3.241). Gillian Barge's Goneril and Penelope Wilton's Regan never reappear, with their deaths ignored for the remainder of the play. Only Nunn's 2008 film accords Barber's Goneril and Monica Dolan's Regan their post-mortem re-presentation, their faces exposed as the stretcher-bearers await Albany's dismissive command. Between 1962 and 2008, therefore, the reinstatement of Lear's daughters as significant onstage presences (albeit in death) suggests a renewed recognition of their importance as women in the play, especially when transitioning from malicious harridans to sensual temptresses.

Rutter's 1997 performance study, with its appraisal of Goneril and Regan as '*sexualized* metaphors,' appears isolated in its reconsideration of the sisters. Indeed, Cristina León Alfar, writing in 2003, still argues that the 'troublesome' Goneril and Regan remain 'among the most neglected of Shakespeare's women in academia' (p. 17).[10] Alfar blames feminist criticism, which seems fixated with the 'problem of the absent mothers' in *Lear*, for the sisters' relegation 'to the margins' (p. 206n.). Alluding to Thompson, Alfar also confirms their continued victimization by prejudiced, misogynistic scholars, who still view them as 'evil' and 'unnatural' because they 'behave like men' (p. 19). This 'entrenched' attitude to 'female evil,' Alfar contends, masks what is truly 'unnatural': Lear's tyrannical and 'grossly self-indulgent system of monarchy' (p. 80). Read not as 'evil' women, as Ugly Sisters of comic pantomime, but as daughters of an egotistical monarch, Goneril and Regan's underwritten, unsoliloquized agendas become clear.[11]

For Alfar, the 'logic' of *Lear 'requires* Goneril and Regan to rebel against traditional feminine passivity *to become* cruel tyrants, to become monarchs' (p. 109). Jena Said Makdisi, writing about the compromises women make when embarking on a political career, echoes this sentiment.[12] Offering Goneril and Regan as exemplars of political expediency, Makdisi asks: 'Can women enter politics without playing by the rules set by the existing system, and therefore becoming not only tainted by it, but an integral part of the game?' (p. 108). Neither 'evil' natures, nor subversive gender transgressions, compel Goneril and Regan to behave so monstrously; they are forced to become 'monsters by playing the monstrous game of power' (p. 108). Although Makdisi's and Alfar's respective studies demonstrate the continuing appeal of 'power' modelling in a post-Foucauldian critical environment, their responses are less polarizing, and certainly less judgemental. Goneril and Regan are, at the very least, now fully visible.

A renewed critical visibility, which accords with the tangible visibility of Goneril and Regan in twenty-first century performance, is likewise evident in Marguerite A. Tassi's 2011 study, *Women and Revenge*.[13] When considering the gender, generic, and ethical implications of *Lear*, Tassi argues that the 'returning of harm for *perceived* harm' is essential for understanding the sisters' anger and vindictiveness (p. 149). Goneril and Regan might be 'dogged female revengers', but they are mere shadows of their earlier *King Leir* counterparts (p. 152). In the anonymous *Leir*, Gonoril and Ragan share the 'conventional stage role of villain-revenger' (p. 160) when plotting against that 'proud pert peat,' Cordella (*Leir* 1.2.2).[14] Shakespeare's shift of attention to the vengefulness of Lear renders the king, and not Cordelia, vulnerable to these 'irrationally' empowered older sisters (p. 152).

The revengeful turning point might be Lear's vicious cursing, but its importance is significantly highlighted, so Tassi argues, in performance.[15] Focusing on the historical and social consequences of 'parental curses', Tassi considers Richard Eyre's 1998 BBC production, in which Barbara Flynn's Goneril 'turns her back to Lear with tears in her eyes as she endures the assault of his curses' (p. 72). Similarly, Nunn's 2008 film shows Barber 'steel[ing] herself against the emotional trauma involved in confronting Lear and withstanding his curse': 'Yet she nearly cries while he is unleashing his fury, and once he departs, she is wracked with sobs, which she must work fiercely to control' (p. 72). These pre- and post-millennial visions invite consideration of the devastating effect of parental curses, and offer if not an explanation, then at least an emotional impetus for Goneril and Regan's subsequent malice.

In line with Tassi's commentary, Barber explores the trauma of Lear's curses in an interview published prior to her accident.[16] Describing how, when McKellen's Lear first cursed her in rehearsals, she 'burst into tears,' Barber explains:

> I've never seen Goneril do that in a production, but then I thought, why not, she wipes away her tears and then swears never to forgive him, and only becomes very hard faced after that initial outburst.

> (Ansdell)

Unaware of Flynn's emotional response in Eyre's 1998 production, Barber nevertheless reacts in accord with Alfar's description of inevitability in Goneril's hatred. Similarly, Barber's comment, that she 'love[s] how Goneril describes her husband as a "milk livered man" [4.2.51] because it's the perfect way to describe this lily-livered idiot who she unfortunately had to marry', confirms how strident female behaviour seems justifiable in performance, if not necessarily in the (male) literary critic's mind (Ansdell).

In the years since Thompson first commented on the absence of Goneril and Regan in *Lear* criticism, feminist and new historicist attitudes have, almost imperceptibly, changed. Gone is Shakespeare as wilful misogynist; in his place appear Goneril and Regan as victims of a political regime dominated by a patriarchal tyrant. In this male domain, the sisters must negotiate the minefield of male intrigue using whatever wiles at their limited disposal. Sexuality and guile, deemed aberrations and subversive tactics by male commentators, offer these women their only hope of survival. Feminist critics, influenced by new historicist practice, explore the political and sexual implications of this subversive behaviour, but such studies remain few and far between. On stage and in film, however, the sexuality of the sisters has acquired its own currency, so much so that Goneril offers its star vehicle status to actors famed for their sexually nuanced performance styles.

Nunn's *Lear*, with its stellar cast, is indicative of this sexualization in a performance context. So important has Goneril become that, with the unexpected absence of Barber, and despite her successful replacement by Jessop, press coverage of the play was delayed to accommodate the 'star's' return. The favouring of the sexualized star over the skilled understudy actor, rather than suggesting a feminist reappraisal of Goneril as a victim, actually suggests a return to the invisibility of Goneril as a cipher, not for pantomimic evil, but for sexual deviance and illicit pleasure. The expunging of Jessop's feat from theatre history suggests an inherent chauvinism in the collective relationship between male directors, producers, and leading performers, who knowingly or unknowingly collude in manipulating audiences and journalists for commercial ends. There are indeed women in *Lear*, but invisibility through masculinization appears no longer to apply to the literary critical domain; instead, it has transferred seamlessly to the profit-driven world of theatre and film production. Only in death need we 'cover their faces'; in theatrical life, Goneril and Regan accommodate their new roles as sexualized, politicized victims, whose subversive sensuality guarantees the renewed exposure of these traditionally neglected Shakespearean women.

Notes

1   Justin B. Hopkins, 'An Anecdote from the Archive', supplement 'Abstract and Brief Chronicles: Creative and Critical Curation of Performance', *Liminalities, A Journal of Performance Studies*, 8, 1 (2012), 1–22. http://liminalities.net/8-1/anecdote.html (accessed 27 January 2013).

2   Jessop declined all requests to discuss this incident.

3   'In praise of ... understudies', Leader, *The Guardian* (3 June 2007). http://www.guardian.co.uk/commentisfree/2007/jun/04/theatre.comment (accessed 27 January 2013).

4   Susannah Clapp, 'A Crowning Glory for McKellen', *The Observer* (2 June 2007). http://www.guardian.co.uk/stage/2007/jun/03/rsc.theatre (accessed 27 January 2013).

5   Private email between Kevin Quarmby and RSC employee, who insisted on anonymity.

6   Ann Thompson, 'Are There any Women in *King Lear*?', in Valerie Wayne ed., *The Matter of Difference: Materialist Feminist Criticism of Shakespeare* (New York, 1991), pp. 117–28.

7   For Barber's sexually malevolent performance, see Kevin A. Quarmby, 'Review of *King Lear* for *Rogues and Vagabonds*' (2007). http://quarmby.biz/reviews/review_Klear1.htm (accessed 27 January 2013).

8   John Turner, '*King Lear*', in Graham Holderness, Nick Potter

and John Turner (eds), *Shakespeare: The Play of History* (London, 1988), pp. 89–118.

9   Carol Chillington Rutter, 'Eel Pie and Ugly Sisters in *King Lear*', in James Ogden and Arthur H. Scouten (eds), *Lear from Study to Stage: Essays in Criticism* (London, 1997), pp. 172–225.

10 Cristina León Alfar, *Fantasies of Female Evil: The Dynamics of Gender and Power in Shakespearean Tragedy* (Newark, 2003).

11 Claudette Hoover, 'Goneril and Regan: "so horrid as in woman"', *San Jose Studies* 10, 3 (1984), 49–65.

12 Jena Said Makdisi, 'War and Peace: Reflections of a Feminist', *Feminist Review* 88 (2008), 99–110.

13 Marguerite A. Tassi, *Women and Revenge in Shakespeare: Gender, Genre, and Ethics* (Selinsgrove, 2011).

14 *King Leir*, ed. Tiffany Stern, Globe Quartos (London, 2002).

15 Lynn Bradley, *Adapting 'King Lear' for the Stage* (Farnham, 2010).

16 Caroline Ansdell, '20 Questions With … Frances Barber', *Whatsonstage.com* (2 April 2007). http://www.whatsonstage. com/interviews/theatre/london/E8821173718472/20+Questions +With...+Frances+Barber.html (accessed 27 January 2013).

32

Not Sycorax

Judith Buchanan
University of York

Present Sycorax

For the New York Metropolitan Opera's 2011–12 season, librettist Jeremy Sams wrote a new opera, 'The Enchanted Island'.[1] In February 2012, the work also reached audiences around the world, beamed into cinemas in live HD. Although based on Shakespeare's *The Tempest*, 'The Enchanted Island' was built upon the pasticcio ('mash-up') principle of reinvention-through-amalgamation, an approach Sams used as the spur for rethinking the emotional and political dynamics of Prospero's island. Generous in its plundering of both musical and narrative sources, the opera draws on Baroque arias from the repertoires of Handel, Vivaldi, and Rameau, and scripts in characters beyond those stipulated by *The Tempest*'s *dramatis personae*, including some who have wandered in, as if unsuspectingly, from *A Midsummer Night's Dream*. In his most significant interpolation, Sams invited on to centre-stage a character who, though suggestively present in *The Tempest* through rhetorical reference, is physically absent from Shakespeare's play: Sycorax the witch.

In *The Tempest*, Sycorax has, we are told, died long before the dramatic action begins. She is invoked by her son Caliban to legitimize his claim on the island (1.2.333); and by Prospero both as a distasteful memory about the island's dishonourable past (1.2.281–4) and as the mechanism for keeping Ariel in grateful servitude ('Hast thou forgot / The foul witch Sycorax ...?' 1.2.357–8). The potency of her symbolic presence, however, is resonant. So much so, in fact, that Ted Hughes was prompted to declare that, in the real operations of the play, the news that Sycorax is dead functions as 'little more than a figure of speech'. Since, as Hughes asserts, Sycorax is 'everywhere',[2] reports of her death can seem, if not exaggerated, then at least circumscribed in relevance. The quality of Sycorax's absence is, therefore, crucially infused with a version of presence. The Caliban of *Une Tempête*, Aimé Césaire's 1969 post-colonial revision of the play, even refuses to accept that Sycorax is dead, choosing instead to believe in her as an ongoing symbolic counter to Prospero's oppressive rule – as alive as the earth itself: 'je sais qu[e la terre] vit, et que vit Sycorax.'[3]

'The Enchanted Island' inherits Césaire's Caliban's touchingly articulated faith in Sycorax's ongoing life, together with Hughes' implication that, in the ways that count, she is not in any case really dead, and converts this into a literal truth. 'I am coming back from the dead', said mezzosoprano Joyce DiDonato in interview, gleefully ventriloquizing the witch she plays.[4] Whereas in both Shakespeare and Césaire, Sycorax's existence had been dependent on other characters' (always) agenda-driven configurations of her, on Sams' stage, she becomes visible in her own right; and where she had been necessarily voiceless in Shakespeare, Sams gives her an emotional and narrative trajectory expressed through soaring arias that touch and move. Moreover, at the opera's close, in an interpretive turn implicitly craved by postcolonial readings of *The Tempest*, Prospero (countertenor David Daniels) kneels

FIGURE 4 *Sycorax (Joyce DiDonato) and Prospero (David Daniels) in 'The Enchanted Island', New York Met 2011/2012*

before her to seek forgiveness for past wrongs and to restore the island to her rule (Figure 4). Unsurprisingly, it is a dramatic tableau that stays in the memory. Not only does it offer a carefully crafted, restorative answering phrase to the treatment Sycorax has received in the back-story of this particular production, but it reaches significantly beyond the bounds of this production also, to speak back feelingly to the assumptions about the patrilineal shape of right endings that have underpinned most of the play's performance history.[5] In this single, charged performance moment, Sycorax is redeemed from a demonizing history, the established power imbalance between Prospero and Sycorax is dramatically revised and decades of critical wrestling with Prospero's colonial and patriarchal impulses find a fantasy resolution.

Sams credited Dryden with the idea of resurrecting and incarnating Sycorax: showcasing her theatrically was, Sams declared, a dramatic ploy simply 'too good not to steal.'[6] Sams' Sycorax, however, has more depth than the relatively shallow spectacle of Sycorax the twin sister (*sic*) of Caliban in Dryden and D'Avenant's 1667 adaptation. As embodied, and sung, by DiDonato, the operatic Sycorax proved a weighty counterbalance to Prospero and a figure of noteworthy pathos in her relationship with Caliban. The consensus in review was that DiDonato's Sycorax stole the show. She was praised for her 'unsparing ferocity', her 'knack for flamboyant theatrics' and for the ways in which she 'cackled, curled and soared with virtuosic flair in the bitchy-witchy spasms of Sycorax'. 'She commanded the stage from her first showcase scene,' wrote the *New York Times*; and in the midst of a 'sea of comedy', concluded *The Wall Street Journal*, DiDonato's Sycorax emerged 'a tragic heroine'.[7]

Absent Sycorax

As it happened, therefore, this particular Sycorax gave a performance of some force and moment. To have created a performative presence for Sycorax at all, however, was no small intervention into the dramatic scheme of Shakespeare's play. Firstly, there is no gender imbalance so startlingly extreme elsewhere in Shakespeare,[8] and a staged Sycorax necessarily dilutes the visual and narrative drama of Miranda's gender isolation. Secondly, incarnating Sycorax could potentially challenge the colourful, rhetorical accounts of her wickedness which, in her absence, Shakespeare's Prospero has taken near perverse delight in relating. For Shakespeare's Prospero, in fact, Sycorax's absence is a convenience – psychologically as well as politically. It licenses him to reach repeatedly, and insistently, for versions of her as the neatly demonizable foil against which he can define himself in reassuringly self-congratulatory terms. The parallels in their situations that anchor this comparison are self-evident. Each arrived on the island with a child following a banishment, and each then established him/herself as magical ruler of the island, with Ariel kept in service by each in turn.[9]

But there, as Prospero makes plain, the acknowledged parallels end, and the clear distinctions begin. The commands

Sycorax issued were 'earthy and abhorr'd' (1.2.273) whereas Prospero is a self-proclaimed figure of 'dignity' (1.2.73); Sycorax coupled with the devil (1.2.321) whereas Prospero's wife was 'a piece of virtue' (1.2.56); Sycorax animalistically 'littered' Caliban whereas Prospero's parental rectitude may be gauged by his claim to 'have done nothing but in care of' Miranda (II.iii.16); Sycorax is the imprisoner of Ariel (1.2.276), Prospero the liberator (1.2.292–3); she is carnality ('earthy', 'grown into a hoop', mothering a 'whelp' 1.2.258–84), he, intellect ('[w]ithout a parallel' in 'the liberal arts' 1.2.73–4); she is dark magic to his good, female magical principle to his male. In Prospero's 'interested' account, the direct comparisons are many, and they matter. His insistence that Ariel should remember the much rehearsed detail of Sycorax's island story, and his half bullying, half needy instruction to Ariel to 'speak' and 'tell' him of it, reveal his own need to have her tale recounted (1.2.150–268). Point by point Prospero asserts, and needs to hear spoken back to him, the fact of Sycorax's villainy, catechizing Ariel in the distinctions between Sycorax and himself until, at the close of the dialogic bout, he finally hears what he needs to hear – his own nobility ('That's my noble master!' 1.2.299) comfortingly rearticulated. Within the simple, if manipulative, schema established by Prospero, hearing his own nobility thus proclaimed temporarily exorcizes the unruly witch presence that haunts him. The ignobility of Sycorax certainly absorbs more of his attention, and specifically of his bile, than her role in the action should properly justify. In fact, the disproportionate degree of attention that the absent witch receives from Prospero suggests the extent of her significance in his framing of self. The acuteness of Prospero's anxiety to be understood as the counter to unruly female sorcery – as, insistently, Not Sycorax – is, therefore, part of the dramatic engine of the play.

By Act V, Prospero's self-distancing mechanisms from the debasement of female magical principle have been firmly established. In his self-consciously magnanimous declaration that 'the rarer action is / In virtue than in vengeance' (5.1.27–8), the extent of his remove from the figure of the vengeful witch is consolidated with apparently irrefutable finality. But the play does not let the Prospero-Sycorax dialectic rest there. Rather it is in precisely this moment, when Prospero's status as noble man might seem most assured, that he is then overcome by an act of linguistic possession that problematizes the very distinction that has seemed key to his knowledge of who he is – and, importantly, of who he isn't. As has been well charted, Prospero's 'Ye elves of hills, brooks, standing lakes, and groves' speech (5.1.33–51), in which he first celebrates the extent of his magical powers and then renounces them, has a near quotational relationship with the 'Ye Ayres and windes: ye Elves of Hilles, of Brookes, of Woods alone / Of standing Lakes' speech of magical vaunting in Ovid's *Metamorphoses* Book VII, 263–77 (as rendered in Arthur Golding's popular 1567 translation). The parallels between speeches are striking and clearly intended to be identified by sufficient sections of the audience to inflect an understanding of Prospero. The highly educated character of some of the earliest (court and Blackfriars) audiences for *The Tempest* licensed it to parade a little well managed erudition on the assumption that swathes of its audiences would catch the allusion. And catching the allusion in this case meant identifying Prospero's appropriated Ovidian speech as belonging to the sorceress Medea.

If Medea has inhabited a surrogate in *The Tempest* before Act V, it has clearly been her fellow sorceress Sycorax. Stephen Orgel points out that even Sycorax's name ('Sy' + 'corax') may be derived from one of Medea's epithets, 'Scythian Raven'.[10] But in Prospero's abjuration speech, Medea's influence in the play is shown to extend beyond the intimate engagement of this dark sorority. In citing Medea, Prospero gives voice, almost despite himself, to a darker sorcerer within – a figure whose voice, inherited from Ovid, is both female and morally suspect. And so it is, through the linguistic allegiance with the Medea/Sycorax composite, that the neurotic energy with which Prospero has kept his witch as foil is now suggestively exposed as having its roots in a deeper recognition of her not as foil but kin. The Medean echo licences the suspicion in an audience that the benevolence of Prospero's 'art' may have been over-egged – setting him apart, as the exercise of that art does, from the rest of humanity, both literally and morally. And it allows Prospero himself unobtrusively to acknowledge an inner darkness to his metaphysics. The imperative he feels then to abjure his powers is intimately related to this recognition: the acknowledged kinship of his own 'rough magic' with the witch's dark arts leaves a disquieting imprimitur upon his person that, having been first, and expensively, owned, must then be resolutely renounced.

Composite sorceress

When Julie Taymor cast Helen Mirren as Prospera – a feminized Prospero – for her 2010 *Tempest* film, it attracted a degree of global attention unprecedented for a Prospero of either gender. How, it was asked, did regendering Prospero in this way change the dynamics of the drama? For reviewer Robert Horton it did 'surprisingly little to affect the experience of the play, outside the curiosity of seeing Mirren tackle the role.'[11] Others, however, were taken with the new maternality a female Prospero could bring to the relationship with Miranda. And Roger Ebert found that regendering Prospero made new, and better, sense of the play as a whole: 'Prospera empathizes with [Miranda] as Prospero never did. Indeed, all the relationships on the island curiously seem more natural when the character becomes a woman.'[12] Moreover, given Prospero's propensity to characterize his own activities through the metaphorical filter of the birthing act (he 'groaned' under his 'burthen' in delivering Miranda to the island, and was blessed with 'an undergoing stomach to bear up' (1.2.156–7)),[13] such passages assume a different authority when voiced by a character for whom the literal burden of delivery is more than a metaphor. A female Prospera can own such imagery as a male Prospero could not.

FIGURE 5 *Prospera (Helen Mirren), branded 'witch', in Julie Taymor's* Tempest *(2010)*

Making words more organically *becoming* to their speaker, however, is not all gain. The unbecoming, after all, can contain its own eloquence. As voiced by a mother, the childbirth imagery may sound more right but, as a result of its non-disruptive appropriateness, the language is required to do less work: it no longer, therefore, signals a competitive rejection of the actual maternal body (hyperbolized in Prospero's rhetoric about Sycorax); no longer communicates an appropriative claim to both halves of the parenting partnership;[14] and no longer contributes to the broader series of transgender performances (linguistic, magical, illusory) that punctuate the action of *The Tempest*.

Mirren's performance as Prospera has depth as a study in passionately invested retrospection. Moreover, her resolute enactment of the decision to redirect the future in defiance of a cruelly misogynist past gives a clear interpretive drive to her rendering of the role. Acts of cross-casting, and, more dramatically yet, of character regendering – as Asta Nielsen's equally gender-bending 1920 *Hamlet* demonstrates[15] – can reinvigorate an audience's sense of the gender-political landscape of a play through the anatomical fact of the actor's body inflecting the reading of character. Placing Mirren at the centre of this drama necessarily, therefore, jostles some of the play's potentialities into rewritten and revivified versions of themselves. However, the film's decisive central act of regendering also prevents it from participating in some of the more fluid gender play already inherent in Shakespeare's *Tempest*. Prospero's island, as Shakespeare configured it, plays host to a series of ludic, compensatory, aspirational, competitive, and tormenting acts of female impersonation: Ariel as water nymph, avenging harpy, goddess; Prospero as birthing mother and Ovidian sorceress. The interpretive possibilities of Prospero's revealing contributions to this protean world of performative transgendering are, inevitably, not available to a central mage for whom female is not an occasional, and purposefully pointed, impersonatory performance but rather a stable identity.

Whereas other productions[16] put Sycorax on screen, Taymor does not. Despite making visible events from Milan's traumatic past, and the imprisoning horror of the cloven pine, she never shows us Sycorax. Nor does she need to: there is, after all, a version of Sycorax on screen throughout. Mirren's Prospera becomes, as was expressed in review, 'something of a sorceress', turning the drama into 'a commentary on the way accomplished women were once (and perhaps still are) branded as witches'.[17] Speaking at the Venice Film Festival 2010, Mirren said:

> Women have been punished for being powerful for many centuries ... [C]hanging Prospero into Prospera ... you can bring in that history of female struggle. Certainly in Shakespeare's day and many centuries before and after, women of knowledge were punished for that knowledge.[18]

And so it is that the play's original sorceress, rescued from the drama's nether regions, here finds a voice, and a presence, at its centre as Mirren's Prospera performatively *incorporates* the figure of the punished witch into her person. It is an act of intimate identification for which Shakespeare prepares us. However, whereas in Shakespeare's play that identification erupts at a late stage, and in spite of earlier repressions, through the linguistic self-alignment with Medea, in Taymor's film it is built into the *dramatis personae* from the start. Shakespeare's roguish witch operating as a guerrilla force from the margins of the play, is, in Prospera, not just de-alterized, but legitimized. There is, of course, still an actual Sycorax referred to in the film, but her impact is reduced by the fact that much of both her story and her symbolic charge has been centrally assimilated by Prospera. In Taymor, therefore, the reconciliation with the demonized other does not come as an ambush from within (as in Shakespeare), nor as a humbling and healing encounter from without (as in Sams' opera). Overwriting Prospera with the suspect sorceress from the start carries its own interest but necessarily sacrifices the revelatory movement – the shocking shift from Sycorax as other to Sycorax as self – that characterizes Prospero's faux-obdurate but actually dynamic relationship with his off-stage nemesis. Taymor's film undoubtedly finds a platform from which to comment, and comment powerfully, on both the historical and contemporary position of 'women of knowledge'. Nevertheless, by implicitly eliding the tensely antagonistic magical poles of the drama into one composite figure, as an adaptation of *The Tempest* it cannot but forfeit some of the darkly stimulating, and specifically gender-dynamic animus of the play's inner life.

Notes

1   Director, Phelim McDermott; conductor, William Christie.

2   Ted Hughes, *Shakespeare and the Goddess of Complete Being* (London, 1992), p. 382.

3   Aimé Césaire, *Une Tempête* (Paris, 1969), p. 26.

4   *New York Daily News* (22 December 2011).

5   See Marina Warner, '"The foul witch" and Her "freckled whelp": Circean Mutations in the New World', in Peter Hulme and William H. Sherman eds, *'The Tempest' and Its Travels* (London, 2000), pp. 97–113 (p. 112).

6 Jeremy Sams, 'Creating *The Enchanted Island*', The Metropolitan Opera Playbill and Liner notes, Virgin Classics/EMI DVD (2012).

7 Marion Lignana Rosenberg, *Classical Review* (1 January 2012); David Patrick Stearns, *The Philadelphia Inquirer* (3 January 2012); Martin Bernheimer, *Financial Times* (2 January 2012); Anthony Tommasini, *The New York Times* (1 January 2012); Heidi Waleson, *The Wall Street Journal* (4 January 2012).

8 On this, see Ann Thompson, '"Miranda, Where's Your Sister?": Reading Shakespeare's *The Tempest*', in Susan Sellers ed., *Feminist Criticism: Theory and Practice*, (Toronto, 1991), p. 54.

9 On their affinities, see Jonathan Bate, *Shakespeare and Ovid* (Oxford, 1993), p. 254.

10 *The Tempest* ed. Stephen Orgel (Oxford, 1987), p. 19.

11 Robert Horton, *The Herald* (17 December 2010).

12 Roger Ebert, *The Chicago Sun-Times* (15 December 2010).

13 See Janet Adelman, *Suffocating Mothers: Fantasies of Maternal Origin in Shakespeare's Plays* (London, 1992), p. 237.

14 Prospero references Miranda's mother only once: to assert his own assured paternity (1.2.56–7).

15 See Ann Thompson, 'Asta Nielsen and the Mystery of *Hamlet*', in Lynda E. Boose and Richard Burt (eds), *Shakespeare The Movie: Popularizing The Plays on Film, TV and Video* (London, 1997), pp. 215–24.

16 Both Jarman's *The Tempest* (1979) and Greenaway's *Prospero's Books* (1991) show Sycorax.

17 Jay Stone, *The Ottawa Citizen* (24 December 2010), Column 1.

18 Quoted by Anita Singh, *The Sunday Telegraph* (12 September 2010), p. 5.

33

'Miranda, where's your mother?': Female Prosperos and What They Tell Us

Virginia Mason Vaughan

Clark University

Two decades ago, in a widely-circulated essay, Ann Thompson wondered whether it is possible 'for a staging of *The Tempest* to convey anything approaching a feminist reading of the text' without substantial rewriting. She observed that, aside from Miranda, women are noticeably absent: Claribel and Sycorax are mentioned but do not appear; Ceres, Juno, and Iris perform briefly but are not human; and Ariel, who is often portrayed by an actress, is an androgynous spirit. While the text seems to deny the 'importance – and even in some cases the presence – of female characters', it also 'attributes enormous power to female chastity and fertility', along with an insistence on male control.[1] Thompson's expressed desire for a feminist interpretation of Shakespeare's *Tempest* may have been answered, at least in part, during the last decade when directors and actors in the United States re-framed Shakespeare's romance – not so much by re-writing (although in two cases new lines have been inserted) but by introducing a female Prospero.

Inspiration may have come from Shakespeare's Globe's 2000 production that featured Vanessa Redgrave. Her cross-dressed, male Prospero was a British landowner, who wore boots and patched shepherd's garb and spoke with a North Country accent. As reviewers noted at the time, Redgrave's Prospero failed to convey the magician's vengeful ferocity, succeeding only in softer moments with Miranda when an underlying maternal tenderness shone through. Still, a noted actress had performed Prospero on a major stage, and in regional theatres of the United States, female Prosperos would soon follow, reinforcing in new ways the role's 'maternal' dynamics.

The following year Director Penny Metropulos's *Tempest*, produced for the Oregon Shakespeare Festival, presented Demetra Pittman as an overtly female Prospero. Metropulos's programme notes claim that 'Gender is not the issue of the production', but reviewer Michael W. Shurgot begged to differ. Pittman's Prospero, he argued, 'was not an angry, avenging monarch'; instead, 'she was mostly weary of human perfidy'. Indeed, it mattered profoundly that Pittman's Prospero was a mother, not a father. Her scenes with Miranda 'resonated a mother's care for her daughter's inevitable entry into the tragic-comic human community that no father could have imagined'. Her rejoicing at Miranda's betrothal, for example, 'captured the anguish of a woman who had given birth and had been betrayed by [in this production] a sister, and who knew that daughters were often political pawns in the hands of European nobility'.[2] Pittman's female Prospero, in other words, highlighted the parental affection between Prospero and Miranda that is often buried in performance; more important, it conveyed a mother's sympathy for a daughter who, like herself, is circumscribed by patriarchy.

Another *Tempest*, directed by Emily Mann at the McCarter Theater Center in Princeton, New Jersey, cast women actors as

Prospera, Ariel, and Alonsa, Queen of Naples. Blair Brown's Prospera was exceptionally feminine, wearing flowing tresses and elegant gowns, while Julyana Soelistyo's Ariel was a pixie spirit. The gender switch, noted one reviewer, allowed 'for a gentler, more feminine aspect to Ariel's pleas for freedom from servitude'. In addition, 'Prospera's maternal warmth temper[ed] her fearful power and magical prowess' (*Daily Princetonian*, 27 February 2003). Another reviewer reported that Blair created a Prospera 'who is a formidable island empress, magisterial and graceful. If her Prospera appears to be short on thunder, she glows with comforting maternal wisdom' (*Variety*, 4 March 2003). Both reviewers approved of the gender switch, but wished that Mann had exploited it more fully.

In a 2011 *Tempest*, directed by Sharon Ott for the Georgia Shakespeare at Oglethorpe University, Prospera's maternal concern stretched from Miranda to include Ariel and Caliban. Reviewer N. R. Helms observed that 'as a mother rather than a magician, Prospera's tenderness revealed her human capacity for pity'. Carolyn Cook's 'Prospera interacted with Ariel and Caliban both as master and as mother'; she acted as 'a gentle master' when offering Ariel 'his freedom along with her love', and as a teacher, when she held Caliban's hand in the final scene. Helms's review implies that Cook's Prospera conveyed the magus's vengeful passions more effectively than Blair Brown had, but tenderness dominated the play's final scenes.[3]

These three productions, all directed by women and featuring a female Prospero, suggest that the obvious parental affection Prospero shows for Miranda in Shakespeare's text resonates more fully when the parent becomes a mother figure. One underlying source of urgency in getting Miranda safely betrothed and off the island – the danger of an incestuous relationship between father and daughter – is erased, allowing for the parental figure to touch Miranda more fondly and demonstrate affection more freely. But the reviewers' criticism of Blair Brown's 'lack of thunder' suggests a downside to the softening of Prospero/a's role, for if there isn't some thunderous rage in the play's first half, the shift to forgiveness in the final scenes falls flat.

By stereotyping the female Prospero in a maternal role, these productions failed to answer Ann Thompson's objections to Shakespeare's text. They did not make *The Tempest* into a critique of patriarchal control or question in any way the play's emphasis on female chastity and fecundity. For that, it would seem, Thompson was right – it takes some re-writing. This is certainly the case with Julie Taymor's filmic *Tempest*, which, after a very short run in 2010, went to DVD in 2011. To be sure, Helen Mirren also captured the female Prospera's maternal dimension, adding a not uncommon touch of testiness between exasperated mother and determined teenage daughter in 1.2. In 3.1's betrothal scene, she holds Miranda by the arms and gently strokes her cheek. The maternal dynamic is extended in sporadic moments to Ben Whishaw's translucent Ariel, but for Caliban, Mirren's Prospera displays nothing but fury until his final exit, when she looks at him with grudging respect.

At the same time, Taymor's *Tempest* offers a feminist critique of patriarchal power by providing Mirren's Prospera a backstory to explain her status as Duchess of Milan in the 1.2 exposition. In lines written by contemporary playwright Glen Berger, Prospera explains to Miranda that her husband, the Duke of Milan, had allowed her to dabble in scientific experimentation, but when he died and left the Milanese throne to her, her brother Antonio had conspired with the King of Naples and his brother Sebastian to stage a coup by accusing her of witchcraft. This narrative is spoken as the screen shows flashbacks of Prospera at her experiments and of Sebastian and Antonio lurking in the palace's dark corners as they wait to entrap her.

These brief shots of Milan's claustrophobic built space establish a contrast between European power politics, dominated by the masculine figures of Alonso, Sebastian, and Antonio, and the sunlit vistas of Prospera's island. Although her underground cave features the 'brave utensils' she needs for scientific experimentation, as the characters wander around the island from one landscape to another, shots of lava beds, ironwood forests, standing pools, and ocean-washed cliffs create a sense of openness and possibility. This is Prospera's world, which, like the half-moon pool of water near her cell, is gendered female.

The flashbacks to Milan that show Prospera as an early modern Duchess, dressed in the tight corset of Renaissance costume, also indicate the gender constraints she endured as Duchess. The Europeans' black costumes, reminiscent of Velásquez's portraits of conquistadors, are confining, especially in contrast to the loose-fitting trousers and tunic that Prospera wears on the island. And it is the corset that she must resume at the film's end when her royal power is restored. As Ariel tightens the stays on her bodice, Prospera murmurs, 'So, so, so' in a tone of resignation. Taymor told me that she intended the corset to signify the confinement of patriarchy. Indeed, returning to Milan and resuming her political power is not a restoration for Prospera but a sacrifice. She is giving up the freedom of her island retreat, the scientific inquiries she has conducted in her cell, the lure of the surf and the breeze, not to mention the freedom of loose-fitting clothing. The shot of her being tightly laced signals the sacrifice Prospera is making for her daughter.[4]

Taymor's film does not deal with the issue of Miranda's chastity overtly, but the visual imagery she substitutes for Shakespeare's masque does convey an alternative view of human sexuality. As Miranda and Ferdinand gaze at the heavens, Prospera prepares a spectacular dance of stars and planets that culminates in the figure of Vitruvian man etched in stars, only in this image it's Vitruvian man-woman because separate male and female figures converge into one. This androgynous vision replaces the masque's mythical vision of Iris, Ceres, and Juno, who promise the young couple 'honour, riches, marriage blessing / ... Earth's increase, foison plenty' (4.1.106–10).

These details suggest that it is not simply the casting of Helen Mirren in the lead role that lends Taymor's *Tempest* a feminist perspective. The directorial choices Taymor made in both location and costume subtly critique the patriarchal system underlying Shakespeare's text. A more systematic feminist critique emerged in 2012 when the Oscar-winning actress Olympia Dukakis portrayed Prospera for Shakespeare and Company in Lenox, Massachusetts, in a stage production directed by her former student, Tony Simotes. Dukakis had pondered the text for many years, directed it in Whitefish, Minnesota, and made it her own. In a lengthy interview, she explained to me why she undertook such a demanding role at the age of 81. Dukakis confided that she had grown up learning about Greek civilization from her father, who taught classics and spent his life studying the ancient myths. But in the wake of first wave feminism and through books by Merlin Stone and Monica Sjöö,[5] she discovered archaeological proof that before the Greeks conquered Asia Minor, worship of the Great Mother, a female goddess of sexuality and power, flourished in the ancient world. Dukakis spoke passionately about the ways Perseus and other Greek invaders silenced and systematically destroyed ancient female religions. To Dukakis, the destruction of women-centred religion constituted a great betrayal, one from which all women who have been silenced by patriarchy need to recover by looking into themselves, recovering and expressing their anger. 'Being denied your "place" is an ongoing reality for women in a patriarchal culture'.[6] Dukakis referred as well to the Sumerian myth of Inanna, a goddess who is separated from her sister, Ereshkigal. Inanna lives and thrives above ground, while her sister is confined to the underworld. Inanna spends her life knowing something is missing. She has to reclaim her anger. She has to discover a mode of being that has been repressed.[7]

This sense of betrayal informs Dukakis's appropriation of Prospero's role. Her conception of Prospera's life in Milan, she told me, was pre-patriarchal, but when her brother steals her crown, a fragmentation of the spirit tears her apart. Ariel and Caliban are, in a sense, archetypal parts of her psyche. Ariel is like Artemis, the side of woman that refuses to be touched and insists on remaining intact and independent. Caliban is the vengeful, lustful side of her nature, a side that takes over for much of the performance.

According to Dukakis, Prospera finds a new kind of power on the island. She connects with the natural world, with the materiality of plants and stones, and with the 'old consciousness, and I think, the ancient mothers who are guiding and empowering her'.[8] Moreover, 'it's the male world she takes on. Prospera intends to use this boy Ferdinand, because she knows if the connection happens, her daughter can get power back. She [Prospera] can't have it for herself, but she can get it for her daughter'. Prospera's obsession with Miranda's chastity is defensive, because she knows if Miranda yields sexually, Ferdinand will reject her: 'She has to learn some restraint'. After the masque of 4.1, Dukakis added new lines to the script to make her point. As Prospera crowns the young lovers, she says, 'For this I raised the tempest ... My daughter will be the queen of Naples, ruler over Milan, vengeance for a crown taken.' She's finally got what she wanted. But suddenly she realizes her daughter's love for Ferdinand and his love for Miranda and she can't take vengeance on him or his father. Dukakis explained: 'Then she is really confounded, and then Ariel comes in and tells her about Caliban and the connection happens, and Caliban – mine own, I have in me the same violence, the same desire – Caliban is going for revenge because he feels the island was taken from him and we have the same thing playing itself out. This is the change I made: I said, "we devils", not "you devils, and I do it right to the audience'. Prospera's anger surges again in Act 5, especially when she confronts her brother, but Ariel's comment that 'you would change your mind, I would were I human', and her own self-recognition force her to forgive. The change doesn't happen suddenly. But it does happen because 'the person she needs to free the most is herself. She has to free herself from this manip-ulation, this conniving, this using, she has to free herself'.

Translating a conception that evolved out of Dukakis's own research and life experience into a performance was no easy task, but several staging choices underlined the dynamics she discussed in our conversation. Dukakis's Prospera, clad in a simple black dress with white jacket, provided a powerful rendition of Prospero's fury in a performance worthy of Medea. While her concern for Miranda was evident, it was not softly maternal, for as she told me, 'mothers can be as brutal with daughters as fathers'. Beside Dukakis, who dominated the small stage, Ariel and her fellow spirits, dressed in gossamer gowns, were all palpably female. The Europeans, whether of the court party or the comic subplot, were all male, and as Don Aucoin observed in his review, this opposition was conveyed most clearly in the confrontation between the 'female forces of the enchanted island and the male forces of civilization'. All of the men who invade Prospera's island – whether it's the aristocrats Antonio and Sebastian or the servants Stephano and Trinculo – want to take power. But on the island, the female spirits reign supreme. The staging of Ariel's appearance as a harpy in 3.3 was most telling: Prospera stood above on a catwalk, 'observing and controlling, while Ariel (the excellent Kristin Wold) and several other female island spirits cow a group of men, forcing them to positions of submissive prostration' (*Boston Globe*, 31 July 2012).

Another interpolation was substituted for the text's epilogue. Prospera came downstage accompanied by Ariel and Caliban on either side; she freed Ariel to the air (as in the text), and then in an extra line or two, freed Caliban as well. Dukakis told me after the performance that she had to free them; she had to in order to free herself. Still, giving up power wasn't easy for this Prospera. Even when Dukakis's Prospera forgave her brother's perfidy, her voice resonated with anger; the production made clear that it was the only choice. As Patti Hartigan concluded in her review, the point is 'to create a sense of equilibrium where both genders can share power and celebrate all aspects of themselves, including ferocity' (*Boston Globe,* 15 June 2012).

Perhaps Dukakis's Greek heritage and background in Greek literature also informed her Prospera. Prospero's lines in 5.1.33–57 which describe the powers he is about to relinquish are nearly identical to the words Medea speaks in William Golding's translation of the *Metamorphoses*, a text that Shakespeare had studied in school and knew well. Like the Great Mother, Medea had extraordinary powers. She, too, was betrayed by a man, Jason, who abandoned her for another woman after she had used magic to aid his quest for the Golden Fleece. Flooded with primordial wrath, Medea took a horrible revenge, killing her own children in the process. As a female Prospero, Dukakis could tap into the darkest passions, making her decision to forgive more difficult, yet more convincing.

None of the performances discussed here can fully satisfy the objections raised by Ann Thompson. Substituting Prospera for Prospero does change the play's dynamics, especially the relationship between parent and child, but to introduce a clear feminist perspective, a little rewriting is required. Mirren's and Dukakis's Prosperas lead us to question patriarchal power, and, at the end, to wonder whether Prospera and Miranda's journey to Milan and Naples will reinscribe them in patriarchal confinement. Perhaps their experiences on Prospera's island will enable them to transform the world they find in Europe into a more equitable space where, in Dukakis's words, 'men and women are sacred and important to the planet and no one is diminished by the other'.[9]

Notes

1   Ann Thompson, '"Miranda, Where's your sister?": Reading Shakespeare's *The Tempest*', in Virginia Mason Vaughan and Alden T. Vaughan (eds), *Critical Essays on Shakespeare's 'The Tempest'* (New York, 1998), pp. 234–43; quotes from 242 and 239, reprinted from *Feminist Criticism: Theory and Practice*, ed. Susan Sellers (Hemel Hempstead, 1991), pp. 45–55.

2   Michael W. Shurgot, '2001 Ashland Season', *Upstart Crow* 21 (2001): 93–101; quotes from 99 and 100.

3   N. R. Helms, 'Georgia Shakespeare at Oglethorpe University', *Shakespeare Bulletin* 30 (2012): 165–72; quotes from 171 and 169.

4   Interview with Julie Taymor, 14 June 2010.

5   Merlin Stone, *When God was a Woman* (New York, 1976); Monica Sjöö and Barbara Mor, *The Great Cosmic Mother: Rediscovering the Religion of the Earth* (New York, 1987).

6   Quoted from Shakespeare and Company's in–house magazine, Summer 2012.

7   See also Patti Hartigan's 'Dukakis channels storm within', *Boston Globe* (15 June 2012).

8   This and all other quotations from Olympia Dukakis (unless noted otherwise) are taken from her interview with Virginia Mason Vaughan on 18 August 2012.

9   Olympia Dukakis, quoted in Patti Hartigan, *Boston Globe* (15 June 2012).

34

Joseph Cornell: A poem by John Thompson for Ann Thompson

For the dust cover of our metaphor book
('dust cover', wonderful term)
we chose a Cornell
box.

It was a book we'd started to write
in Tuscany,
Neither of us speaking a word of Italian – vines
and olives, most beautiful of all landscapes.

As for Cornell, we'd seen a miraculous
show,
and neither of us would be
quite the same afterwards.

Comparable
to the Janáček
in Berlin,
World Shakespeare Congress

before the Wall
came down,
Katya
so poised, so moving, so perfect.

Was it our first conversation
or our second
you told me about
The Two Noble Kinsmen?

Nor did we fail
to rise to the challenge
of Douglas Sirk,
Imitation of Life in Paris on Christmas Day.

Cornell never
made it, travel wise,
to Europe, save in dream.
We've made it to the States

or wouldn't have seen
his boxes,
shared that experience of
balance, wistfulness, peace.

LIST OF CONTRIBUTORS

Iska Alter (Hofstra University)

Catherine Belsey (Swansea University)

Judith Buchanan (University of York)

Dympna Callaghan (Syracuse University)

Kate Chedgzoy (Newcastle University)

Hannah Crawforth (King's College London)

Trudi Darby (King's College London)

Keir Elam (University of Bologna)

Ailsa Grant Ferguson (National Theatre)

José Manuel González (University of Alicante)

Suzanne Gossett (Loyola University Chicago)

Jean E. Howard (Columbia University)

Anne Isherwood (King's College London)

Farah Karim-Cooper (Shakespeare's Globe)

David Scott Kastan (Yale University)

John Lavagnino (King's College London)

Russ McDonald (Goldsmiths, University of London)

Kathleen E. McLuskie (University of Birmingham)

Clare McManus (University of Roehampton)

Gordon McMullan (King's College London)

Sonia Massai (King's College London)

Gretchen E. Minton (Montana State University)

Lucy Munro (King's College London)

Lena Cowen Orlin (Georgetown University)

Reiko Oya (Keio University)

Lois Potter (University of Delaware)

Kevin A. Quarmby (Oxford College of Emory University)

Fiona Ritchie (McGill University)

Elizabeth Schafer (Royal Holloway, University of London)

Hilda L. Smith (University of Cincinnati)

Neil Taylor (University of Roehampton)

John O. Thompson

Virginia Mason Vaughan (Clark University)

Valerie Wayne (University of Hawai'i)

H. R. Woudhuysen (Lincoln College, Oxford)

INDEX